Glassblowing

Glassblowing

by Frank Kulasiewicz

WATSON-GUPTILL PUBLICATIONS/NEW YORK
PITMAN PUBLISHING/LONDON

Copyright © 1974 by Watson-Guptill Publications

First published 1974 in the United States and Canada by Watson-Guptill Publications,
a division of Billboard Publications, Inc.,
One Astor Plaza, New York, N.Y. 10036

Library of Congress Cataloging in Publications Data
Kulasiewicz, Frank, 1930–
   Glassblowing.
    Bibliography: p.
    1. Glass blowing and working. I. Title.
TT298.K84 1974   748.2   74-12446
ISBN 0-8230-2120-3

Published in Great Britain by Sir Isaac Pitman & Sons Ltd.,
39 Parker Street, Kingsway, London WC2B 5PB
ISBN 0-273-00856-0

All rights reserved. No part of this publication
may be reproduced or used in any form or by any means—graphic,
electronic, or mechanical, including photocopying, recording, taping,
or information storage and retrieval systems—without
written permission of the publishers.

Manufactured in U.S.A.

First Printing, 1974

To Carol Lynne

Contents

ACKNOWLEDGMENTS, 9

INTRODUCTION, 11

Freeblown Glass Vs. Lampworking, 11
Areas Covered in this Book, 11
The Revived Interest in Glass, 12
Equipment, 12
Materials, 12
Summary, 12

1/ STUDIO FACILITIES, 15

Shop or Studio, 15
The Furnace, 17
Firebrick, 18
The Furnace Base, 20
The Furnace Walls, 22
Casting the Burner Block, 24
The Furnace Roof, 26
A Firebrick Pot, 27
A Clay Pot, 27
The Furnace Front, 28
Finishing and Binding, 30
A Shelf and Door, 32
The Burner, 34
The Burner Support, 36
Insulating the Burner Block, 37
Completion of the Burner, 38
Other Furnaces, 40
Lead Glass-Melting Furnace, 41
Crucible Furnaces, 42
The Glory-Hole, 44
Annealing, 46
Building a Gas Annealing Oven, 48

The Oven Walls, 49
Binding the Walls Together, 50
The Roof Arch, 51
Completing the Front and
    Removing the Arch Form, 52
Making a Door, 53
Attaching the Door, 54
Building the Burner, 56
A Hanger and a Heating Oven, 56

2/ TOOLS, 59

Hoods and Venting Fans, 59
Loading and Cleaning Tools, 60
Tongs, 60
Metal Stands, 60
Reflecting Shields, 61
Mittens and Gloves, 61
Annealing Oven Tools, 61
Forming Tools, 62
Blow Pipe, 62
Stainless Steel Tubing, 63
Holder or Stand for Pipes, 64
Marver, 64
Glassblower's Bench, 64
Pucellas, Jacks, and Tongs, 65
Paddles, 65
Blocks, 66
Pontils, 67
Gathering Irons, 67
Tweezers, 67
Shears, 68
Special Tools, 69

3/ Firing, Melting, and Annealing, 71

Checks Before Lighting the Furnace, 71
Furnace Adjustments, 72
A Test Firing, 72
Lighting the Burner, 74
Adjustments After Lighting, 75
Turning Off the Furnace, 75
Loading the Furnace, 76
Melting Glass, 77
Adjustments After Melting, 78
Cleaning the Furnace, 78
Annealing Glass, 80
The Oven Burner, 80
Lighting the Oven Burner, 81
Using the Oven, 82
Turning Off the Oven, 82

4/ Glass, 85

Natural Glasses, 85
Commercial Glasses, 85
Glass Qualities, 86
Kinds of Glasses, 86
Potash/Lead Glass, 86
Boro-Silicate Glass, 86
Opal or Opaque Glass, 89
Sand/Soda/Lime Glass, 89
Batch Melts, 89
Materials, 90
Conversion Factors, 91
Developing Your Own Formula, 92
Changing the Oxide Relationship, 92
Changing the Chemicals Used
 to Introduce Oxides, 92

Recipes for the Soda/Lime Glass, 93
Converting a Batch Composition into
 a Theoretical Oxide Recipe, 94
Ingredients Not Calculated, 94
A "Better" Glass, 95
Suggestions, 95
Second Melts, 99

5/ Working Freeblown Glass, 101

Materials and Organization, 101
The Pace of Glass, 101
Keeping the Glass and Pipe Hot, 102
The Glassblowing Procedure, 103
Gathering Glass, 107
Marvering and Blowing the Bubble, 108
Necking the Bubble, 109
Blocking and Additional Gathers, 110
Forming on a Blow Pipe, 111
Attaching the Pontil, 112
Making Closed Shapes, 116
Making Open Shapes, 116
Removing the Pontil and Annealing, 118
Some Words of Advice, 119

6/ Stems, Handles, and Other Additions, 121

Casing, 121
Stemware, 122
Hollow Stemware, 124
Handles, 125
Hollow Handles, 127
Angel Swings or Bridges, 128
Wings, 129
Trailed Glass, 130

Multi-Chambered Vessels, 131
Cold Glass Additions, 132
Impressed Decorations, 133
Lily-Pad Design, 134
Prunts, 135
Multiple Forms, 136
Steam Bubble, 137
Paperweights, 138
Simple Molds, 139

7/ Color In Glass, 141

Methods of Adding Color, 141
Factors that Influence Color, 141
Furnace Atmosphere, 142
Composition of Colorant, 142
Base Glass, 142
Oxidizing and Reducing Agents, 142
Types of Colorants, 142
Sequence of Color, 142
Chromium, 143
Cobalt, 143
A "Strike" or "Flash" Color, 143
Copper, 144
Gold, 144
Iron, 144
Manganese, 144
Nickel, 153
Silver, 153
Sulphide, 153
Cadmium-Selenium, 153
Carbon Amber or Sulfur Amber, 155
Titanium, 155
Uranium, 155

8/ Decorating and Finishing, 157

Types of Decorations, 157
Esthetic Considerations, 157
Safety Considerations, 157
Application of Decoration, 158
Metallic Decorating Materials, 159
Staining Metals, 160
Copper Staining, 160
Irridescence, 162
Mirroring Glass, 164
Sulphide Surface Colors, 165
Flocking Glass, 165
Removing the Glass Surface, 165
Cutting and Finishing Machines, 167
Cut Glass (Ground), 166
Engraving, 170
Sandblasting, 171
Etching, 170
Frosting, 172
Polishing, 173
Finishing Glass, 174

Appendix, 177

Glossary, 206

Bibliography, 209

Suppliers List, 211

Index, 214

ACKNOWLEDGMENTS

I am grateful to my friends and associates both in and out of the glass field for their help and encouragement. To the many American glass artists, known to me personally or through correspondence, I am grateful for the privilege of using photographs of their creative endeavors.

I am particularly indebted to Roberto Rios Ugartechea for allowing me the free run of Inco Glass Company in Mexico, to Masamitsu Okada for his generous time and help in my travels through the glass factories in Japan, to Junshiro Sato for an afternoon at Kagami Crystal Factory that I will long remember, to Erwin Eisch of Germany and Sybren Valkema of Holland for their early encouragement of my interest in glass, to Robert Florin for use of his photographs, to Mrs. Emma Jones for her many hours of reading and discussion preliminary to this book, and to my wife whose quick finger on the button made most of the demonstration photographs in this book possible.

Introduction

Mexican Vase. Lead glass, 4" x 8". An excellent example of double casing produced at a handworking factory in Mexico. The clear casing is very visible in the photograph, but if you look closely you will see the partially successful attempt to case color on color before the crystal casing.

The aim of this book is to supply elementary technical information on the tools, equipment, and techniques needed to establish studio facilities for beginning freeblown glass work, especially to persons who are already interested in glass but who cannot find the needed guides. There are few publications that treat the area of glassblowing from the individual craftsman's or student's point of view, therefore I also hope that this book will further the growth of freeblown glass as a contemporary craft in America. I want to encourage the craftsman or student to develop both knowledge and sensitivity toward the medium by the best means possible—actually working with the material.

It is not my purpose to make a case for freeblown glass, or glass used in any other way as a crafts medium. Nor is it my purpose to impose or review individual esthetic theories and values espoused by other craftsmen or teachers in the field.

Freeblown Glass Vs. Lampworking

A definition of offhand or freeblown glass is presented here to avoid use of the ludicrous term "handblown" glass. Freeblown glass refers to the various processes used to develop hollow forms from molten glass under the direct visual and tactile control of the artist producing his own ware.

"Offhand," "freeblown," or "blown in the air" glassworking is different from "lampworking" or "flameworking" blown glass. The latter processes are not done from melted glass in a furnace, but rather with the use of glass tubing. We will be using a furnace filled with molten, hot glass. The lampworker uses a small burner to reheat his glass tubing (or rods) until they are soft enough to manipulate, tool, or blow.

Areas Covered in this Book

I will deal with designing and building furnaces and tools, safety considerations, calculating chemicals, and melting glass, as well as techniques of forming, decorating, coloring, and developing an understanding of what glass is. Reference tables, recipes, glossary, bibliography, and information on commercially available equipment are also included.

Step-by-step photographs will show you how to build the equipment and work the glass. In addition, photographs of a variety of glass pieces by many American artists working in many different ways will illustrate

Mr. Nino E. Buffoni demonstrating another form of glassblowing usually referred to as "lampworking" or "flameworking." This is different from the kind of glassblowing we will do in this book in that Mr. Buffoni works with cold glass tubing that he reheats to blow and form over a small burner. Photo by Paul Williams.

differing philosophies and esthetic theories.

The Revived Interest in Glass

As you start working in glass you will meet difficulties. I want to help you circumvent the unnecessary obstacles that I went through when I developed an interest in glass. As I look back now on the renascence of interest in glass in America, it was very much the situation of the blind leading the blind. Even though we were all enthusiastic, each one of us spent a great deal of time going in circles and retracing our steps before getting off the beaten track. During this renascence of glass, from time to time there was a minor breakthrough in working, equipment design, or understanding. For a while this became "the answer" and had, as with so many "answers," to be recognized as only a way or as one step in a way.

There were (and are) those who had little to offer and (wisely) kept silent, faking some great secret—mimicking a historical situation of years earlier when "secrets" were indeed important in glassworking. In great abundance was the "esthetician," who really knew very little technically, and the "technician," who spoke in the trade jargon to such a great extent that he was able to pass himself off as an expert.

Equipment

The American glass craftsman involved in the recent renascence of glass often came from a ceramics background. Controlling fire, mixing chemicals, and the manipulation of form is common to both media, and a sensitivity to one increases knowledge and sensitivity toward the other.

The simplicity of equipment design suggested and proved in ceramics by people like Paul Soldner was sometimes forgotten when potters began to work in glass. Money has been spent on a variety of expensive safety and control devices ("purple peepers," super-sensitive solenoid valves, high-voltage sparks, elaborate clocking devices, etc.), all because the potters forgot that the only way they kept their commercial kilns working was to bypass these electrical monstrosities. From studios I have visited all across the country I know there is a small fortune in useless equipment that glassworkers were talked into buying before they applied the simple skills they had learned in related areas.

The equipment that generally works best is that which you design and build yourself. As far as equipment designs, what I offer you here is simple—perhaps too simple. But you can easily add to this equipment as you find the need for more expensive refractories, larger ovens or furnaces, etc. The important thing is to start.

Materials

Even craftsmen who had extensive experience in mixing their own glazes and clays, and had managed to get these two completely different materials to join together without cracking, did not seem to know they could get glass to stick to glass! Mixing sand with soda ash and lime, and then melting this into a glass, was some kind of technical witchcraft beyond the normal craftsman's understanding.

Summary

Besides starting you off in glass, there are at least three things I would like to influence in your work. I want to convince you that simplicity and ease is best when it comes to most of your equipment. Further, I want to convince you that glass is not something you need to consult an engineer about before you mix chemicals and melt. And, lastly, I want you to be able to stand on your own, and not rely on any "establishment" or trend to tell you what kind of glass to make.

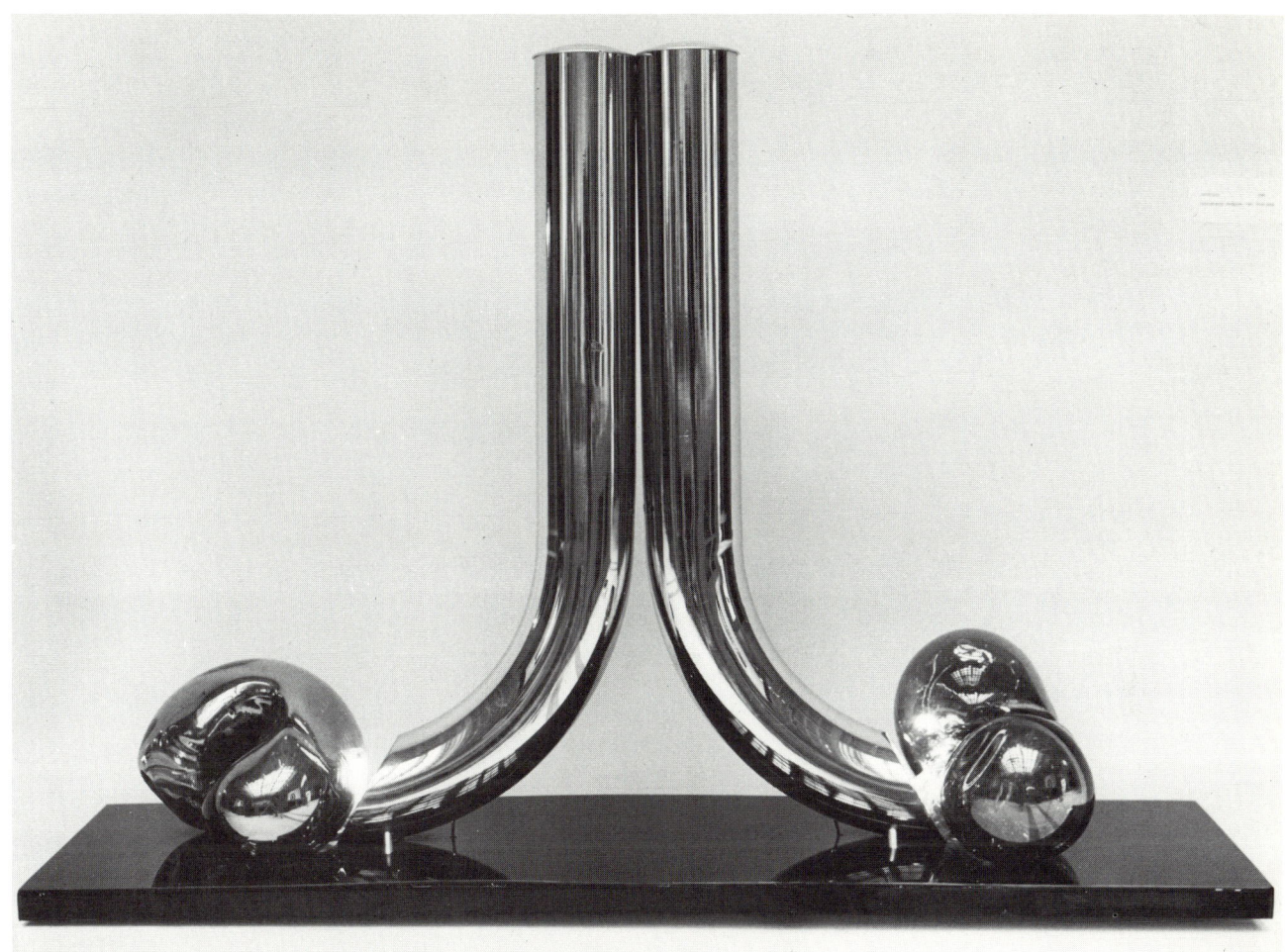

Untitled *by Boris Dudchenko. Freeblown glass, chromed steel, lights, and plexiglass, 48″ x 32″ x 12″. The artist works toward combining the warm, hand-made quality (like frozen motion) of blown glass with the machine-made, hard-edge coldness of metals and plastics. This untitled construction consists of two blown shapes (mirrored inside) two tubes of chrome steel, and mirrors and blinking lights all mounted on reflecting black plexiglass.*

1/Studio Facilities

Long Necked Bottle by Robert Biniarz. Freeblown silica borate glass with silver, copper, cobalt, and nickle, 5″ x 12″. An elegant and graceful form that varies from clear glass at the wide lip and narrow neck to opal and opaque multicolor swirls and spots in the main body. Most of the decorative effects were done during forming by selective additions of chemicals on the marver and skilled handling of the furnace atmosphere.

As an artist, you have control over the design of the glass you create. To a large degree this control and creativity holds true for your equipment and tools as well. It is not only possible, it is advisable, for you to design and build some of your own. You will reduce your costs, and even more important, you will have more effective equipment for your needs. Furnaces and ovens can be produced from standard refractory bricks, and many tools can be made from readily available materials. The modern artist/craftsman feels his needs are unique, therefore his equipment should also be unique.

In this chapter I will show a step-by-step method for building a small furnace and an annealing oven. Both have proven effective for beginning work in glass, but they are subject to your modification. Unlike industrially produced equipment, which is usually welded together, this equipment can easily be changed when you feel the need. I have also included information on other furnaces, ovens, and "glory-holes" that may be helpful. These designs have been influenced by various working situations, budgets, and safety considerations, as well as by the artist's individual creative development.

SHOP OR STUDIO

An outdoor area, preferably fenced (chain link or other "open" fencing) and roofed with fire-resistant material, is ideal for glass work in warmer climates. In cold climates an indoor work area next to the covered outdoor area may be necessary. If the furnace and oven are indoors, however, costs and complications are greatly increased. A building housing a furnace should be fire resistant and well ventilated, and you may be required to use expensive, delicate, and often undependable electronic control devices that seriously increase costs and decrease ease of operation. I don't believe that you have to be an engineer to fire your furnace or to work with glass.

Indoors or out, the work area of your studio should have few obstructions that might cut down your freedom of movement. The floor should be level, and a concrete slab is helpful. About 300 square feet (20 x 15) is a minimum amount of space (for one furnace used as the "glory-hole," one oven, one bench, etc.). Some craftsmen work with less, but for a beginner, the larger the free space the safer the shop.

Utilities. Water, natural gas, and electricity are needed for the facilities described in this chapter. The furnace and oven will require at least 100,000 Btus of natural gas. If you need new utility lines for the shop it would be wise to install large service lines for additional equipment at a later time. Pounds pressure for the gas lines is helpful and economical in some areas, but is usually legal only outdoors.

Electricity should be adequate for blowers, fans, and lights. Remember that having many electrical outlets does not indicate a large amount of electricity. Your service line and fusing plan are the important considerations. If possible, you should have lights, burner blower motors, and fans on three separate circuits. All heavy-duty equipment with large motors (grinders, saws, compressors, etc.) should be separately fused if possible.

Ventilation. Outdoors this usually takes care of itself. When the furnace is indoors it must be vented with a hood. This vent system should preferably work on a natural-draft principle rather than by electrical exhaust fans because it is important for the exhaust to continue working during any power failure. With an indoor furnace area, the flow of air should be directed from the outside over the work bench and artist (but not on the glass being worked), toward the furnace. If a hood vent is used, then the air intake for your burners should not be located under the hood.

Mixing, Grinding, and Storage Areas. You will need storage space for chemicals, glass, etc., and a working area for mixing and grinding—the more space the better, with plenty of shelves and tables. Mixing and grinding areas are best located indoors in an area separate from furnace. A 6 x 10 foot space can hold a small mixer, chemicals, scales, etc., but there is a safety factor involved. Crowding too much in a small space leads to the problem of dust from chemicals. You should provide exhaust ventilation and use a face respirator. A larger space, if available, is more desirable.

Special Items. Safety showers and refrigerators are optional items that appear in some of the better studio layouts. The shower is seldom (luckily) used, but it is a definite plus in case of hair or clothing fires. It is usually located close to the furnace and glory-hole.

Refrigerators are used constantly to provide ice for minor burns. This ice treatment, if applied at once, is most effective for the minor burns that do occur. Needless to say, if cold drinks are stored in this refrigerator make sure they are of the nonalcoholic type.

If possible, avoid putting electronic safety controls on your equipment ("purple peepers," "violet peepers," high-voltage electronic sparks, flame rods, air-pressure sensors, etc.). These are often recommended by electricians on a routine basis, but for your purposes they are not only unsuitable, they can be undependable. Some (electronic spark transformers and rods, pressure sensors and turn-offs, etc.) are even dangerous in this working situation.

Location. Some consideration should be given to the location of the shop. Orientation to your neighbors (and their temperament) is of particular importance. Exhaust gases, chemicals, abrasive compounds, etc., will not help your neighbors' gardens or trees. It would be best to come to an agreement before investing money in equipment. It is also wise to consider the noise factor. The furnace will be on 24 hours a day, and the soothing blast of a well-working burner might be music *only* to your ears.

Despite all of the above, it must be noted that a great many of the glassworking facilities of the backyard or garage type work very well.

The Furnace

The furnace is the heat container used to melt the glass. It is also often used to reheat the vessel while working with glass. There are commercial furnaces available on the market; however, I feel that your first furnace should be one you build yourself.

The furnace I suggest you build has design features that are possible only because of its size. For example, on a larger furnace the roof would have to be arched (or suspended), the door might be larger, the burner placement in the roof would be impractical, etc. This is a good beginner's furnace, and it can be used effectively as a "test" furnace for glass formulas or as a color furnace if you later get a larger furnace. It is designed so that the "pot" (the container that holds the molten glass) can be removed without dismantling the whole furnace. This feature makes melting experiments far more practical and accurate. The materials needed for this furnace are listed in the appendix on p. 178, and this chapter will demonstrate how it should be built.

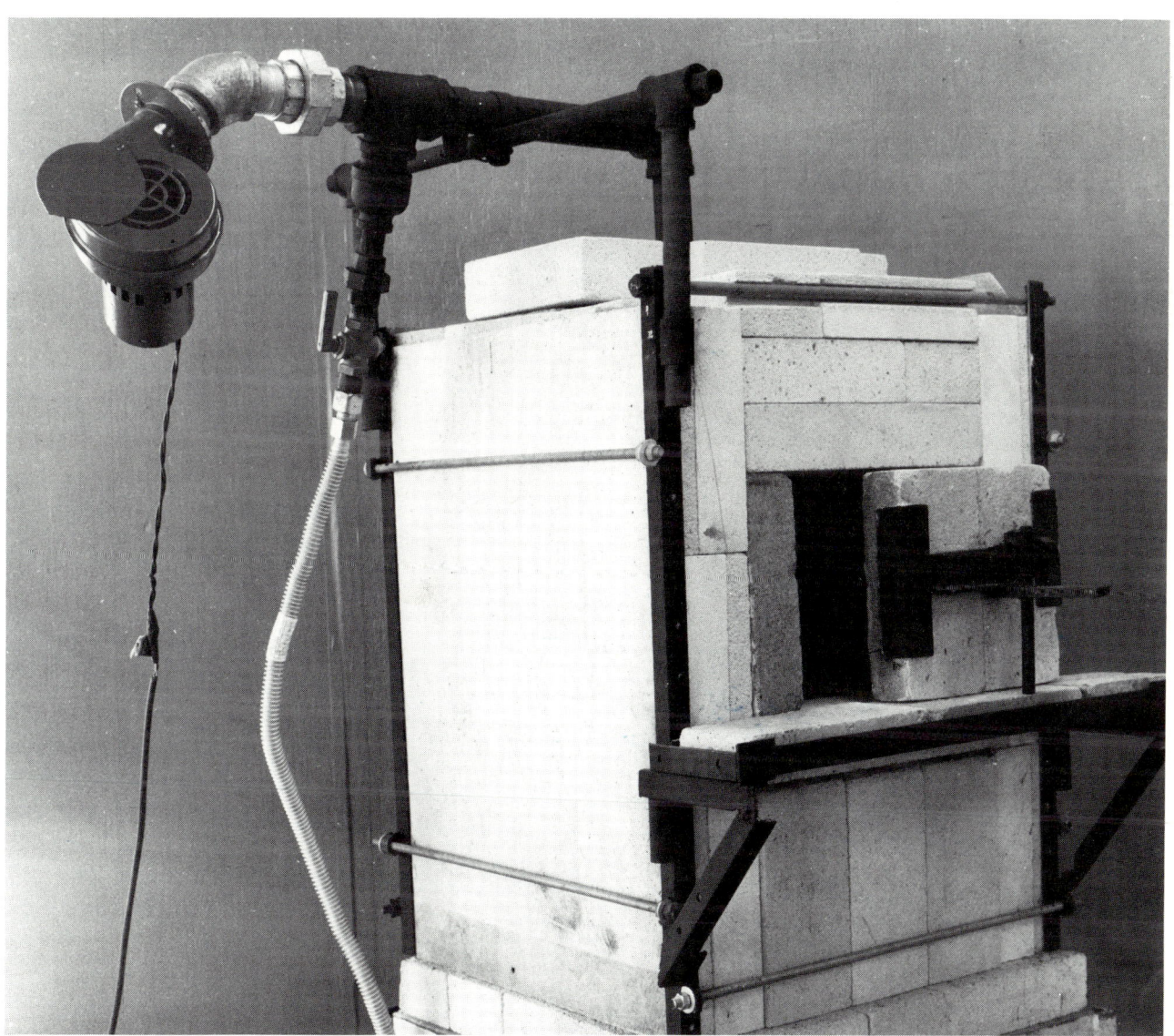

A view of the furnace that you will build. The electrical connection is only temporarily in place for test purposes.

STUDIO FACILITIES 17

FIREBRICK

Firebrick is made of special high-fire materials that are used in the production of heating equipment. There are two basic types: hard firebrick (usually simply called firebrick), which is dense, heavy, and strong; and insulating firebrick, which is light, porous, and easily chipped or broken.

A variety of sizes of "standard" brick shapes can be found on the market. The basis for these different shapes is the "straight," which is a brick 9″ x 4½″ x 2½″, and is the building unit used for most heavy-duty heating equipment. Either multiples or fractions of these dimensions can also be used. This straight can be halved in four ways to produce: a "soap" (9″ x 2½″ x 2¼″), a "No. 1 Split" (9″ x 4½″ x 1¼″), a "feather edge" (9″ x 4½″ x 2½″ tapering to 0″), and a "half-straight" (4½″ x 4½″ x 2½″). The first three shapes can be bought, the fourth has to be broken. You would probably cut all of these shapes from insulating brick straights. Shapes larger than the straight are referred to as "square-edge tile."

Insulating Firebrick. Insulating firebrick is available in a range of temperatures. The temperature ratings (2000°F. to 3000°F.) refer to the temperature at which the material crumbles or melts. The lower the rating, the less durable the material, but the better it is as an insulator. As the temperature rating goes up so does the price. In my furnace I used 3000°F. bricks; however, 2300°F. are initially more economical, are better insulators, and are more likely to be available from local suppliers. The quality of the insulating brick from a particular manufacturer will be consistent in most parts of the country because the producers ship the brick from a central plant.

It will be necessary to saw some special sizes of insulating brick when building your furnace. You will need a carpenter's square, a sharp nail, and a hacksaw.

Hard Firebrick. The quality of hard firebrick may vary depending on the clays available in the area of production. These bricks are too heavy to be shipped long distances unless special qualities are required. For this furnace you can use any brick that is better than fireplace brick quality for the walls. A brick of 50% alumina or more will hold up better for the roof and door tiles. Special glass-melting brick (such as Zircon and Mullite) are expensive, and for your first meltings they are probably not economical. The brick for your pot can be of fairly low alumina content that will break down rapidly (the molten glass actually dissolves the brick).

Firebrick is difficult to cut unless you use heavy industrial saws with masonry blades. Some companies will do this cutting for a modest charge; however, it is possible for you to break the brick into the approximate size you need with a hammer, chisel, sharp nail, and carpenter's square.

Insulating Brick

1. Mark your cut line, as straight as possible, with a nail. If you need a half-straight size use a hard firebrick straight lined up evenly as a guide.

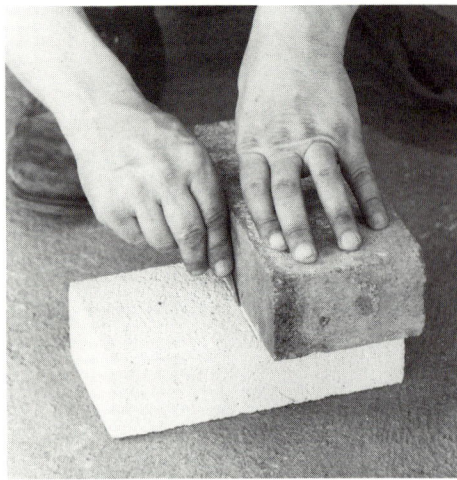

Hard Firebrick

1. Start by scoring a line in the brick with a sharp nail and a carpenters square.

Standard firebrick shapes. From the left: a straight, a soap, a No. 1 split, and a feather edge.

2. Then continue the score line around the brick on all sides using a carpenters square as a guide.

3. Line up your hacksaw in the score line made by the nail, and proceed to make a straight cut.

4. Cut all four sides of the brick to the depth of the saw blade before cutting any deeper. Then alternately saw all four sides until the brick is halved.

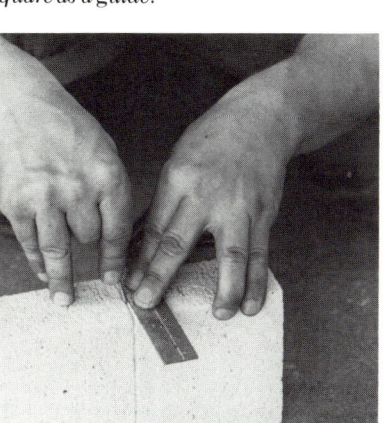
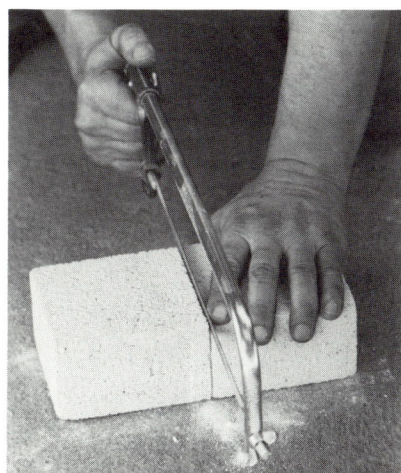
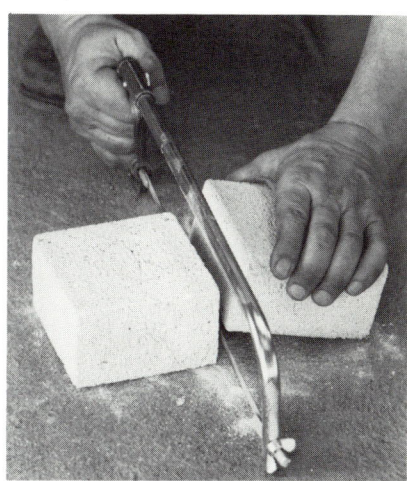

2. Score all four sides of the brick, making sure the score lines are kept straight.

3. Using just enough impact to chip the brick, follow the score line using a hammer and chisel.

4. Continue until the brick breaks. If the edge is too rough you can grind it against rough concrete or another brick.

The Furnace Base

The following series of photographs will show you how to construct a base for your furnace. Although the furnace shown was built on a metal rolling stand, you might find it easier and more economical to build on a base of cement blocks, as shown in the variation below.

1. If you wish the furnace to be portable, you can weld a steel frame in the desired size and add strong wheels.

1. One of the simplest ways to make a furnace base is to arrange ordinary concrete blocks as shown.

2. Arrange eight straight firebricks on top to provide air circulation under your furnace (to help protect the concrete from heat).

2. Place transite (or metal) on the portable frame. (You do not need firebrick underneath since the stand provides air space.)

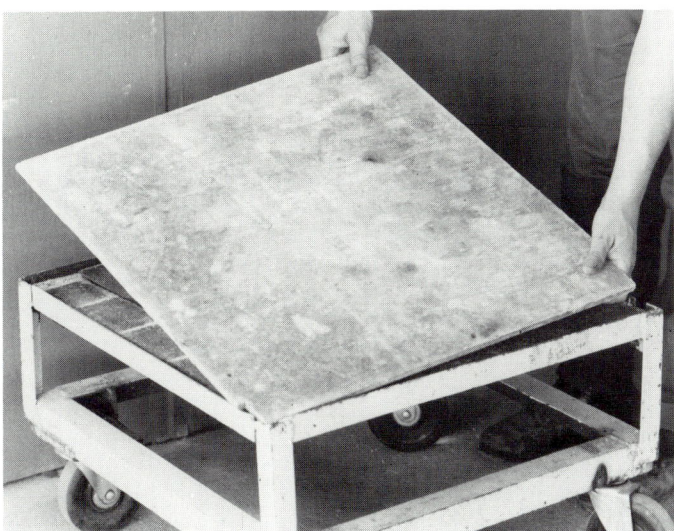

3. Then arrange a layer of insulating brick on the transite in the same way as with the concrete base.

3. Place a piece of transite (or metal) at least ½" thick on top of the firebrick.

4. Next place a layer of insulating brick on the transite. You need 12 straights and one half-straight.

STUDIO FACILITIES 21

The Furnace Walls

Stack the bricks evenly to form the double wall of the furnace. The edges of the bricks are usually square, unless damaged in transportation. Do not use broken edges in contact with the row above or below.

Inside Hard Firebrick Splits

Row 1
Left: split upright, split horizontal.
Back: three splits upright.
Right: split horizontal, split upright.

Row 2
Left: top of split from Row 1, split.
Back: tops of splits from Row 1.
Right: split, top of split from Row 1.

Row 3
Left: split, half-split.
Back: split, half-split.
Right: half-split, split.

Row 4
Left: split upright, split.
Back: split upright, split.
Right: split, split upright.

Row 5
Left: top of split from Row 4, split.
Back: top of split from Row 4, split.
Right: split, top of split from Row 4.

Outside Insulating Brick

Row 1
Left: straight upright, straight horizontal.
Back: straight, 3½″ piece, straight.
Right: straight, straight upright.

Row 2
Left: top of straight from Row 1, 2½″ piece, straight.
Back: 7″ piece, straight.
Right: straight, 2½″ piece, top of straight from Row 1.

Row 3
Left: straight, 4½″ piece.
Back: straight, 3½″ piece, straight.
Right: 4½″ piece, straight.

Row 4
Left: straight upright, 2½″ piece.
Back: straight, 7″ piece.
Right: straight, 2½″ piece, straight upright.

Row 5
Left: top of straight from Row 4, straight.
Back: straight 3½″ piece, straight.
Right: straight, top of straight from Row 4.

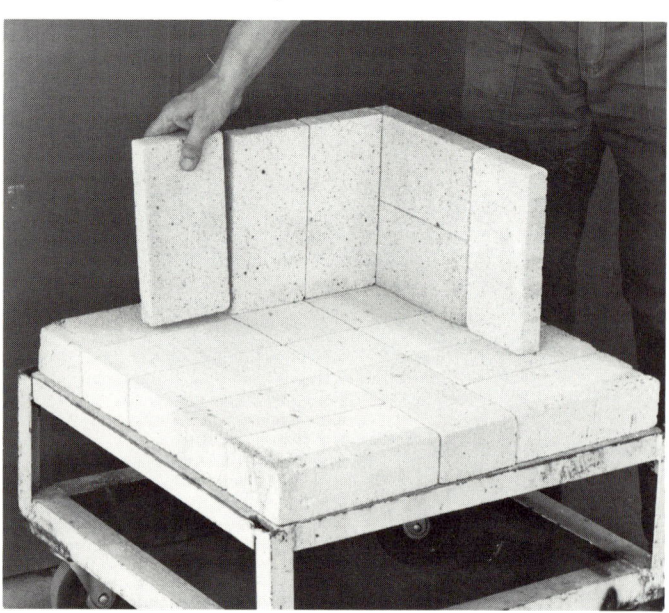

1. Begin building the hard brick inner furnace wall out of splits. Note that the side wall overlaps the back wall.

3. Continue building the inner and outer walls as shown, adding first an inner layer, then an outer layer.

2. Build the outer wall out of insulating brick. Keep it flush with the front edge of the hard brick. It will be necessary to cut bricks to fit.

4. These are the walls as they near completion. The unfinished side will be completed in the same way as the finished side.

5. The completed sides and back walls of the furnace.

Casting the Burner Block

Before building the furnace roof you have to cast a block to hold the burner in place. Although there are other ways to make the burner block, I have found the following system works very well. The castable refractory used for this block should be rated at 2800°F. or more. The price on these castables increases with the rise in temperature rating.

1. A 6″ x 1¼″ pipe with a 1¼″ pipe coupling attached (well-greased) is centered in the space between two 18″ x 6″ x 2½″ square-edge tiles. Firebrick straights are lined up with the outer edge of the tiles, and the ends are closed with two extra firebrick straights.

3. After the castable has set (follow the directions on the bag for the proper time and temperature), loosen the pipe by turning it in place (if necessary use a pipe wrench) and remove the greased firebrick and tile.

2. All inside surfaces of the firebrick and tile are greased, with extra applied to joints that might leak. Mix the refractory castable according to directions on the bag and pour into the mold. Fill the castable to the upper levels of the firebrick.

4. Remove the pipe from the top of the block and the coupling from the bottom. It may be necessary to tighten the pipe in the coupling to break it loose from the castable. After the block has hardened you are ready to continue construction of the furnace.

The Furnace Roof

The opening of the furnace roof will be closed with two 18″ x 6″ x 2½″ square-edge tiles and the burner block you have just made. Additional insulating bricks will make the roof level and will insulate the burner block.

1. Place two square-edge tiles on the walls of the furnace, one flush with the front wall. Allow a 3½″ opening between the front and back tiles.

2. Lower the burner block in place between the tiles. All four sides of the block are supported, either by the furnace walls or by the square-edge tiles.

3. Now place two insulating bricks in place on both sides of the burner block to level the roof and insulate the burner block tile.

A Firebrick Pot

You are now ready to put a "pot" for holding the molten glass into the furnace. Break firebrick splits (or tank brick splits) into four pieces, each 2½" long. It is best to break the ends off two splits so each 2½" piece will have one straight edge for tighter joints.

There should be space between the outer pot walls and the inner furnace walls, as well as space under the pot. This space will be filled with high-fire grog—packed in place—before the furnace is heated. This layer of grog helps you to remove the tank without having to rebuild the entire furnace. However, you may find that a 12" x 12" x ¼" piece of transite under the pot is easier to build than a layer of loose grog. Either can be used. The use of the feather-edge is optional. It simply makes the glass flow to the back of the pot for easier gathering.

A Clay Pot

Almost all high-quality lead crystal produced is melted in clay pots. If you want a clay pot instead of firebrick, you can build one out of "pot clay," or a mixture of one-half (dry volume) high-fire fireclay and one-half high-fire fireclay grog with just enough water to make it plastic. Build the pot ½" bigger than you want in all outside dimensions (it will shrink during drying and firing), dry slowly, and fire to stoneware temperature (2400°F.) in a ceramic kiln.

Longer-lasting tanks can be made out of high-alumina, mullite, or zircon castables (there will be little or no shrinkage, so adjust accordingly). These materials are not very plastic, however, so do not lend themselves to easy working with hand methods.

This is a clay pot that could be used in the furnace.

1. This is a cut-away view of the pot you will build showing the placement of the floor splits and feather edge. The left side of the photograph represents the front of the furnace. Begin the bottom by placing two splits on the transite or grog. Put the feather edge on top with the large edge facing the front of the furnace.

2. Begin the walls by placing one of the 2½" pieces and a split on the transite flush with the edge of the splits toward the back of the furnace. Place a split on each side of the tank floor splits. Then place a 2½" piece and a split toward the front of the furnace. Build the second row of splits and broken splits in reverse order, so the corners overlap the first row (splits and piece on each side, split in front and back).

3. Here is what the completed tank should look like. The tank should be set back ½" from the front edge of the furnace. If the joints can be seen through, tie a piece of string around the tank to hold it together until the grog is packed in place.

The Furnace Front

The walls, roof, and pot of your furnace are now in place. The front of the furnace—the door opening, shelf, and door—still needs to be added. This demonstration will show you where to place the bricks to build the furnace front.

1. Place three firebrick straights across the front of the furnace, keeping them flush with the inner edge of the hard brick wall. There should be open space between the outer tank wall and the front wall of the furnace to be filled with grog.

4. Place a firebrick straight on each side of the door opening flush with the edge of the tile, and place another 13½" x 4½" x 2½" tile on top. Next lay an insulating brick and an insulating half-straight on top of the tile.

5. Next you need to line the sides of the furnace and door with bricks. Place one insulating brick straight and one insulating brick split on each side of the furnace.

2. *Place three insulating brick straights in front of the firebrick. If there is a slight difference in the height of the brick use a small amount of castable to level the bricks or the entire door frame may be out of plumb or unstable.*

3. *A 13½" x 4½" x 2½" square-edge tile serves as the bottom of the door opening. Line up the tile with the outside edge of the insulating brick underneath.*

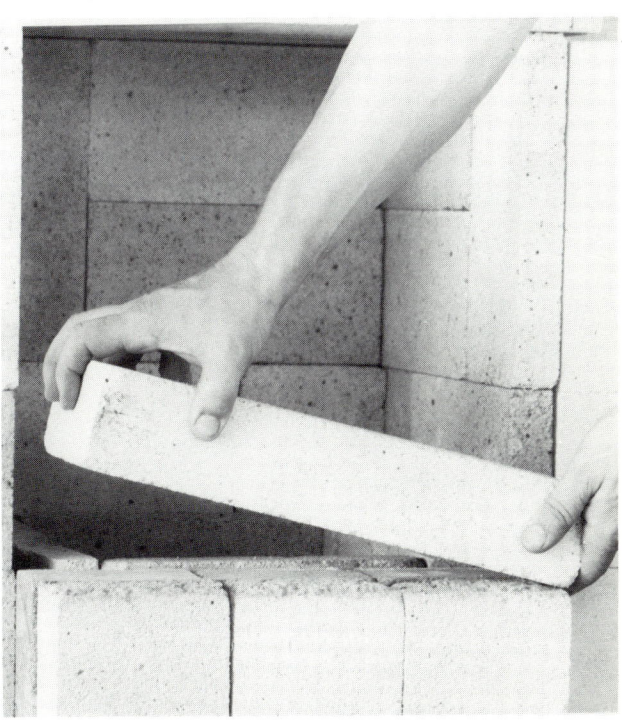

6. *Put the split toward the door in the second row. Finish the third row on both sides with an insulating brick straight toward the inside and a split toward the outside.*

7. *Using a saw or rough file, groove an insulating brick straight and a half-straight as shown, and put them on top of the door opening. The top tie rod will fit into the groove and will be inset to keep direct exhaust heat from hitting the rod.*

STUDIO FACILITIES 29

Finishing and Binding

Before binding the furnace together it is a good idea to cut insulation brick to fill the spaces on the furnace roof. This could be done after the transite and angle irons are in place. Then you need to finish off the roof and bind the furnace together. Note: some craftsmen have used metal banding machines to bind their furnaces. Another way is to use wire and turn buckles.

1. A close-up of the side of the roof shows the T-shaped burner block supported by the tile and the furnace wall. Insulating brick will fill up the remaining empty space.

2. Here the roof of the furnace is complete. Insulating brick, cut to fit, has filled up the space on either side of the burner block.

5. Be sure that all rods are level so the furnace will be properly alligned. Initially, the nut on the rods should be tightened by hand.

6. Here you can see the front and top of the furnace with transite, corner angles, and top tie rods in place.

30 GLASSBLOWING

3. This shows the furnace front, with transite propped up on the side for fitting purposes, before the corner angle irons and tie rods are added.

4. The top front rod goes through a ⅜" hole drilled in the angle iron and lines up with the insulating brick groove. The side ³⁄₁₆" rods go through ⅜" nuts that were welded to the angle iron.

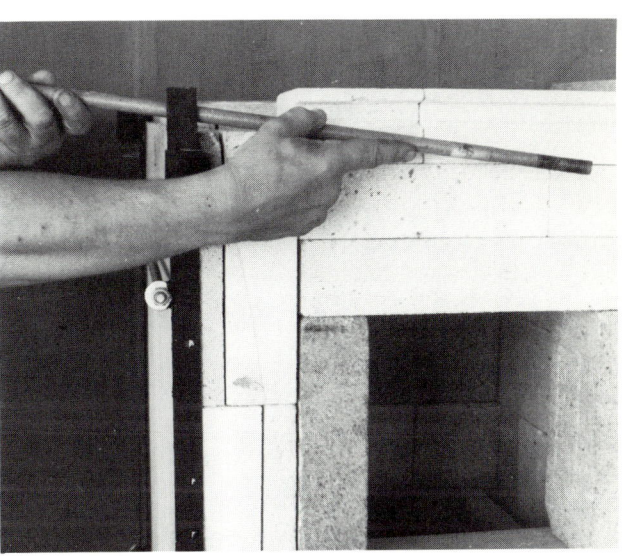

7. Now you should install and hand-tighten the bottom rods in the same manner as for the top of the furnace. Visually check the allignment of all the rods.

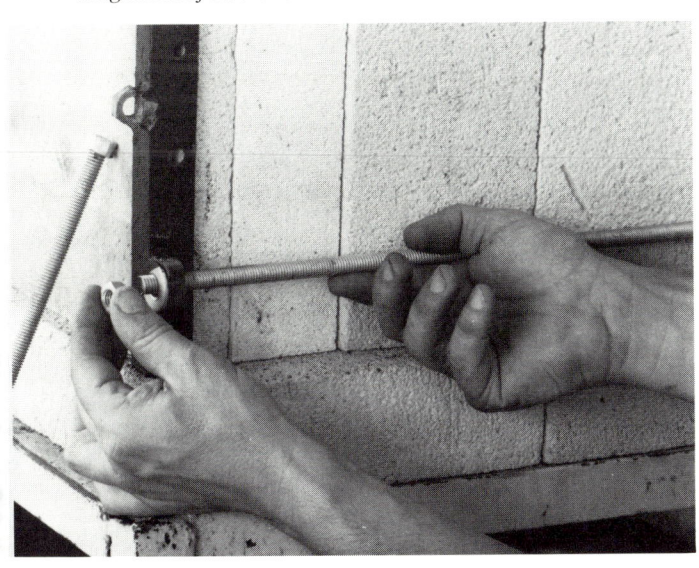

8. Now tighten the rods until the bricks are brought into firm contact with each other. Do not overtighten or the brick corners will break and the rods bend.

A Shelf and Door

A simple shelf attached to the front of the furnace can be made by stacking brick or cinder block to the proper height, then banding or wiring firebrick in place. Or a frame can be welded directly to the corner angle irons; however, this makes rebuilding or changing the pot difficult.

The simplest type of door can be firebrick, stacked by using long-handled tongs. The system is not the most stable, but it has been used often with success. Other solutions are a hanging frame holding the brick in place or hinged doors of various types.

In this, as in many furnaces, the door opening acts as the exhaust so it is seldom closed completely. Since vapors from the furnace quickly coat the door, it should not be brought in contact with either the door frame or the furnace wall or they may bind together with a coat of glass.

The door you will build is made of two insulating bricks held together by pieces of angle iron clamped by a ½″ bolt. The nuts holding the bolt are welded on, and the metal handle is welded to the clamp. The welded-on upright piece serves to hold the door upright.

1. *Sections of ½″ pipe are welded to the front of the furnace angle irons to serve as a sturdy rest for the shelf support. The ⅜″ x 2″ solid rod on the shelf support fits into the pipe.*

4. *Here is a view of the furnace with angle irons, tie rods, and shelf in place.*

32 GLASSBLOWING

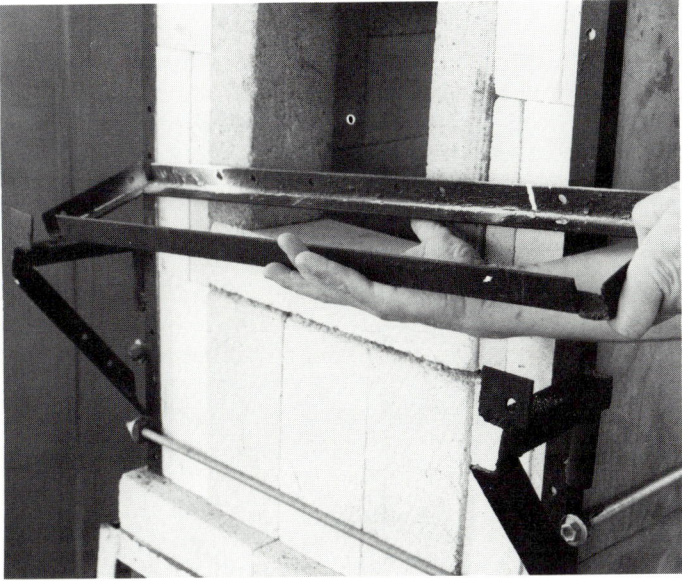

2. *The angle iron frame (about 24" x 5") is now put in place on the supports. The shelf frame and shelf supports are not attached to one another.*

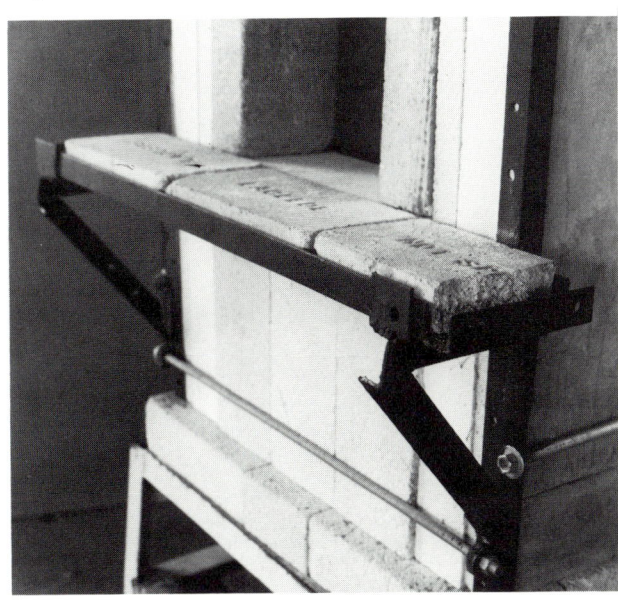

3. *Firebrick splits are cut to fit to complete the shelf at the front of the furnace.*

5. *A close-up of the furnace door shows how the two insulating firebrick straights are clamped together.*

6. *This type of door is lifted and set in place (always wear an asbestos glove). Make certain the metal upright always rests on the shelf or the door will fall. The door should not touch the door frame or wall.*

STUDIO FACILITIES 33

The Burner

There are many types of burners you can construct. Pipe burners made for ceramic kilns ("Madison Burners" for lack of a better name) require a kiln or chimney draft to suck the gas and air into the burner and into the kiln. Venturi burners are designed so the gas flow sucks air with it. Forced-air burners use the flow of air past the gas orifice to suck gas into the burner. Although the first two types of burners can be used on some glass equipment, they are not suitable for this furnace.

Your requirements are for a comparatively short, hot flame burning in a small enclosed space using low-pressure (household) natural gas. The forced-air burner is ideal for this situation. In general, you should avoid multi-burner air manifold systems. They are complicated, expensive to install, and lack versatility once they are in place.

The fewer the bends in the air (or mixed air/gas) pipes of the burner, the more efficient the burner. A straight pipe from blower to furnace is ideal, but not practical for this furnace. The extra 45° elbow in this burner cuts down on the air supply, but it acts as protection for the motor in case of power failure. I have had power failures for up to four hours with this burner and had no problems as long as the gas supply has remained on and burning.

Air Blower and Motor. A small, low-pressure air blower is recommended for this furnace. The motor should be of the inexpensive and replaceable type (it should not require more maintenance than a few drops of oil every couple of weeks). I have used small, economical motors non-stop for over six months (some were worn out much more quickly). Use a simple plug-in extension cord with the motor for maximum flexibility. Make sure *all* electrical appliances are grounded.

Orifice Size. With a forced-air burner the orifice size is not critical. If the orifice is too large, adjustment of the gas flow is difficult but not impossible. For this burner and this furnace (up to an altitude of 2000 feet above sea level) try an orifice of 13/64″. If the orifice is small you can simply drill it larger.

1. The plumbers pipe fittings used for the burner are, from the left: a 8″ x 1¼″ nipple, a 90° 1¼″ elbow, a 12″ x 1¼″ nipple, a 1¼″ to 1½″ bushing, a 1½″ T, a 1½″ short nipple, and half of a 1½″ union. Extending from the T is a ¾″ cap ground slightly and drilled with the orifice hole, and a ¾″ x 5″ continuous-threaded pipe passing through: a 1½″ short nipple, a 1½″ to ¾″ bell reducer, and half of a ¾″ union.

2. When the gas supply unit and mixing T are joined, the orifice must point in the direction of the gas/air flow, toward the furnace. This is critical in the burner design, so mark the location of the orifice in relation to the pipe by scratching on the threaded ¾″ pipe, bell reducer, and short nipple.

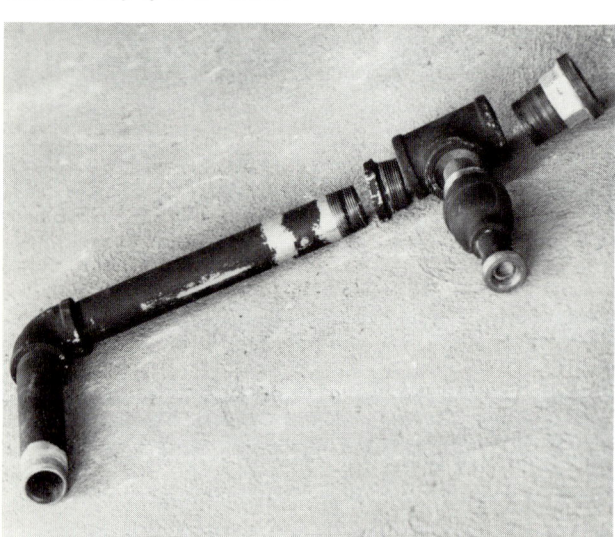

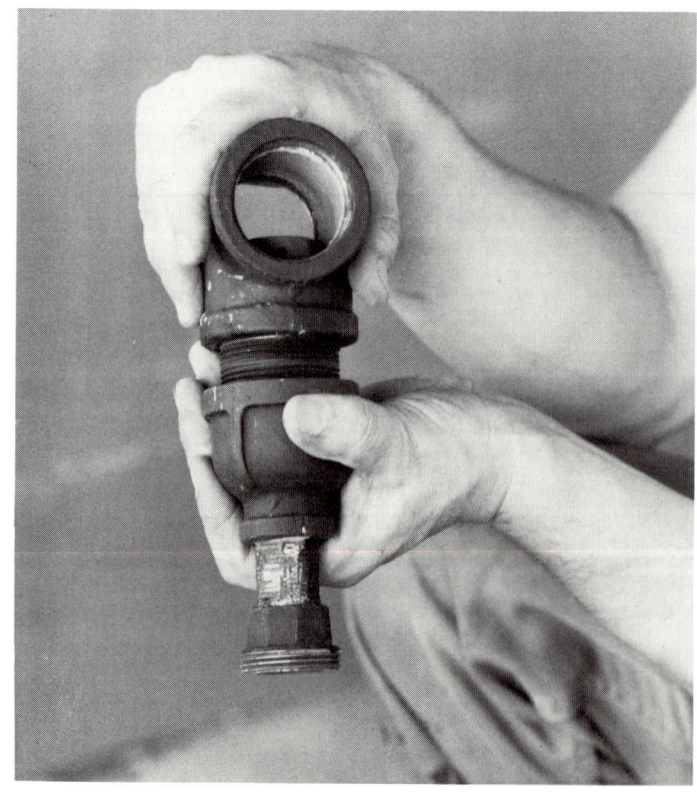

3. Slide two pieces of metal band (or plumbers tape) over the 12" nipple and drill holes in the band for 3/16" bolts. Another 3½" band is used to join the pipe bands. Assemble the burner, making sure the pipe connections are tight. Place two straights as shown and push the burner into the burner block about 1½".

4. The burner is in position on the straights. This brick support has been used by some craftsmen as a permanent mount, however, I feel a sturdier mount is safer.

The Burner Support

This burner support consists of two *electrical* ¾" couplings welded to the left-front and left-back angle irons, with two ¾" x 10" continuous-threaded pipes through the couplings. There is a ¾" T on top of each pipe; a 27" x ½" pipe goes through the T's and through the 3½" metal loop on the bottom of the burner.

1. Here both burner supports are in place. The following steps will show you details of the burner support assembly.

2. Adjust the threaded pipes and T's so the holes in the T's are about even with the bottom of the burner.

3. Put the ½" pipe through the T's and the metal strap on the burner. If necessary, adjust the T's up or down by turning the threaded pipe.

4. The burner should rest on the ½" pipe and the brick supports, and it should be level with the top of the furnace. Tighten the nuts and bolts and remove the bricks.

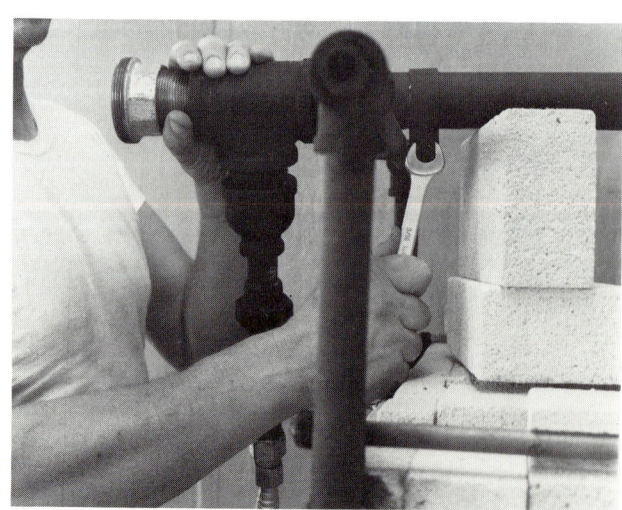

Insulating the Burner Block

The burner block is made of a refractory material that conducts heat and should be insulated. To do this you need four insulating straights and two pieces of insulated brick (5½″ x 4½″) with a 1¾″ hole cut or filed as shown. These are placed on the roof around the burner. These six pieces should not be permanently attached because you can cool a hot burner by manipulating them.

1. Insulating brick cut to fit around the burner are being put in position.

2. Here is a close-up of the burner and burner block insulation.

Completion of the Burner

To finish the burner attachment connect a flexible ¾″ gas utility hose to a ¾″ short nipple, a ¾″ gas cock, another ¾″ short nipple, and then to the remaining half of the ¾″ union. Use pipe compound on all iron-to-iron connections.

Bolt a 1½″ pipe flange to the blower flange. If the holes do not line up you will have to drill new holes in the blower flange. Screw a 1½″ short nipple into the flange, then a 45° elbow, another short nipple, and the other half of the 1½″ union. If the blower does not have an air control cover you should attach one as illustrated. This burner can be made without the ¾″ union on the gas line or the 1½″ union on the air, but I feel they make construction easier.

1. Carefully line up the two halves of the ¾″ union, and hand-tighten.

4. Tighten the union by hand. (It is not necessary to wrench-tighten the union.)

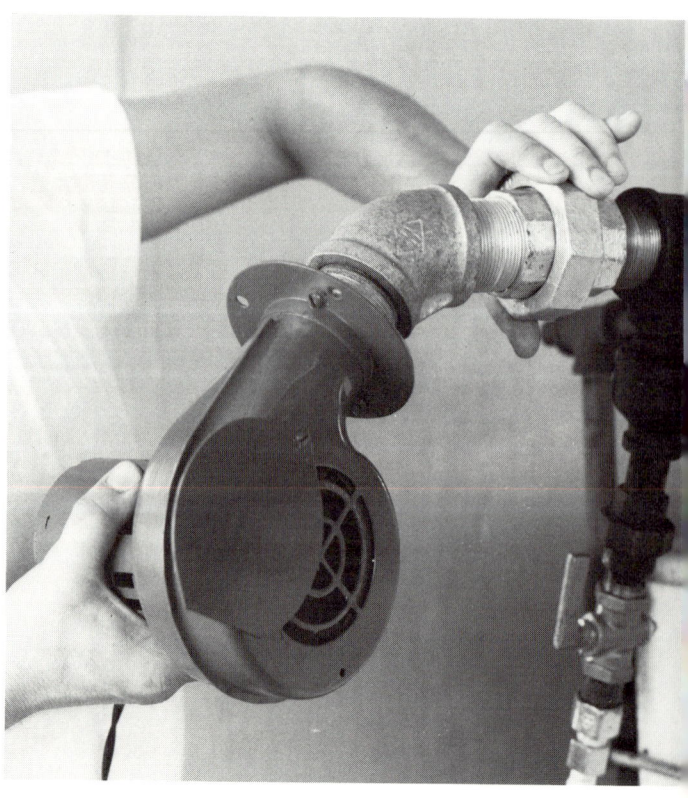

2. *Now use a pipe wrench and crescent to tighten the union without changing the direction of the orifice (this must remain pointing toward the furnace).*

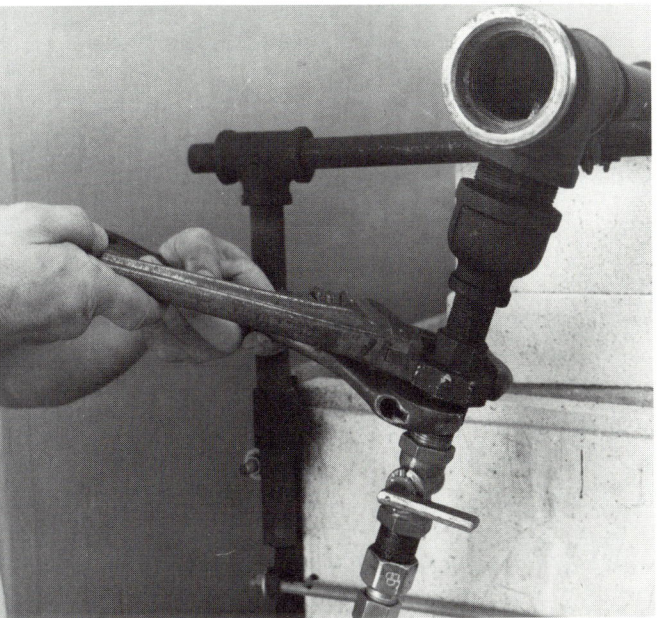

3. *Line up the blower assembly with the burner.*

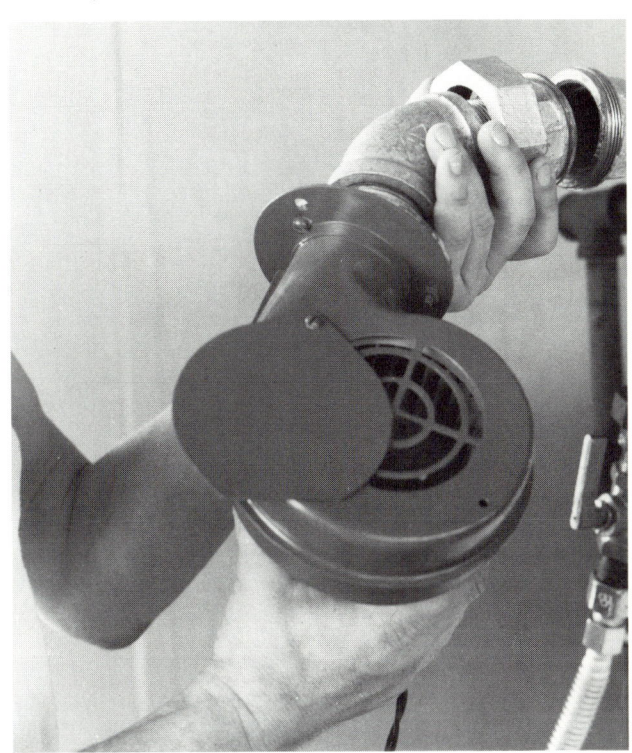

5. *To adjust the amount of air, loosen the screw, move the metal plate, and tighten the screw again.*

6. *This is a view of the completed burner, blower, and support.*

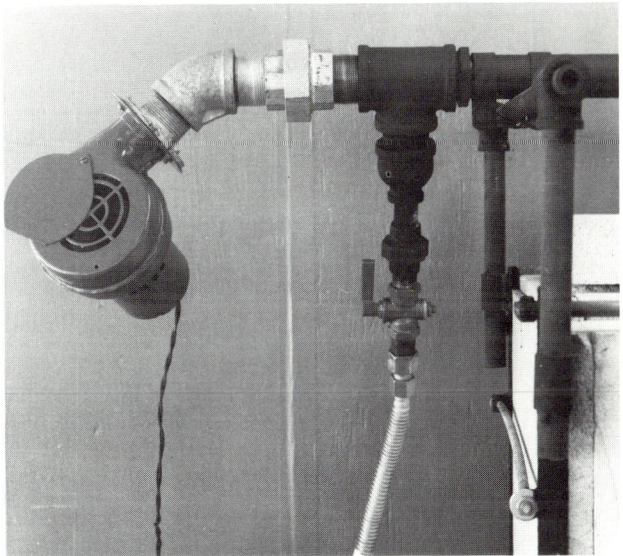

OTHER FURNACES

With a larger furnace the burner is more effective if it heats from the front or side and is mounted closer to the glass surface. In this furnace the roof is arched independently and supported by a metal frame and tie rods. The tank for the molten glass is about six times as large as that in the small furnace and is rectangular. This furnace is fired with high-pressure natural gas (5 pounds pressure). The walls are made in two layers—the inner is 2½″ of hard firebrick and the outer wall is 4½″ of insulating firebrick.

A larger furnace that I designed and built.

Lead Glass-Melting Furnace

I designed and built a furnace especially for melting glasses that contain high amounts of lead oxide and therefore could not be exposed to direct flame or combustion gases. It was a large furnace, and when melting lead glasses it contained two tanks. This furnace was also used for melting non-lead glasses, in which case it held three tanks. For those readers who do ceramic work, this furnace is related to the muffle-type kilns where, again, the flame does not strike the ware being fired.

The burner entry was from the left front and just above the glass level. The firebox circled the rim of the tank area and exhausted at the right front of the furnace. Below the firebox was a hard firebrick shelf. On the shelf over the tank was a clay cover, arched at the top, rectangular and open in the front, which effectively kept the flame from the glass surface. The walls were 4½″ of insulating firebrick, the roof a high barrel arch that radiated the heat through the clay tank cover to the center surface of the glass area. Using grog around the tanks enabled me to change the size and number of tanks without rebuilding the furnace.

A large lead glass-melting furnace that I designed and built.

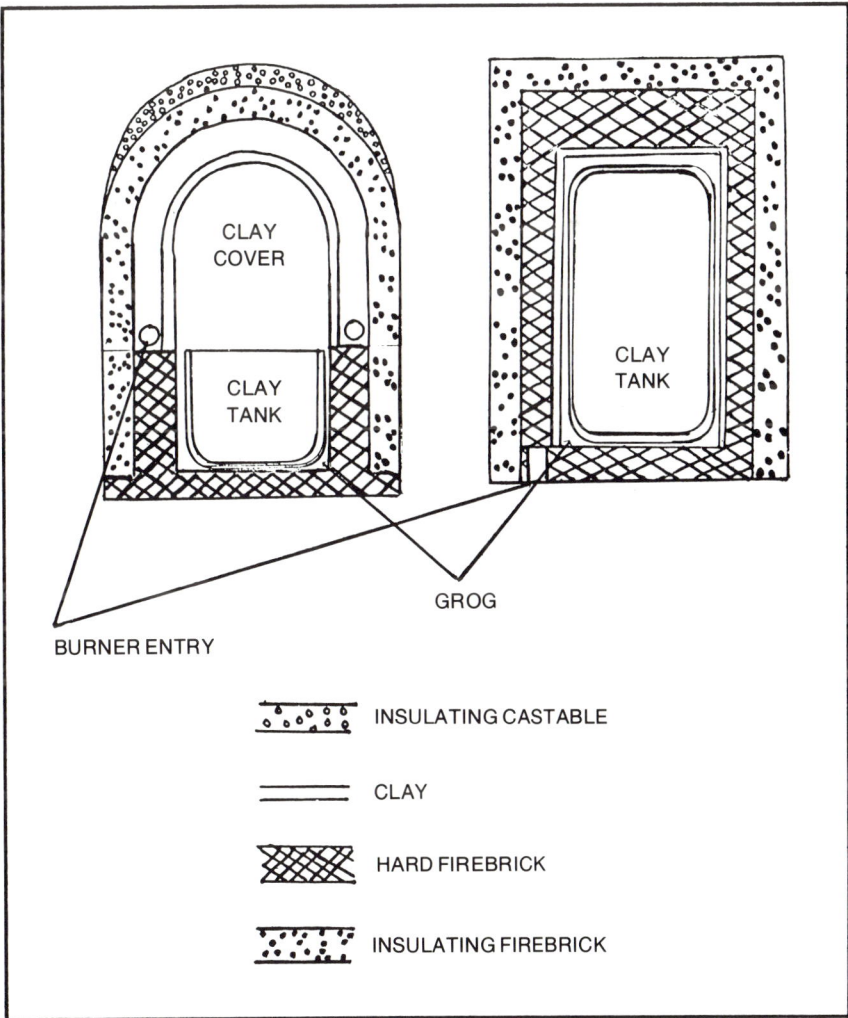

The plan for the furnace shown above.

STUDIO FACILITIES 41

CRUCIBLE FURNACES

Crucible furnaces vary in size (depending on working needs and intended use), but they are usually smaller than the furnaces previously described. They can be designed to hold one or more crucibles. The crucible material that comes in contact with the glass is usually heavily grogged clay. In many furnaces the crucibles are designed and placed so they can be easily and quickly removed. A leaky crucible can rapidly ruin a furnace. It is best to avoid a direct flame on the side or bottom of the crucible since this may cause thermal shock and crack the crucible wall. Start firing the crucible furnace with the same care you would take in firing pottery—the clay crucible undergoes the same expansion stresses as a piece of ceramics.

Here are some considerations for the design of the crucible furnace, when and if you feel the need for this type of furnace: (1) design to allow additions of glass and colorants to the crucibles while the furnace is being fired, (2) provide for a good view of the molten glass surface, (3) provide for visual inspection of sides and bottom of the crucibles (to check for cracks and leaks), and (4) cover the floor of the furnace with grog so it will not be ruined by leaking crucibles.

Types of Crucible Furnaces. I built a downdraft crucible furnace for colored glasses. The design is rather unique: two small burners enter high in the back wall and are positioned so the flame burns around the crucibles, exhausting at the floor level in the back wall. There is no flame aound the top of the crucible, and this makes gathering glass much safer. A clay cover is over the top of the crucible, and the bottom of the crucible rests on several inches of high-fired clay grog. Because no flame makes contact with the glass, special glasses (such as lead glasses) can be melted in this furnace. The furnace walls are 2½" hard firebrick (1¼" on the back wall) on the inside and 2½" insulating brick on the outside. Transite, angle iron, and tie rods bind the furnace together. The top of the furnace is made out of high-fire refractory/insulation castable. The small holes in the front of the furnace (they are also located in the sides) are for visual checking for crucible cracks or leaks.

A simple updraft crucible furnace like the one shown could also be built. The top is partially covered (when gathers are not being made) with firebrick splits since the exhaust is through the top opening of the furnace.

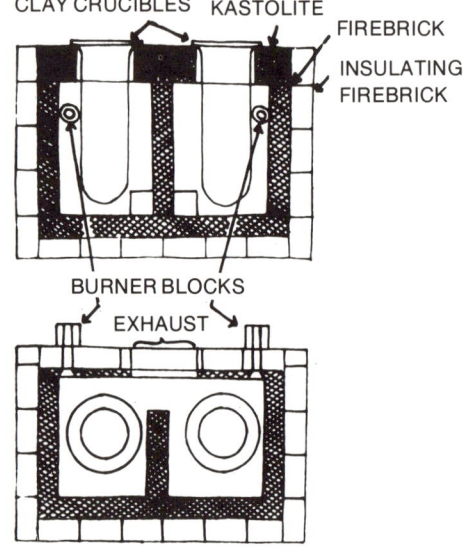

(Above) The plan for the furnace shown below.

(Left) A downdraft, double-burner crucible furnace, designed for special glass melts.

(Left) A small updraft crucible furnace I built for glass test melts.

(Below) These are clay crucibles made for the furnaces shown.

STUDIO FACILITIES 43

The "Glory-Hole"

Traditionally an auxiliary furnace, or glory-hole, is used for reheating the glass vessel during the working process. It may also be used to preheat pipes and pontils before they are used in gathering or forming. In one Mexican factory I saw a glory-hole used to clean ("pop-off") excess glass from pipes and pontils.

The term "glory hole" is usually used for this piece of equipment, although the term "dog house" is used in other countries. In the Mexican and Spanish factories the term obviously relates to the shape of the furnace.

The Value of a Glory-Hole. There is a difference of opinion concerning the value of a separate reheating furnace (glory-hole) in contemporary glass work. Some feel strongly that the glory-hole can be dispensed with by designing the furnace to serve both functions. Others maintain that the glory-hole is needed even if the furnace is designed to be used for reheating. Both have valid arguments.

I feel that initially you should use the furnace described in this chapter as your glory-hole. Later you may feel that a separate reheating unit would be a help. The major points against the glory-hole are the added cost and space required in the shop. Some arguments in favor of its use are: (1) a concentrated hot flame is available without affecting the temperature of your glass melt, (2) the prevention of accidentally dropping multicolored vessels into the clear or light-colored glass, (3) placement of the furnace burner closer to the surface of the glass for more efficient heating, (4) larger vessel production if the glory-hole is designed with a larger door, (5) more people using a furnace at the same time, (6) properly placed glory-holes cut down on the cross traffic—thus adding an important safety feature to the shop, (7) the glory-hole does not stay on continuously, but is lit only when work is done (the melting furnace stays on continuously in most situations).

Types of Glory-Holes. I have seen a variety of shapes and designs for glory-holes in my travels in Japan, Europe, Mexico, and the United States. These included a large, square, four-holed, bottom-fired design at the Toledo Museum shop; a refractory-lined drum stood on end with a hole in its side at a factory in Colorado; a single-opening square design fired from the top at a factory in Mexico; a "dog house" shaped furnace, opened at each end, bottom-fired, at other Mexican factories; metal drums turned on

their sides fired from the top, sides, bottoms, insulated and not insulated, opened at one end or both; and a simple open-flame burner with no container used for reheating at the bench. In most of these situations the craftsmen were fairly well convinced that theirs was *the* way.

My Glory-Hole. My glory-hole is a drum lined with 4½″ insulating firebrick and 1″ refractory/insulating castable. It uses two burners fired from the back-bottom and front-side. The flame from the back burner circles the drum interior until exhausting from the front. The front burner enters at a 90° angle from the left side of the furnace near the door and is controlled by an on/off foot switch. The back burner heats the castable so the entire surface acts as a radiating heat reflector. The front burner is turned on when intense local heating of a part of a vessel is desired. The front burner can be quickly adjusted to produce strong reducing flames for special effects (lusters on the glass surface, irridescent effects, etc.). The burner placement reduces excessive heating of the burners (as is likely with burners mounted in the top of the glory-hole) and prolongs burner life. The burners can be used jointly or separately, and the door is hinged to provide either a 9″ or 17″ round opening. The glory hole, as a general rule, is used mostly for special effects, and although it is invaluable for these uses, I feel that you can start without one by using your top-fired furnace as an effective substitute. When you feel the need for something better, the information provided above should help you in your design.

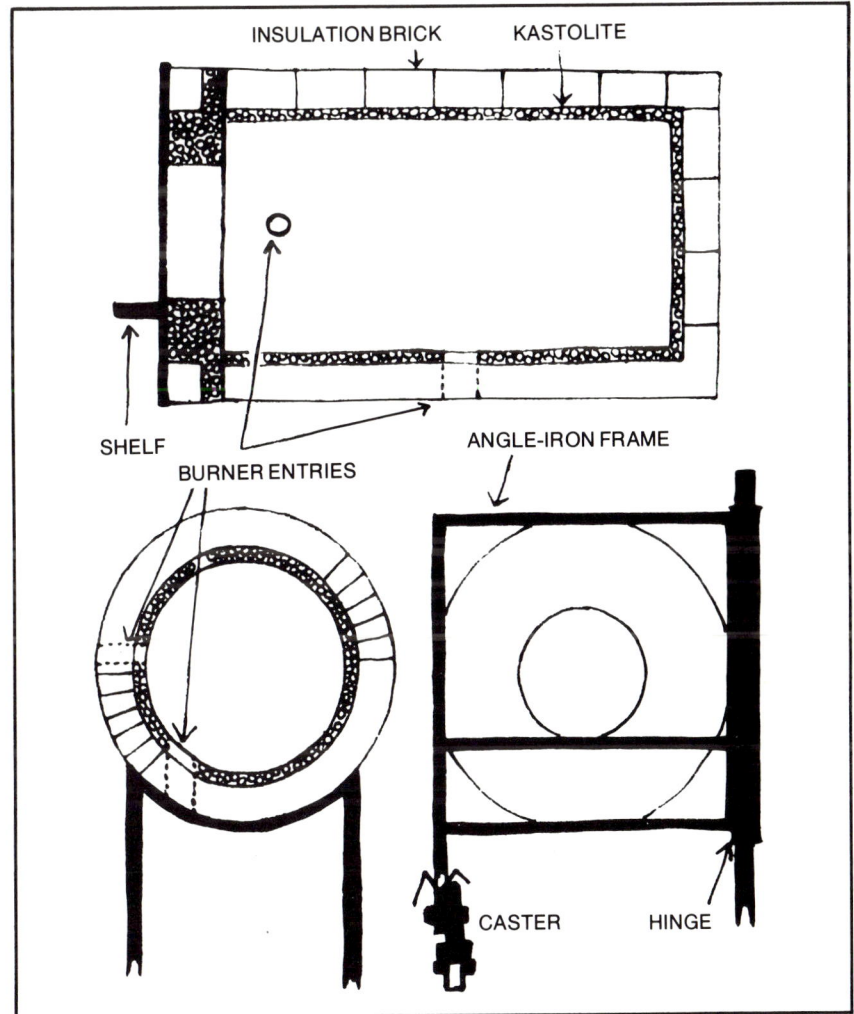

(Far Left) Here is a view of my glory-hole. The front section is hinged to the right so it can be opened to a 17″ circle for larger objects. The opening shown is 9″.

(Left) A diagram of my glory-hole.

Annealing

Glass is annealed to relieve the strains that occur during normal working procedures—such as heating and cooling various parts of the vessel, gathering molten glass over cooler glass, cold, wet tools chilling the outer surface of the glass, etc. The glass is held at the annealing temperature for a length of time that is related to its size and thickness, then brought slowly through the annealing range to prevent formation of new strains, and finally brought down to room temperature. Without proper annealing the glass may crack—in the annealing oven, soon after removal from the oven, or after a period of months—depending on the degree of strain in the glass and its subsequent handling.

Needless to say, putting the glass in a sunny window in an air conditioned room is a rigid test of the success of your annealing. Keep in mind that this is likely to be the kind of handling at least some of your glass will get.

Annealing Temperature. Annealing temperature will vary depending on the type of glass (in general, about 50°F. below the deforming point) and on the design of the vessel. Thicker, larger, or uneven-walled pieces need longer annealing than thin, even-walled pieces that may even need no annealing at all. Pieces held at the upper limits of the annealing range need less annealing time than those annealed at the lower limits. All of this suggests a working procedure (see Chapter 3 for instructions on using your oven). Since heavy, large, thick-walled, or unevenly blown ware (or solid glass, such as paperweights and doorstops) require longer annealing periods, these pieces should be blown early in the work day so they have a longer period in the annealing range. Work toward smaller, thinner, evenly blown pieces as the work period progresses.

Annealing Methods. There are a number of annealing methods with historical precedents. One method uses the furnace for heating vermiculite or asbestos fiber to pack around ware in a fireproof container. Another

A simple, top-loading, electric annealing oven that I have used with two electrical heating coils.

method uses buckets or cans of burnt lime in which the hot ware is buried. Buckets or cans can also be heated by a secondary heat source (the ware is then stacked inside without insulating materials). You can also make use of the exhaust heat of the furnace by placing the ware on top of the furnace, either out in the open or in fireproof containers. From discussions with other craftsmen, these processes can be classified as faulty.

Types of Annealing Ovens. Although there are a number of fuels available for use in an annealing oven, you will probably have a choice between gas and electricity. Both have advantages and problems. Electricity offers great control over temperature and time relationships, gives a constant atmosphere that does not affect the glass surface, and lacks turbulence and air currents that can strain the ware. Electricity is expensive and good controls (Variacs and other types of variable transformers) are delicate and expensive. With gas much of the above is reversed; gas is more economical and controls are somewhat cheaper, however many designs for gas annealing allow for possible changes in the oxidizing/reduction atmosphere that may affect the glass surface, and the gas flame can cause turbulence in the oven.

You also have a choice between a top loader and a front loader. The oven I suggest you build is a front loading, gas-fired design. The basic shape and design of this oven could also be used for electricity, in which case the burner entry and exhaust holes would not be needed, and a solid, flat roof made of 3″ thick insulating block could be used. Electric ovens should have electric supply lines separate from other equipment lines to prevent damage to appliance motors. It is best to have each element on a separate circuit breaker. Electricity is either on or off unless some type of variable transformer is used (this expensive piece of equipment acts to the electrical current in the same way that a gas valve works in controlling the gas supply).

My front-loading electric oven is made with special blanket insulation and a variac heat control device. It uses only one heating element and goes to 1000° F. in less than 15 minutes.

Building a Gas Annealing Oven.

Since you already have a gas supply for your furnace (and for some of the reasons discussed earlier) I suggest you use a gas oven. The step-by-step photographs should help make construction of the oven clear. This oven can be built on a rolling metal stand, however you will find it easier and more economical to build on a base of cement blocks.

1. One of the simplest ways to build the base for the oven is to arrange 15 ordinary concrete blocks as shown.

2. If you want the oven to be portable, you can weld together a steel frame and then add wheels.

3. Arrange firebrick straights so there is air circulating underneath. This will protect the concrete from the heat. Then put a piece of transite, at least ¼″ thick, on top of the brick or frame (brick is not needed if you used a metal frame).

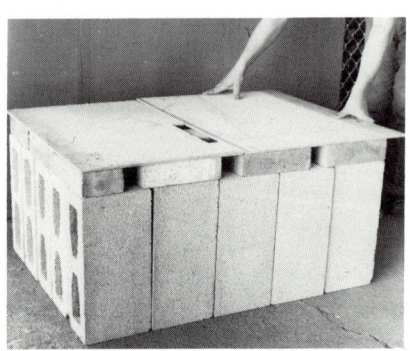

4. Arrange a layer of insulating firebrick on the transite. Note the placement of three insulating brick soaps (you should cut these) and the space left for a tie rod in the middle of the oven floor.

5. Arrange another layer of insulating brick on top of the first layer. The outer row of bricks and the brick near the burner entry are 2300 F. The remaining bricks are 2000° F. It is somewhat simpler, however, to use all 2300 F. insulating brick.

6. Another view (from the front) shows the design of the burner entry and firebox. The marked bricks will receive the open flame and should be at least 2300 F. insulating brick. Note that the brick directly in front of the burner has been shaped with a file for better flame dispersal.

THE OVEN WALLS

The walls of the oven are built mainly out of insulating brick straights. The photographs show the steps in building the walls, allowing for overlapping corners where possible, and suggest placement of the door opening, burner ports, and exhaust vents at the rear top of the oven.

1. Here I am beginning to build the walls out of insulating brick straights.

2. The first row of bricks completely circles the oven (12 straights) since the door opening does not start until the second row.

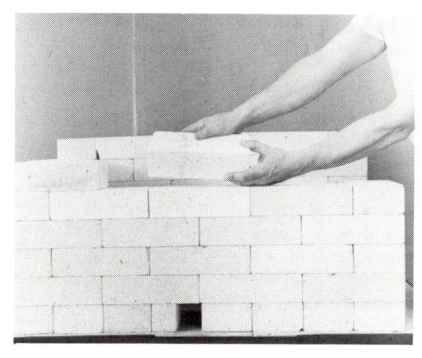

3. A side view of the oven showing the fourth row of bricks being added. Note the overlap of the bricks at each corner.

4. A detail of the front of the oven showing how the door is made. The design of the door requires a half brick (which you must cut) every second row.

5. The right wall of the oven. Again every second row requires cutting a half brick to complete the door opening. Note the half brick exhaust vent in the back of the furnace on the fifth row.

6. This is a detail of the burner entry and "firebox" from inside the oven. The bricks in the floor and wall marked with the "X" must be at least 2300° F. insulating brick.

STUDIO FACILITIES 49

BINDING THE WALLS TOGETHER

Angle irons and tie rods are used in each corner of the oven and in the middle of the side walls to bind the furnace together, and to support the arched roof. Transite, at least ¼" thick, or metal sheets are used in the back and sides of the oven. Although this method of arch support is unusual, I have found that for low heat application it is simple and satisfactory.

1. To bind the oven, prop up the angle irons and insert top tie rods. The nuts are then hand-tightened on the sides and back of the oven.

2. The bottom tie rods are also loosely put in place, first in the front of the furnace, then in the back.

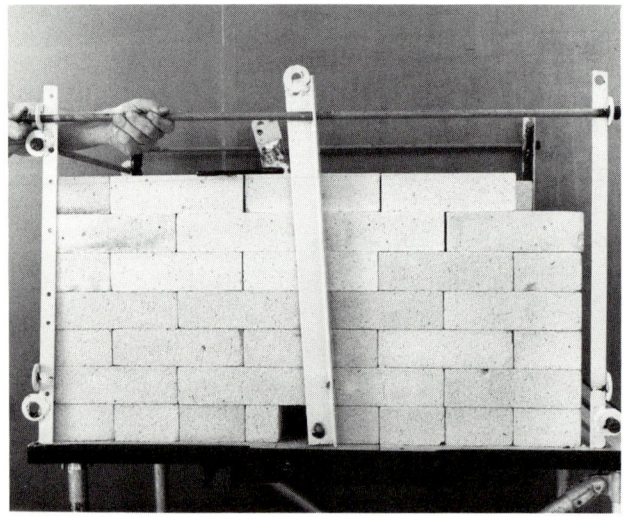
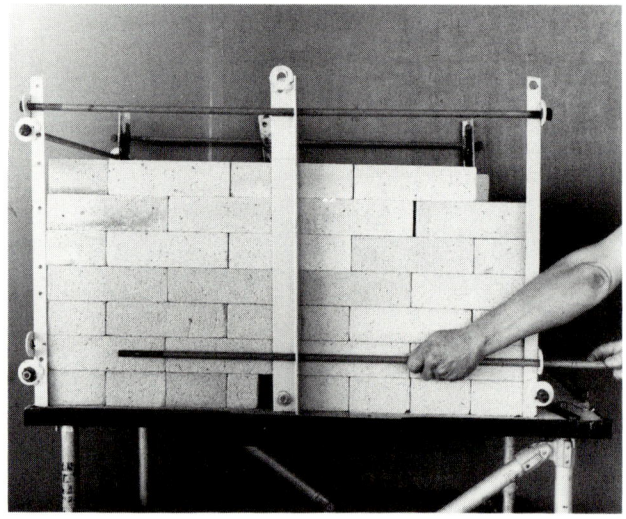

3. Transite is slid into place in the back and sides of the oven (note the exhaust hole in the back piece). The transite on the sides of the oven will act as the outer support for the roof arch.

4. Add rows six and seven to the back wall. Three straights have been placed on each side wall (on their sides as shown) as back-up for the insulating brick feather-edge you will cut for the arch support.

The Roof Arch

The roof of this oven is a sprung arch. Although 2000°F. block insulation can be used for roofing an electric oven, 2300°F. 4½" thick arched insulating brick holds up better in a gas-fired oven. I feel it is worth your while to take the extra effort to cut the wooden arch form and spring the arch. For most of the arch you will use No. 1 arch brick—a standard brick, 9" x 4½" x (2½"–2⅛"). Because of the number needed it is easier to buy them than cut to fit. The key bricks are standard No. 2 arch brick, 9" x 4½" x (2½"–1¾"). These you can easily cut (or file or grind) yourself.

1. A wooden arch form has been cut to fit and is being positioned on the brick and wooden supports. The top of the arch should be flush with the top edge of the feather edge and side straights.

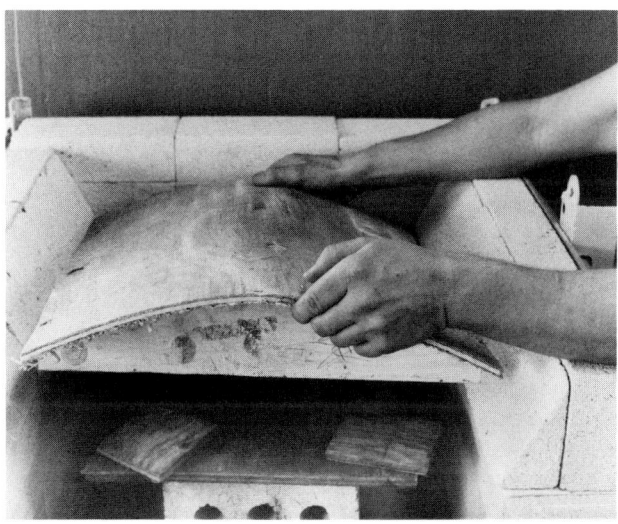

2. No. 1 arch insulating bricks are put in position on top of the arch form.

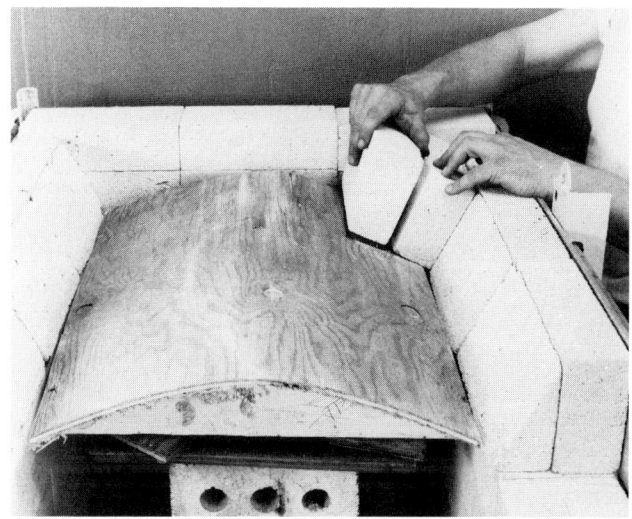

3. Four arch insulating brick are put on each side of the center line for each row of the arch.

4. Cut two insulating brick straights and a half straight to form the key bricks in the arch. The second exhaust hole is left in the top of the roof 4½" from the back of the arch.

COMPLETING THE FRONT AND REMOVING THE ARCH FORM

The front of the furnace was built for fitting purposes before tightening the tie rods. After fitting, enough of the oven front is removed to allow the arch form to be taken out (the middle and back tie rods will hold the arch up temporarily). This arch form can be used for other pieces of equipment, so do not burn out or otherwise destroy the form.

1. Complete the left side of the door with an insulating straight and a piece of cut insulating brick.

2. Complete the front with (starting from the left) a cut insulating brick 2½" x 4½" x 1", an insulating brick straight, a 2½" x 4½" x 13½" square-edge (hard firebrick) tile, and a cut insulating brick 2½" x 4½" x 3½". Finish the seventh row with three insulating brick straights.

3. Put the top front tie rod in place (a door latch has been added to the rod). Now tighten (with a wrench) all the nuts on all the tie rods until all the iron angles and the transite pieces are firm against the furnace walls and the arch-support brick.

4. Leaving the rest of the tie rods tight, remove the front top rod. Next remove the furnace front. Remove the supports from under the arch form, then pull the arch form down and out of the front of the oven. Replace the front of the furnace, tie rod (be certain the door latch has been put over the rod), and retighten the rod.

Making a Door

This oven will use a simple hinged door, with insulating brick fitted in an angle iron frame and 1″ pipe acting as a hinge in 1½″ pipe. This door is easily opened and closed, and because of its overlap on the oven front it makes an effective heat barrier.

1. First a 1¼″ x 1¼″ angle iron, a 1″ metal "strap," and five pieces of 1¼″ x 1¼″ x about 2″ angle are welded together to form the door frame. Then 1″ pipe about 2″ long is welded on as shown.

2. Insulating brick straights are slotted to fit into the angle iron and metal strap (as shown), leaving enough space for a piece of ¼″ transite between the insulating brick and the angle iron supports.

3. More slotted insulating bricks are fitted snugly in place. This is a view of the inside of the door. Note the "peep-hole" in the second brick.

4. The last row of slotted insulating brick is pushed in place. The inside of the door is facing upward in this photograph.

5. A piece of transite fits into the space between the brick and angle irons on the outside of the door.

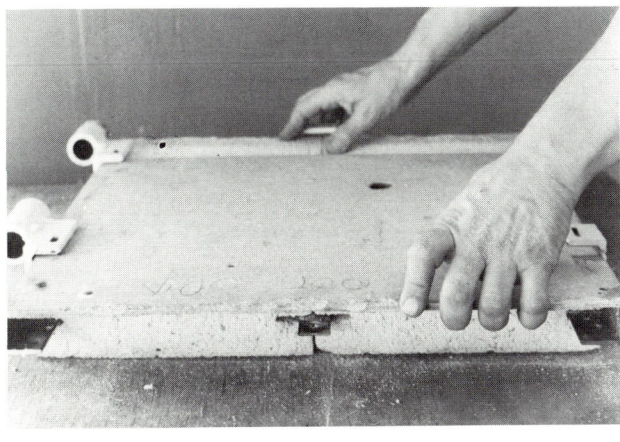

6. A piece of 1¼″ x 1¼″ angle iron is bolted on at each side and in the center to support the top of the door. Note that this top iron should be "snug" against the insulating brick.

STUDIO FACILITIES 53

Attaching the Door

It is important for the door to fit tightly against the door frame, or even fit into the frame slightly. This will prevent cooling drafts from entering the oven and causing thermal strains in your ware. The photographs show one method of hanging the door. You could also hang the door from rollers and slide it open and closed. Although I have put a "homemade" heavy-duty hinge on the door in the first building stages, you may wish—on this first oven—to fit the door in place and then weld the hinge parts in the proper location.

1. A welded door support frame (with 1½" pipe welded in place to act as hinge) is positioned on the top tie rod on the right side of the oven and then bolted in place.

3. If you built the oven on cement blocks you can position the frame support this way. The two cement blocks holding the angle iron are filled with concrete after the door has been fitted in place.

2. If the oven has been built on a metal stand, the middle and bottom of the door support are bolted to the metal stand.

4. The door hinge (1″ pipe) fits into the support frame pipe hinge 1½″ pipe).

5. This is a close-up of the section of pipe and hook on the top tie rod that acts as the door lock.

Building the Burner

A burner similar to that used for the furnace can be used for the oven. You have no need for concentrated heat in the oven, therefore the blower and motor can be left off. The orifice can be much smaller (7/16th or less). To make heat control more effective I suggest two modifications in the burner design. Since smaller amounts of gas are used in this oven, regulation of the gas becomes more critical. A needle-valve gas cock with at least 6 full turns from open to close is therefore much better than the standard gas cock with only ¼ turn from closed to open. Although more expensive, this valve is a requirement for easy, effective use of the oven. This burner is not forced air (no blower or motor), so I advise you to use a 1½″ "cross" rather than a 1½″ T pipe fitting. Because this nearly doubles the air opening, it will increase the amount of air coming into the burner. Both the air intakes should be fitted so they can be closed off when the oven is sealed.

A photograph of this burner is shown on page 83. Basically, gas enters through the needle valve, the ½″ gas pipe, and the reducing bushings (welded or braised to the ½″ pipe) to the orifice cap and orifice through the left of the 1½″ "cross" pipe fitting. The orifice must point upward toward the oven burner entry. The air entry at the bottom of the "cross" can be closed with a 1½″ plug when the burner is not being fired. The same holds true for the air opening to the right of the "cross." The top of the "cross" has a 1½″ x 2″ nipple, a 1½″ to 1¼″ reducing 90° elbow, and a 1¼″ by 6″ nipple fitted just to the front edge of the burner port of the oven. Instead of welding the gas pipe to the bushing, you can use a continously threaded ½″ pipe, a bell reducer, a short 1½″ nipple, a 1½″ to 1¼″ bushing, and a standard 90° 1¼″ elbow, etc. (as with the furnace burner). This is all a matter of choice or availability; changes in the burner, except for the needle valve and "cross" fitting, rarely change the burner performance.

A Hanger and A Heating Oven

When working glass it is sometimes helpful to put aside the vessel on the pontil or pipe for a few minutes while doing some job that requires both hands (or is easier to do with both hands), such as opening a furnace door, adjusting a burner, preparing a pontil, or blowing a second vessel for a multiple piece. In most instances a couple of nails driven into a convenient post or beam will do. I often use an adjustable test-tube holder and attached metal angle support for such activities.

To keep the vessel from cooling too quickly while hanging in this holder it is helpful to have a box made of some insulating or refractory material to keep air from circulating over the pipe head and vessel. I have found that a secondary heating oven placed below the holder is a help, particularly when doing multiple-section objects. The burner and insulating brick walls on three sides help keep the vessel hanging in the oven hot for longer periods of time. This gives me a chance to concentrate on producing another section or performing other activities that require extra time. The front door opening of the oven has hard firebrick (straights and soaps) around the door, and all soft insulating brick that might be hit by the pipe or pontil is protected by metal strap or angle. The pipe or pontil fits into the metal slot in the front of the roof section.

(Left) A pontil or pipe holder that is useful for hanging a vessel so you can free both your hands. It was made from a test-tube holder fastened to a shelf support.

(Above) A small heating oven used in conjunction with the pipe holder. A small burner and the insulation brick walls and roof help keep the vessel on the pipe hot while the artist works on other tasks.

2/Tools

Family Group by Frank Kulasiewicz. Freeblown opaque and opal glasses, 12" x 12". A small group of related shapes made of white, grey, and purple phosphate glasses. The forms are all modifications of large blown bubbles with a smaller bubble on top. One has been flattened and the "neck" elongated, another has been flattened and a hole punched in the center (with the tool used to form hollow handles), etc. These are mounted in an epoxy base.

There are many types of tools available commercially, however the unique needs of the individual craftsman often demand that he design and produce his own, or use older tool designs in a new way. In this chapter I will cover two types of tools: those tools (or pieces of equipment) that are needed for using the ovens and furnaces described in the previous chapter, and tools that are used in forming molten glass.

Hoods and Venting Fans

Gasses and heat are continually exhausted from the door of the furnace, therefore, a hood placed above the furnace provides both safety and comfort. Hoods are usually made of lightweight sheet metal. They are generally at least 2 feet high, are tapered toward the exhaust pipe, and are fitted to extend at least a foot beyond the furnace perimeter. The furnace can extend almost up into the hood. If the exhaust system works with an electric motor and fan, these should be located at a distance from the furnace (or be of a special sealed, heat-insulated design). A system that makes use of natural draft and is not dependent on electrical power is far more desirable.

The metal vent hood used over the furnace at the University of Wisconsin in Madison. This system works with an electric exhaust fan.

TOOLS 59

Loading and Cleaning Tools

A long-handled shovel is used to load glass into the furnace. Because of the heat in the furnace, the thin metal in commercial shovels does not last long. I therefore made one out of a piece of heavy pipe cut and shaped with a heavy square rod for the handle. Smaller loading tools, such as the spoon-shaped shovel, can be made for loading into crucible furnaces.

Cleaning tools consist of a scraper and shovel with working heads made of heavy steel. Their dimensions should relate to the size of the furnace. Although other craftsmen find a shovel successful for cleaning out the furnace, I have not found it satisfactory. The scraper is excellent for cleaning the excess glass off the furnace surface, however I prefer a large, heavy-duty gathering iron for actually removing the molten glass. It must be noted that for an accurate test of glasses it is almost essential that a new, clean refractory liner be used in the furnace because there is often a fairly large amount of glass left in a furnace even after careful cleaning.

Metal Stands

Metal stands of various types are needed for working at the furnace. A metal fulcrum at the front of the furnace is essential for supporting pipes, pontils, and gathering irons being preheated for use. A 6" to 10" wide metal stand is used in conjunction with the fulcrum attached to the furnace. The stand, and the tools it supports, should be placed to the side of the furnace so it is out of the way of the craftsman.

A metal yoke, either with rollers or a Y-shaped piece of heavy metal, can be used for other forming operations away from the furnace. I made these mostly of scrap metal, and one uses an old automobile wheel as a very effective and stable base.

From the left: a cleaning shovel and a scraper for cleaning the furnace tank, a small spoon-shaped loading tool for putting glass into hot crucibles, and a large shovel used to load the main furnace.

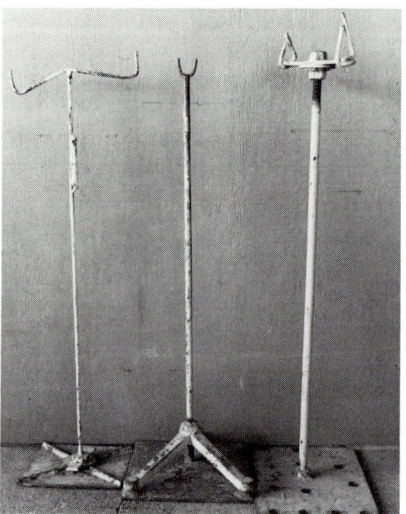

Some of the metal stands I have made that are used to support pipes being preheated at the furnace.

On the left is a set of tongs for moving a crucible in and out of the hot furnace. The set of tongs on the right are standard fireplace or barbecue tongs that serve a variety of uses in the glass shop.

Tongs

Long-handled tongs made to fit can be used to remove and change crucibles. I made a set out of heavy pipe and steel bar stock. The size of the jaws relates to common crucible sizes that I use. The other set of tongs illustrated are sold for fireplace use and serve a similar "all purpose" function in the glass studio (moving hot bricks, opening furnaces, uncovering crucibles, etc.). Several sets are good to have around the shop at all times.

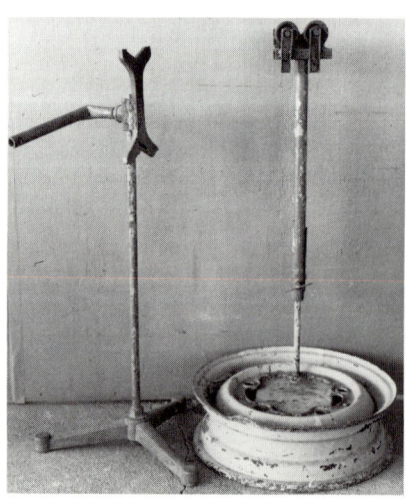

These metal yokes for forming operations were made mostly of scrap metal.

Reflecting Shields

Much of the heat generated by the furnace interior is radiant heat, and reflectors can cut down the amount of heat that you have to contend with when working. The photograph shows how I used a set of reflectors to throw the heat back at the furnace. I painted pieces of transite with silver paint, then attached them with rollers to a metal pipe rail set two feet or so from the furnace. The screens roll out of the way easily, so they can be manipulated without inconvenience during the work cycle. Lightweight galvanized sheet metal is also an effective heat shield, as are lightweight screens made of insulating materials (blanket or block).

Annealing Oven Tools

If your oven is small enough (or your arms are long enough), asbestos mittens are probably the best way to place ware into the oven. When using gloves or mittens it is important to protect your arm by wearing cotton sleeves of dense weave and not synthetic fabrics. Exposure of many synthetic materials to heat melts the plastic, which then sticks to the flesh and causes serious burns.

If the oven is too deep for safe, fast placement by hand, use a set of can holders (the type used in grocery stores for cans on high shelves). Remove the rubber from the jaws and replace it with asbestos cloth (old, worn asbestos gloves work well). This holder gives firm, safe control of the ware being put in the oven. If you cannot get a set of these use a wooden paddle with long handle and a "push stick," but realize that it takes some practice to learn to handle the latter.

Polariscope. A simple polariscope is effective for checking ware for annealing strains after removal from the oven.

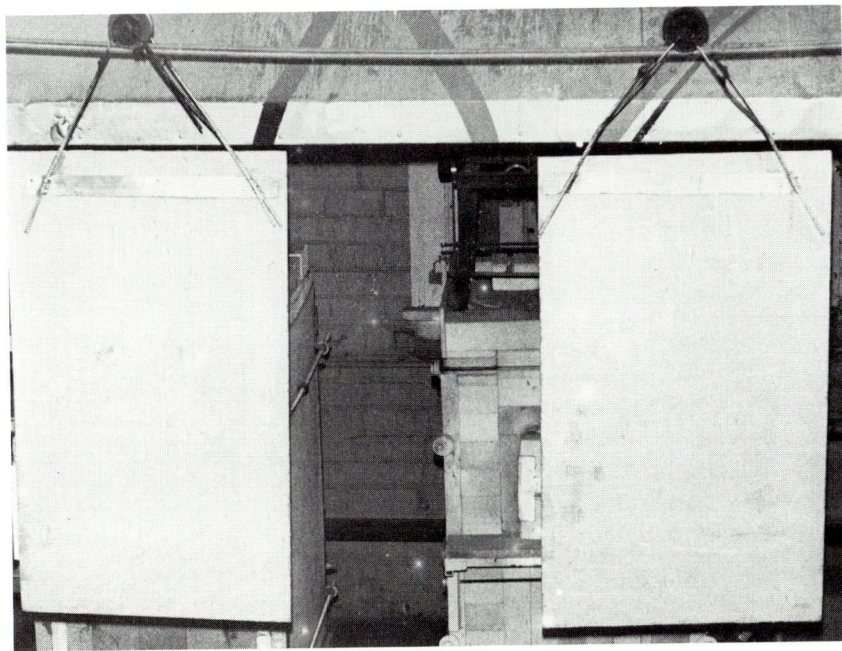

This illustrates one way of mounting reflectors on a pipe so they can be easily moved out of the way on rollers.

Mittens and Gloves

Protective asbestos gloves are essential around the shop. Although it is impractical to wear gloves while actually working the glass, they are necessary for moving any hot metal (handles on doors, etc.) and when handling hot vessels (placing ware in ovens, etc.). These gloves should be the type that are lined with insulating material. They wear out rather fast in most situations, so several pairs should be around the shop at all times. Ordinary cotton work gloves can be used on the left hand when gathering from the furnace as protection from radiant heat.

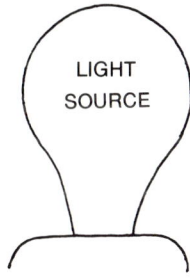

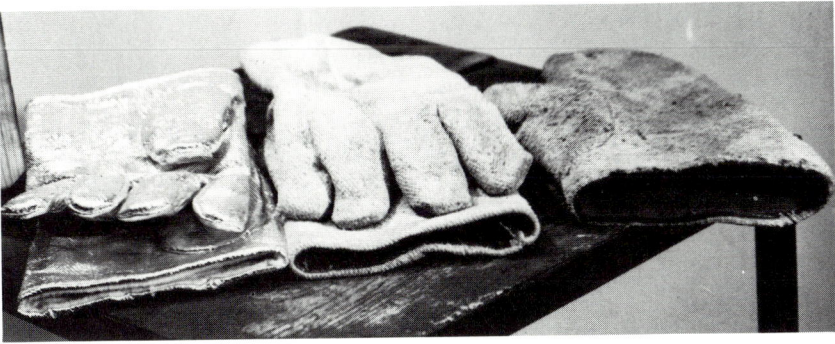

From the left: a pair of asbestos gloves with a special heat reflecting outer surface, a pair of insulated asbestos gloves, and a pair of insulated asbestos mittens.

A simple method of seeing strains in glass is to use two pieces of polarizing glass. A light source is placed below a piece of white paper (or some type of diffusing glass sheet). Above this is mounted one lens. The ware is held above the polarizing lens and the second lens is held above the ware. The top lens is rotated until the strains in the glass, which appear as Newton rings ("rainbow"), are visible.

TOOLS 61

Forming Tools

"Forming tools," as applied to tools used in freeblown glass, include blocks, jacks, blowing irons, gathering irons, and pontils—even the glassblower's bench. All these tools play a role in "forming" the hot glass. I will present the tools in the ordinary order of use. In practice, a tool may be used repeatedly (as with the glassblower's bench), in a different sequence (gathering irons) or not at all (as with shears or "specialty" tools).

I will try to show some of the possibilities in the number and kinds of tools that can be developed for glassblowing. A complete listing, however, is impossible, since artists in glass are constantly inventing, improving, and finding new ways to use their tools.

Metal Tools. The various metal tools that are brought into contact with the vessel being formed tend to mark the glass surface. Although this marking may be a part of a desired design effect, in most instances it should be avoided. Some of the methods used to accomplish this are: using wax on the hot tool, avoiding excessive pressure against the hot glass, frequent reheating of the vessel, and rotating the vessel as contact is made with the tool.

Wood Tools. The artist can produce simple, inexpensive wooden forming tools for his specific creative needs. Traditionally, wooden tools are cut from close-grained fruitwood trees (cherry, pear, etc.) during the time of year when the wood contains the most moisture. The cut sections are kept in water until made into the tool. Some tools (such as forming blocks) are then "burned-in" by rolling very hot, molten glass against the interior surface until it is coated with charcoal. The tool is then kept in water for the remainder of its useful life—except when actually in use. Longer tool life is one advantage of hardwood tools, but softer, less close-grained woods can also be used.

Only the blocking tool needs to be used soaking wet. In theory the wood does not make contact with the hot glass. Instead the hot glass produces a layer of steam on contact with the water in the tool and the glass moves against this steam blanket. Water chills the glass, reduces the working time between reheatings, and creates stresses in the glass. Although this is the purpose for using water in early gathering operations, continued use of large amounts of water in late forming when glass is cooler and thinner is not desirable. The tool should be only wet enough to prevent rapid burning of the wood.

Blow Pipe

This is the essential tool in offhand glassblowing. At its simplest it is a metal pipe about 4 to 5 feet long. The length of the pipe depends on the physical characteristics of the artist, the kind of furnace, and the type of ware being produced. The end of the pipe ("head") that makes contact with the molten glass should be stainless steel to reduce both contamination of the glass and corrosion of the pipe.

Blow pipes are usually made of two pieces of metal—the pipe itself (ordinary or heavy wall plumbing pipe) and the stainless steel head. The shaft of the pipe extends *tightly* into the head about 1", and the two pieces are welded together so they are airtight. I have also done some three-piece pipes, but I doubt if the extra weld and machine work offer any advantage (in theory the extra piece of metal between the head and shaft acts as a heat barrier). You could also make two-piece, all stainless steel pipes (these do away with the problem of loose, hot fire scale inside the pipe).

The mouthpieces on these pipes have been closed down somewhat and machine-tooled to shape. This extra work is not really required—all that is needed is a mouthpiece that is smooth and has no sharp edges to cut the lips of the blowers.

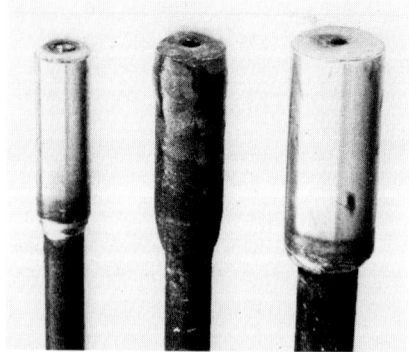

(Above) This is a close-up of the stainless steel "heads" of some of the blow pipes I have made.

(Right) Blow pipes made of common black pipe with stainless steel heads. The pipe to the far right is made of three pieces—a stainless steel head, a heavy-walled piece of iron tubing, and a section of ¾" black iron pipe.

Stainless Steel Tubing

Although somewhat more expensive, seamless stainless steel tubing with heavy walls is a way to avoid the trouble of producing your own pipes. They are as good as most commercial pipes available. The tubing comes in a variety of sizes and I have used tubing varying from 3/8" to 3/4" in diameter. A large opening makes blowing the first bubble easier for the beginner, but is a hindrance in producing a symmetrical vessel.

(Above) A close-up of the heads of the stainless steel tubing showing glass that has stuck to the tube after cooling and the large hole in these pipes.

(Left) It is also possible to use stainless steel tubing for blow pipes. Since these are all one piece, the heads are the same size as the rest of the pipe, although some have been shaped on the lathe. Tape has been wrapped around the pipes near the mouthpiece.

TOOLS 63

Holder or Stand for Pipes

Although not essential, I have found that a piece of large-diameter pipe (4″ to 6″) welded to a large channel iron or plate steel makes an excellent storage stand. The pipes are stored with the heads down, and the metal pipe acts as an effective container for the sharp pieces of glass that sometimes fly off a cooling pipe with explosive force. Safety considerations make having a few of these holders worthwhile.

Pipes are stored upright in this metal stand made of black pipe welded to a metal base.

Marver

The marver is a thick (¼″ or thicker) piece of flat steel (although marble and graphite are also used) at least 12″ square, cleaned, polished, and mounted on a sturdy table 3 to 4 feet off the floor. My preference is for a horizontal marver. Most of the Mexican factories use a marver mounted about 5 feet off the ground and set at an angle reminiscent of the marvers used on some historical German stand-up benches. After seeing the skill with which the Mexicans use this marver it becomes obvious that there are many "correct" ways to work!

Some craftsmen find that coating the marver with oil or wax aids in rolling hot glass smoothly. Personally I do not advise this—the glass will roll in place on the marver and pick up impurities. The 2″ x 4″ block of wood is used to support the pipe for blowing the initial bubble and is not a requirement on the marver.

The marver has two primary uses: to cool and form the first gather of molten glass before a bubble is started, and to chill and shape the small amount of glass that is used as a bond when attaching the pontil to the bottom of the vessel. It can also be used for a variety of other operations including "marvering in" powdered colorants or lumps of glass, flattening the sides of vessels to produce "free forms," and impressing decorations in the glass.

A marver is a ground and polished piece of thick sheet steel supported by a sturdy table.

Glassblower's Bench

The glassblower's bench is, at its simplest, a seat that has two parallel, horizontal arms extended forward on which to roll a pipe or pontil. The bench extends beyond the arm to the right to provide storage space for hand tools. It should be sturdy, made either of 2″ x 4″ wood or of metal. If the bench is made of wood, the arms should have a metal rail on the upper surface. It is also a good idea to have the forward edges of the arms bent up, or to in some way provide a stop for pipes to prevent their falling to the floor.

If you build your own bench (which I recommend), you can adjust the dimensions to your own comfort. I remember my first visit to a shop in Juarez, Mexico. The worker's benches were so high off the floor that a skilled Mexican glassblower 6 feet tall sat with the tips of his toes barely touching the floor! I learned later that the owner of the factory was more interested in the spectators being able to see the operations than in the comfort and safety of the workers. The benches I have built vary from 15″ to 22″ off the floor.

Some commercial benches are quite elaborate (and expensive) with movable, padded seats, lockable, built-in tool cabinets, adjustable arms, etc.

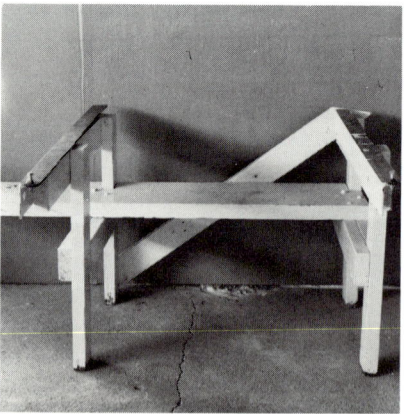

I made this wooden glassblower's bench out of lengths of 2″ x 4″ (and other heavy lumber). Note the metal angle iron on top of each arm and the bolt at the forward edge of the arm to stop pipes from rolling off.

Pucellas, Jacks, and Tongs

There are a number of tools that are made of spring steel with two metal "blades" connected at the top. Although these tools look somewhat like shears they are not cutting tools—they are used to indent or stretch a form. Their names are often used interchangeably, however tongs are really tools with flat or rounded blades, while pucellas have knife-shaped arms or blades.

These tools are best lubricated with wax. This is done by running the hot blades through a lump of wax on the bench after they have been in contact with the hot glass. To a large degree the frequency of lubrication depends on the preference of the worker. There are some elaborate formulas for these waxes (with poetic names like "Milton's Mud" or "Rainbow Crud" given them by glassworkers), none of which work any better than beeswax.

Paddles

Wooden paddles serve a number of functions in glassworking: centering and supporting the gather, flattening and chilling the bottom of the vessel to insure a thick base, and indenting the center of the base in preparation for attaching the pontil. Wedge-shaped paddles can be pushed into a vessel on the pontil to open a bowl form. Paddles with a concave edge can be used to close in and elongate a vessel. Double paddles can be used to make pedestals, etc.

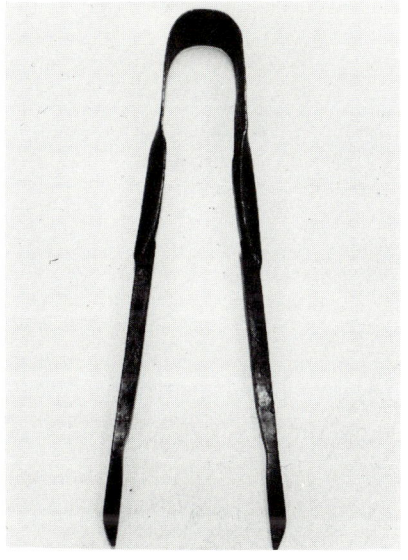

A set of large jacks with knife-shaped arms that have been worn from use. This set was made by one of the factories in Juarez, Mexico and is typical of their tools.

This is a medium-size set of jacks I made from spring steel and round steel rod. They were made primarily for forming handles and the like. The arms are purposely not of the same diameter.

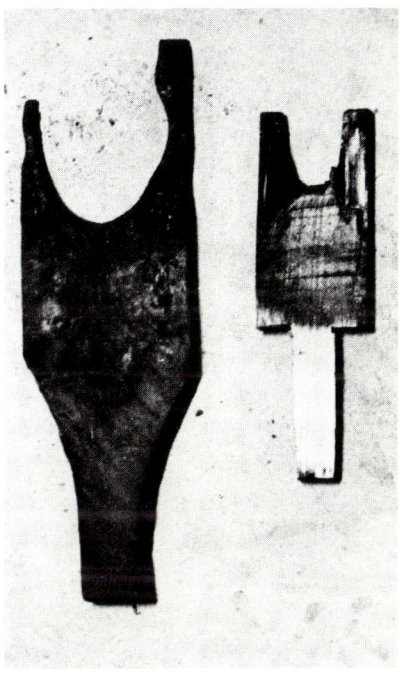

Paddles with concave edges used to close in and elongate glass forms. These paddles can often take the place of metal jacks when working glass.

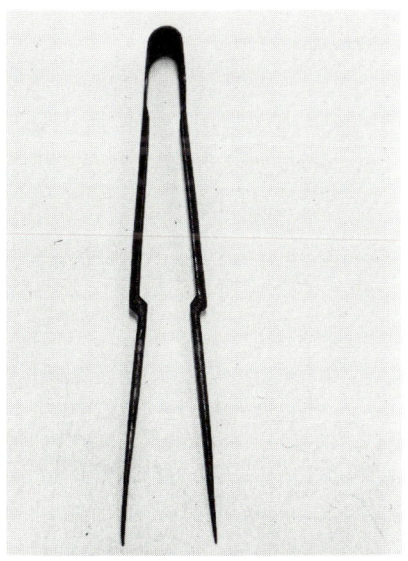

A medium-size set of jacks with round arms made commercially in Germany.

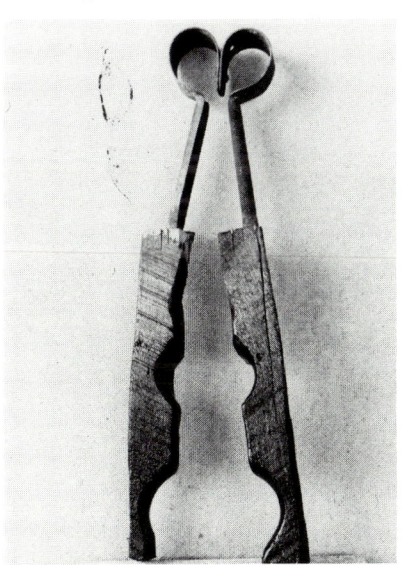

A set of wooden jacks made from an old set of garden shears with pieces of cherry wood for the arms.

Blocks

Gathers of glass made after the initial gather are usually centered and chilled in blocks. The hot glass is rolled in a forming block (half-mold) of the correct size to center the gather, remove irregularities, and chill the glass. This "skin" of chilled glass helps prevent blowing through the bubble.

Forming blocks are usually made from cylindrical sections of tree limbs. One of the flat surfaces becomes the top of the tool, which is then gouged out to form a concave indention, or forming surface. The block can also be roughly hollowed out with a lathe and the finishing work done with a wood chisel and by burning. A sturdy, comfortable, and balanced handle is best attached by drilling a hole in the block, then inserting the handle. Less satisfactory is nailing the handle to the bottom of the block. Larger blocks can be mounted on permanent stands.

Since wear is expected in these tools, it is economical to use a large piece of wood even for smaller blocks. As the tool wears, the hollow will grow larger. In this way small blocking tools gradually become large blocks as the large blocks wear out.

Wet newspaper can be used as an easy substitute for a large stand block. Newspaper is usually the only tool used for blocking in most Mexican factories. Graphite and cast-iron forms are also used in place of wooden blocks in some shops.

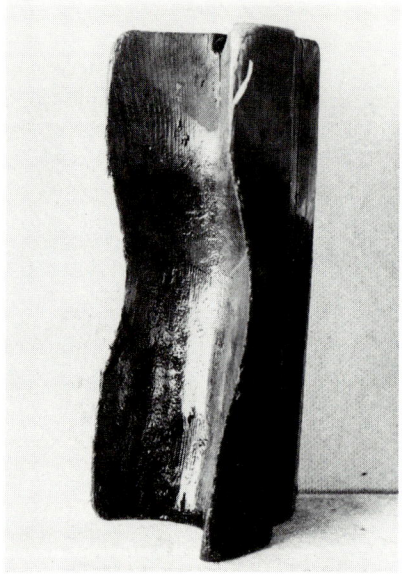

(Above) A long, open block used mostly for long forms. There is no attached handle since it is cradled in the hand.

(Left) A fairly new medium-size block that was made by turning the rough form on a wood lathe, finishing with a hand chisel, and burning with a hot glass gather.

(Bottom Left) A large gather being blocked in wet newspaper in a Mexican factory. In most Mexican factories newspapers are used instead of the more expensive wood blocks.

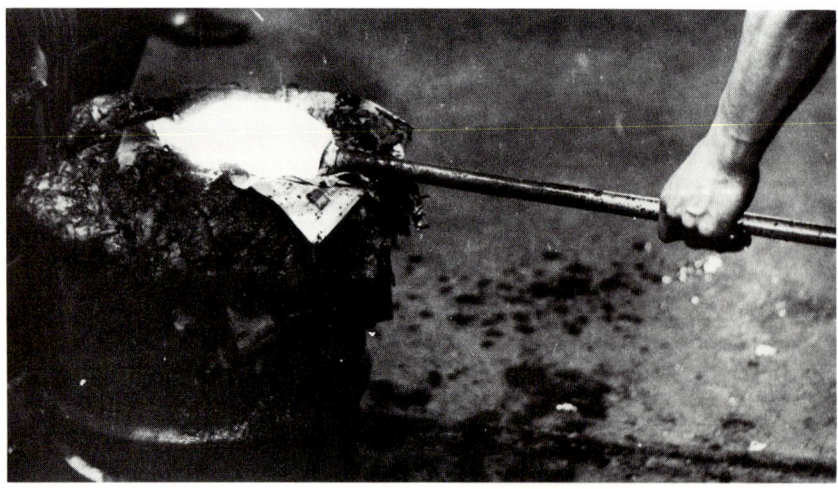

Pontils

The pontil is a steel rod used to hold the vessel during and after removal from the blow pipe. It is attached to the bottom of the vessel with a small amount of molten glass used a bond. The shaft can vary in length and thickness depending on preference and use. The head that contacts the glass should be stainless steel. In practice, a spare blow pipe is sometimes used as a pontil.

A clean pontil mark is often regarded as the trademark of a skilled craftsman. If the separation has not been clean, small pieces of the glass bond will remain on the vessel after the piece has been removed from the pontil. These can often be chipped off with a knife. This marking can be ground off if it is sharp or if the vessel base is not level.

Gathering Irons

Gathering irons are used to bring molten glass from the furnace to the vessel when adding handles, feet, decorations, etc. Pontil rods may be used as gathering irons since they are similar in construction and design, but the head of the iron is often larger to facilitate easy gathering of larger amounts of glass. Some specialized commercial irons have heads made of hollow balls of stainless steel. Other commercial irons use disposable ceramic gathering heads. In the photograph, the longest, heaviest iron with the large head is used primarily as a cleaning tool for the furnace.

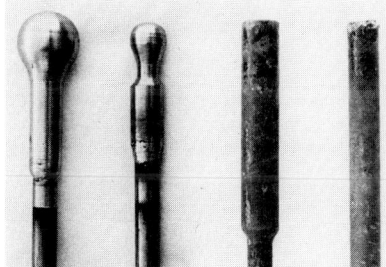

(Above) On the left is a close-up of the stainless steel heads of two gathering irons. On the right is a close-up of stainless steel pontil heads.

(Right) The round-headed iron is a large gathering iron, the two irons in the middle are pontils, and the iron with the large head is for cleaning glass out of the furnace.

Tweezers

Tweezers are primarily used for pinching and pulling the hot glass, however, many artists use a small pair of pliers for these activities. Hardware stores offer a never-ending location for "exotic" tools that can be adapted to pull and pinch the hot glass. Besides the obvious fireplace tongs there are varieties of corn-cob tongs, etc., that for pennies offer the ingenious craftsman tools that would, in another time, have been "trade secrets"!

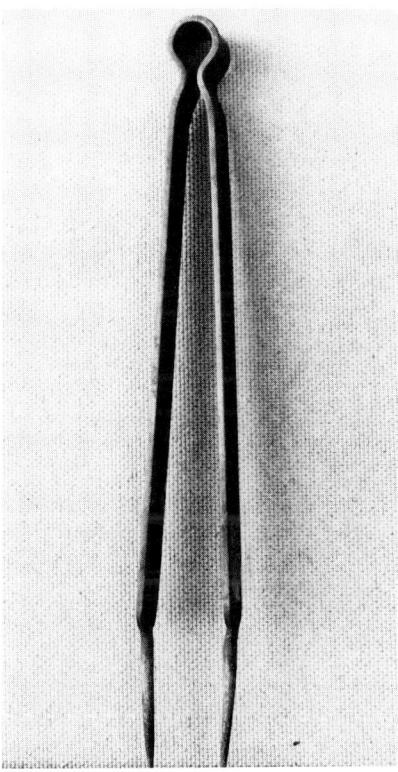

A commercial set of tweezers used to pull and twist molten, plastic glass. This set was made in Germany.

Shears

Metal shears are used to cut hot glass for decorations or handles, to even up the lip of a vessel improperly broken off the pipe, and for other related activities. The trimming shears look like (and can be substituted by) tin snips. The photograph shows a pair of 12″ tin snips that I have used for years. I have purchased tin snips at three times the price of this pair, and commercial German glass-trimming shears at six times the price, and none have worked as well.

For the beginner, a far better investment than trimming shears would be handle shears (sometimes called cutting shears). The cutting edge is squared (or in some cases round) so when cutting handles the glass is not flattened (as it would be with trimming shears). Even more specialized are combination tong/handle shears that have a special formed "tip grasp." They guide the gathering iron in place for a handle and then, with barely a change in position, can cut the required amount of glass for the handle to start the forming operation. Just as interesting is this operation performed with the same smoothness and skill using a large pair of scissors (cloth-cutting scissors, no less). I saw this done in a Mexican factory by a 16 year old who had not been taught that you need expensive shears for the process! For the craftsman working the glass alone, the tong/handle shears are seldom used enough to justify the expense.

A pair of commercial tin snips that have worked particularly well for me as a cut-off tool.

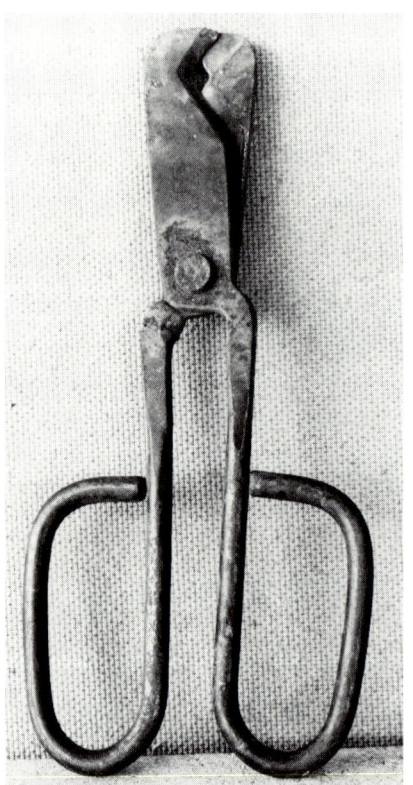

A pair of German-made "handle" or cutting shears. Note the "square" cutting edge that flattens the molten glass to a lesser degree than the straight cutting shears.

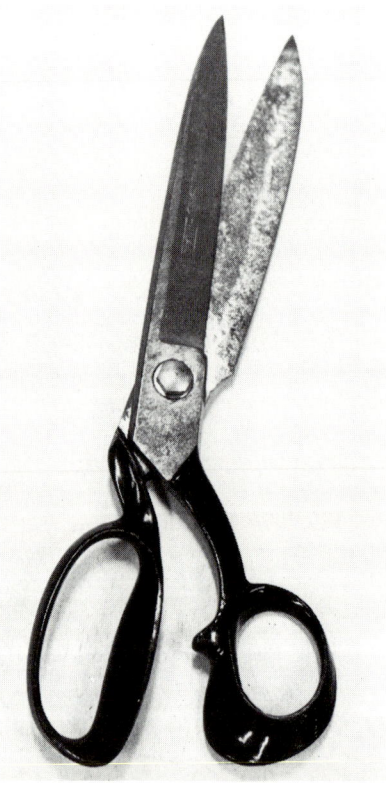

A large pair of scissors used for a great deal of the "fancy" cutting on glass animals, clowns, etc. (much loved by American tourists) made by Mexican glassblowers.

SPECIAL TOOLS

Although there are specialty tools available commerically, there are needs that are served by the artist producing his own tools. I am including several tools that I have made for a particular forming technique.

Hollow Handle Punch. This tool is used to punch a hole through two walls of a vessel to produce a hollow handle. It is made from a pair of pliers, a large heavy nail, and a rod with a piece of ¼″ pipe welded to it. The vessel is caught between the pipe and nail point, and pressure is applied until the nail passes through the pipe, joins the walls, and punches a hole. This hole is then heated, enlarged, and formed (if so desired).

Neck Puller. Two sets of neck pullers are shown. One pair is made from a set of barbecue tongs, and the other from a small section of ¾″ pipe cut in half and welded to heavy rod and to a pair of pliers. Both these tools are of help to beginners who are having difficulty pulling a neck with jacks. They can also be used to pull a great many specialized forms, such as hollow stems and feet.

Foot Tool. This is a tool used to form a pedestal base on stemware. It is a modified form of two wood paddles hinged with a handle. The size of the base, as well as its thickness, is controlled both by pressure on the tool and by the amount of glass used. Some of the variations that I have seen in glass studios and factories have included: grooves in the edge of the tool for forming and pulling the stem, paddles connected with a simple leather hinge nailed to the wood, and simplest and most direct, several layers of wet newspaper held between the fingers.

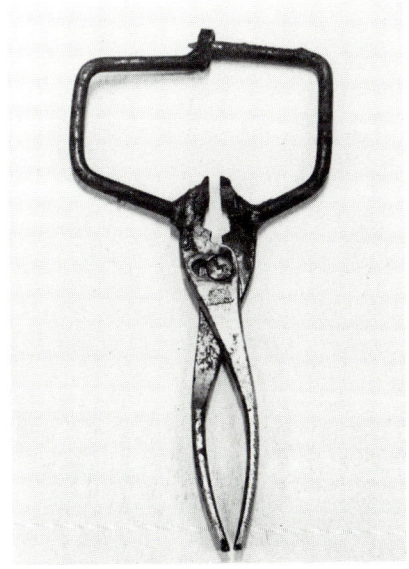

The hollow handle punch is a special tool made with a nail, a tiny piece of ¼″ pipe, and a pair of pliers.

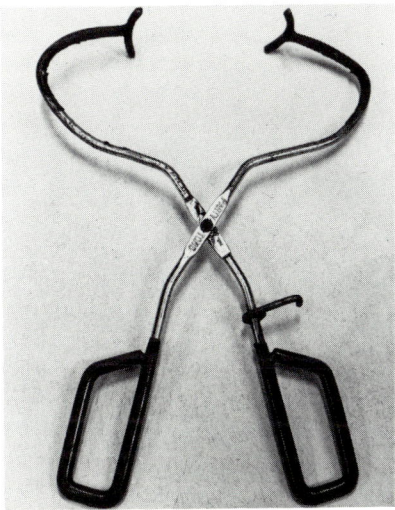

A set of "neck pullers" I made from barbecue tongs. The name adequately explains the function of this tool.

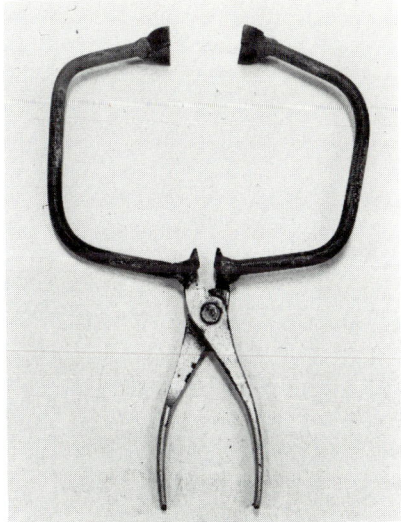

Another set of neck pullers made from pliers, heavy rod, and a section of ordinary black pipe (¾″ in this case, however, any standard-size pipe could be used depending on what size neck you wish).

One of many possible designs for a tool to make the pedestal base on stemware. Basically two pieces of metal that are hinged together, it is used to pressure the soft glass into the form you want.

TOOLS 69

3/Firing, Melting, and Annealing

Motorcycle Decanter by William Bernstein. Free-blown and tooled soda lime glass, 8" x 12". A blown bottle with decorative handles that has a blown stopper tooled and formed while hot into a sculptural glass motorcycle. This is a delightful flight of whimsy possible only to the artist who knows and loves the material he works with.

In this chapter I will show you how to use the equipment you have built—how to safely light your burners, adjust your heat, melt your glass, control your oven and anneal your glass. I will give suggestions on the equipment that has worked for me. These are starting points for you and not the complete and only answer. It may well be that in your use of the equipment you will find a better way than mine. If yours works *and is safe*—well and good.

CHECKS BEFORE LIGHTING THE FURNACE

There are several important points to check before lighting the burner. Some of these have been covered in the previous chapter; however, they bear repeating.

Gas Line. Be sure there are no leaks in your gas line. With the gas on but the burner valve closed, check all connections by painting on a solution of liquid detergent and water. A leaky joint will blow bubbles of gas. *Never* check for a gas leak using a lit match or other flame.

Gas Valve. Check to make sure your gas cock does not leak and that the handle turns without too much force. Again use soapy water for checking, and be certain to soap the bottom of the valve as well as the handle (top).

A new valve is generally ready to use; however, you may have to turn it several times to "break it in," or you might have to adjust the nut that holds the valve together. There is not much chance the valve will need lubricating, but be aware that these gas cocks do need to be greased periodically. It is impossible for me to give you a set "number of turns" or a set time for greasing because heat, humidity, and the type of grease all play a part. If the valve seems more difficult to turn after several months of use, or if it begins to leak gas around the stem, this could indicate a need to lubricate. The valve must be taken apart to grease so the gas must be turned off *before* it reaches the gas cock.

Air Control and Blower. The air control cover should stay stationary when the motor is running and vibrating. To check this, run the blower with the cover set in each position and note any movement. If there is movement, you may be able to tighten the set screw (but do not tighten to the point where you strip the threads), or you can use masking tape to hold the cover in place. Follow the directions on the motor concerning lubrication. Do not over oil.

Furnace Door. The door on the furnace should be easy to move while working (wear an asbestos glove). Before you start your furnace make sure the door is firmly bound, fairly well balanced ("feels good" in your hand), and stands upright with no chance of either falling off the shelf or falling forward in contact with the outside of the furnace. *Never* slide the door. Lift and place it in position each time.

Furnace Adjustments

You will be dealing with three adjustments that control the firing of the furnace: (1) the amount of gas going into the burner, (2) the amount of air going into the burner, and (3) the amount of exhaust gas coming out of the furnace.

Often, at least when first starting the furnace, adjusting any one of these requires a change in the others. The first is controlled by the gas cock (valve) and the amount of gas available in your line, the second by the cover on the blower intake and the amount of air your blower can put out, the third by the furnace door and the size of the door opening.

There are other variables that can also affect the firing: the temperature, wind, and atmospheric conditions outside the furnace; the size of the furnace interior; the materials you put in the tank. These and a host of other factors may or may not prove to be important in your particular situation.

"Hot" and "Cold" Burners. A cold burner fires and behaves completely different from a hot burner—even though it is the same burner. When engineers and other people concerned with heating equipment use the terms "hot" or "cold" burner, they are really making a reference to the condition of the heat container (or furnace), not the burner. In theory, the burner should remain cool to the touch several inches from the burner port. Remember, it is the furnace condition that requires adjustments in the burner as it changes from a "cold" to a "hot" burner.

Markings on the Blower. Figure 1 is a picture of the air control on the burner with the marks I use for controls—3, 2, 1, 0, a mark below 0, and a mark at the halfway point on the blower. A round electrical cover could be used for the blower instead of the square one. You may also find that a different set of markings is better for your situation. All of this is offered as a *starting point only* in the use of your burner.

I will make suggestions throughout this chapter for adjustments based on both time of firing and visual (or audio) conditions of the equipment. There will be variations in each working situation, so sooner or later you will make adjustments to fit your equipment. Two blower motors made by the same manufacturer—same model, type, and size—can sound and behave differently when used in the exact same situation! Obviously any other variable has its effect as well.

A Test Firing

Plan to make a test firing of your new furnace before you actually load it with glass. When you start, be very careful lighting the furnace burner (detailed instructions begin on p.74). Minor adjustments in the air/gas/exhaust relationship can cause the flame to be extinguished, as can wind or other atmospheric changes outside the furnace.

Do not light the furnace in bright sunlight. You want to be able to see the flame and the changes in color of the furnace interior. I usually light the furnace early in the evening.

When the walls of the furnace, tank, door, and burner block are orange-red hot you are usually in good shape. This does not imply, however, that common sense and caution are ever to be forgotten.

Safety Reminders. Wear protective glasses, a long-sleeved, tightly woven cotton work shirt, and an asbestos glove on the right hand. If for any reason the flame blows out, turn off the gas *at once*, leave the door fully open, and wait 10 minutes before relighting. Also, try to determine why the flame went out so you can correct the situation the next time.

Cleaning and Inspecting the Furnace. After the furnace is cold (one day or so), you should inspect the interior. Vacuum out any loose materials that may have fallen into the tank from the burner, burner block, or roof. Check the interior for any new cracks, particularly on the roof. This can be done with a flashlight and mirror if necessary. If you can, reach up into the burner and burner block to check for other loose material that may be ready to fall into your glass tank.

This is a close-up of the blower (intake air control) on the furnace burner. Starting from the right, the markings are: closed, a line (unmarked) halfway between closed and 0, 1, 2, 3, and a halfway mark on the blower. These markings are only a starting point for your work with your burner. You may find a different system of marking better for you. If the screw on the cover does not hold the cover in place, you may find masking tape helps keep the cover from vibrating.

FIRING, MELTING, AND ANNEALING 73

Lighting the Burner

To safely reach the burner port in the furnace roof, you need to make a "lighter." This is easily made from a wire coat hanger. It should be long enough (at least 18") so your hand stays safely outside the furnace. Put a piece of paper in the bent end. With the furnace door fully open, the blower motor off, and the air-control cover fully open, light the paper in the wire holder and position the flame a couple of inches from the burner port.

Turn the gas cock on slowly until the gas lights, then remove the lighter. Position the door so the furnace opening is about a third closed. The gas valve should be about half open—more or less. You want a general flame burning primarily inside the furnace, with some burning taking place outside the door. The flame should not be burning at the burner port. After about five minutes, close the air cover on the blower and hold it tight against the blower as you turn on the blower motor. Then slowly release the pressure on the cover so some air gets into the burner.

After about 10 minutes, turn the gas up to about three-fourths open, and open the air to the mark below 0. Your flame should still be a general flame burning inside the furnace and not at the burner port. It may fluctuate anywhere from near the burner port to the furnace tank. There will probably be a current of flame "rolling" back to the top of the furnace from the edge of the tank.

1. Fold a piece of paper, and firmly force it into the bend in your lighter. With the furnace door fully open, the air control on the burner fully open, and the gas off, light the paper and position it a couple inches below the burner opening in the furnace roof.

2. Turn the gas valve on slowly until the furnace lights. Remove the lighter and extinguish the flame. Adjust the gas so the valve is about at the halfway point between off and on. Close the door about 1/3rd of the furnace opening.

Furnace Adjustments

In 45 minutes turn the gas to full, the air to the 1 mark, and open the door all the way. The furnace interior may show some firebrick edges beginning to turn cherry red by this time. Allow the furnace to fire about 35 minutes with these settings and then close the door to cover two-thirds of the opening, and open the air cover to the halfway mark. The flame will now be burning mostly in the tank, and both the tank and the furnace walls will be red in a short time. Allow the furnace to fire at these settings for about 45 minutes. "Close" the door (remember to leave about ½" to 1" of space between the door frame and the door and continue to fire for about 15 minutes. Adjust the gas to about two-thirds fully open. There will still be a large amount of flame burning outside the furnace door at this point.

A Steady Fire. In about 15 minutes turn the gas back to a little above the halfway point and set the air to 1. Ideally the furnace should be firing so 1" or more of blue flame is visible at the door. You can adjust for this by moving either the gas cock, the air control, or the door. The burner should then stop any "popping" sound and begin a steady "roar."

Turn back the gas slightly when the flame coming out the door becomes yellow. Try to adjust the controls so about 1" of blue flame barely appears at the edge of the door. In less than five hours, cut the air back to 0 and cut the gas back accordingly. At this point even small changes in the gas will change the flame. With the door in the "closed" position you should be able to fire to orange heat without full gas or air in less than 14 hours from the time of the initial lighting. Do not be disturbed by variations in this firing schedule because there are many variables that can make a difference.

Some Suggestions. Experiment with the burner to get the feel of what it will do. Do not expect instant results when you make an adjustment. Instead, check for changes in about 15 minutes. A hint of slightly blue flame around the edge of the door is usually the hottest way to fire. Keep the furnace on for a couple of days to experiment with the controls and to force any loose material from the burner block, roof, and burner into the bank. With a new furnace, this loose material will have to be removed sooner or later, and sooner is better—certainly before you put glass into the tank.

Turning Off the Furnace

To turn the furnace off, close the door of the furnace, turn back the air cover to "closed," and turn off the gas. Because of the burner placement in the top of the furnace it is not advisable to turn the air blower off completely. Some air should continue to blow through the burner pipe. Keep the door closed to prevent the furnace from cooling too rapidly. Fast temperature changes are hard on the furnace refractories. The door can be fully opened for rapid cooling only after the color is out of the furnace. I usually open the blower full at this point; however, if you are in no hurry you can turn the blower off instead.

Loading the Furnace

Now you will actually load and melt glass in the furnace. Relight the furnace as described earlier, and make sure it is quite hot before you begin to load.

The glass is loaded into the furnace using a specially made shovel. The loaded shovel is put into the furnace and then turned over so the glass falls into the tank. Note the metal angle iron on the ledge that is used as a fulcrum and also to prevent breaking the edges of the refractory that could be knocked into the glass tank. Continue to load until the glass level is a little below the top of the tank.

Batch chemicals will bubble up a great deal before melting down. Do not add the next load until this bubbling has stopped and the molten glass has settled to about three-fourths of the volume of the original batch. It will be about four hours before you can add the next load, although the kind of glass, amount of cullet (old glass), etc., has some effect on the melting speed. Your second load can be piled in the tank until it is above the tank level in the center of the tank (but never at the edges). This may continue for several loadings.

Note the glass level in the tank. If one corner is lower than the other, be certain to watch that corner to prevent a spillover. Stop loading when the melted glass level is about ½" from the top of the tank. You may find that after loading the furnace you will have to adjust your burner. I cut back on the gas and open the door slightly.

Loading Scrap Glass (Cullet). If you are using scrap sheet glass (cullet) you will probably find long-handled tongs better to use than the loading shovel. Break the glass if necessary so the pieces are small enough to fit the furnace (always use some kind of eye protection when breaking glass).

When the cullet is put in the hot furnace it will break with explosive force and shoot the glass out of the tank, against the furnace walls and door, and even out of the furnace. Unfortunately, most of the glassworkers I know soon lose patience with this method of loading sheet scraps. They end up throwing pieces of glass into, and sometimes "at" the furnace. I doubt if I need to give an opinion on this method of loading.

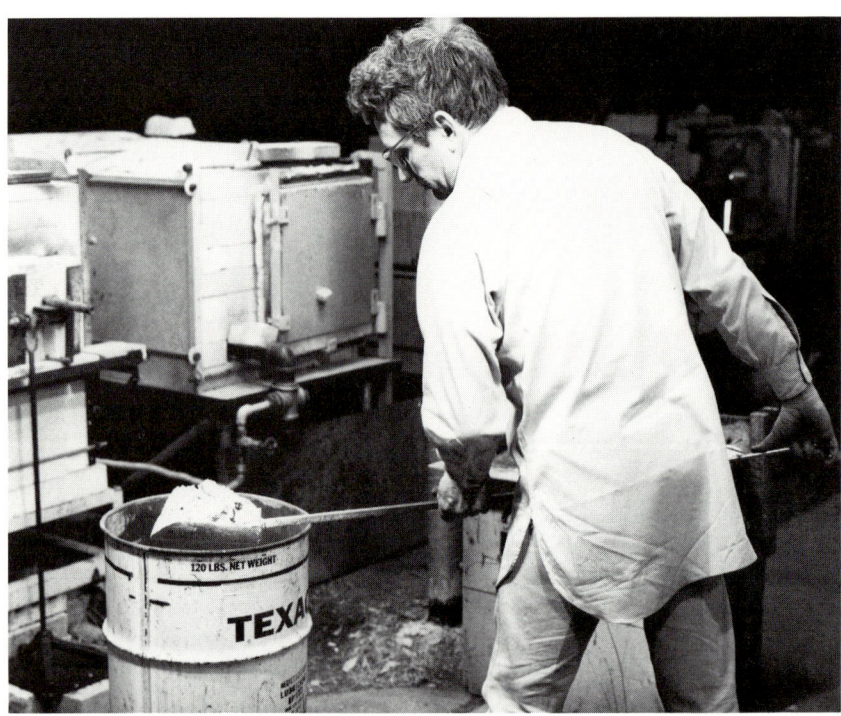

1. When the furnace is at orange heat all the way to the bottom of the empty tank you can start loading glass. Place your container of glass near the furnace, open the door of the furnace wide, and put a piece of angle iron on the shelf. Have your loading shovel near at hand, and be sure to wear a heavy cotton shirt, glasses, and a glove on your left hand. Pick up a load of glass on the shovel.

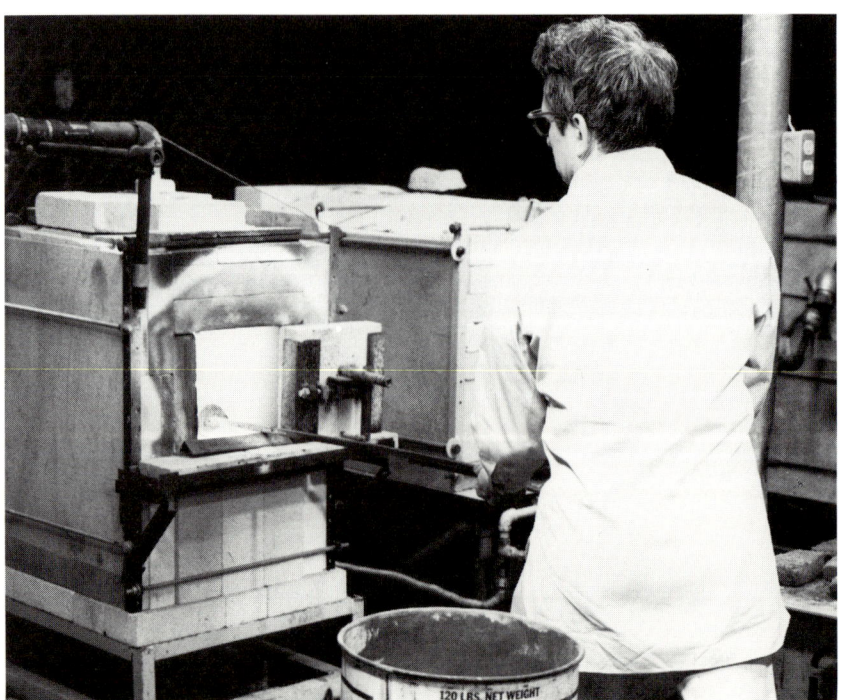

2. Put the head of the loaded shovel into the furnace above the tank and turn the shovel over, dumping the glass into the tank. Continue this process until the level of the glass batch is slightly below the top edge of the tank. If necessary, use a pontil or rod to smooth out the chemicals so you can get an accurate estimate of the level in the tank.

Melting Glass

When you load either batch or cullet into the hot furnace, the melting process starts almost at once. In the case of the batch chemicals there are several phases in the melting. These often occur at the same time in different parts of the tank, but I will treat these phases in a theoretical sequence for the sake of simplicity.

Evaporation of Free Water. Many of the chemicals used in glass absorb water from the air (sodium and potassium nitrate, potassium carbonate, etc.). Since this is "free water," or water not chemically joined to other chemicals, it changes to steam at the boiling point of water (100°C). You will note bubbling taking place as soon as the materials are placed in the furnace. Puffs of dust will appear as water from below the surface moves to the top of the batch. This bubbling is important—it is the start of mixing caused by the heat of the furnace. Ideally some kind of bubbling action should continue through most of the melting process.

Catalytic Action of Chemicals. The chemicals that make up glass have different melting points. Often a small amount of one chemical can lower the melting point of other chemicals. This is one reason why sodium and potassium nitrates are helpful in the batch—they melt at low temperatures and encourage other materials to melt. The second important reason for using these nitrates is that they are strong oxidizing agents. They give off oxygen, which helps to "burn" organic impurities in the batch and give a clearer and cleaner glass.

Evaporation of Chemical Water. The next phase in the melting process is when water that is chemically bound to the materials is driven off by the heat of the furnace. Carbon dioxide is also given off at about the same temperature, as well as various sulfer oxides. All of these continue the rolling and tumbling action of the chemicals that assist in mixing the glass.

Liquid Phase. Now there are a multitude of localized melted chemicals and groups of melted chemicals in the tank. These materials are not yet formed into "a" glass—instead there may be many types and kinds of "glasses" in various stages of formation.

Homogeneous Liquid Phase. The individual "solutions" have now become a homogeneous molten glass without lumps of free batch (crystalline) materials. There may or may not be seeds (bubbles) at this state. With continued high temperatures the glass ingredients themselves will begin to vaporize and the sodium, potassium, and lead oxides will form a glass coating on the door, walls, and roof of the furnace, as well as appearing as seeds in the molten glass.

Another phenomenon might be noticed at this later state of glass-melting. The products of the fire—carbon dioxide, fuels, etc.—will begin to go into the glass solution. When these gases reach a supersaturation point, they might also begin to bubble out in the form of seeds.

Fining Phase. Glass that is "fined" is *relatively* free from small bubbles, called seeds. A fined glass for one purpose might not be fined for another. Glass for decorative light covers and glass for camera lenses obviously have different requirements in order to be classified as "fined."

The fining process begins when the glass is loaded into the furnace and continues until (and beyond) the complete solution of all the chemicals. Some materials aid the fining process in the last stages of glass-melting (arsenic and antimony are two such important oxides). In theory these chemicals are oxidizing agents, and very minute amounts are used. Books on glass refer to the bubbles from the fining agents carrying all the other bubbles to the surface and then out of the glass.

If you do not want the melted glass to be oxidized, chlorides or bromides may be used for a similar "sweeping" action (table salt, or sodium chloride, is one such fining agent). The folklore of glassmaking is filled with stories of the methods used to fine glass. One of the most interesting is to put an iron rod through a fresh potato and then plunge the potato end of the rod to the bottom of the glass tank! I should add, as a safety precaution, "Stand back!"

Since fining is a continuous process that depends on so many variables, it often becomes a matter of esthetics. This judgment is also probably true of other glass "faults" that fall short of physical damage to the object produced.

Reboil. Glass that has fined sometimes becomes filled with seeds when the heat is turned up prior to starting a new work cycle. The cause is most likely the rapid vaporization of the glassy oxides—sodium, potassium, etc.—or the refractories in the tank dissolving from the molten glass. The chemicals that melt the glass can melt similar glass chemicals in other forms. Most refractories used in the furnace contain silica (SiO_2) and alumina (Al_2O_3) which dissolve under high temperatures. The tank in the furnace may therefore be the generator of the seeds in the glass.

Glass rarely becomes seed-free in instances where high heats are continued for long periods of time. If the seeds are caused by excessive dissolving of the refractories it may indicate "cord" (glass of a different composition) and "stone" (pieces of undissolved refractory) formation.

The above stages in melting glass have been grossly simplified and presented so you have some idea of what is happening as you load and fire the various chemicals in your furnace. There is a story of a beginning student in glass who learned about these melting stages in a different way. He filled a clay crucible (in a furnace) nearly to the top and put a refractory lid on it. Soon the lid began to rise on a "head" of bubbly glass until it was perhaps 8" above the crucible. Since the lip was outside the furnace the glass "froze" in place—literally sealing the crucible top airtight. The chemicals below continued fining, and the gases that could no longer escape into the atmosphere "blew" the crucible apart and spewed the hot glass all over the inside of the furnace and firebox! This is one way to learn what happens during the melting process, but it is rather extreme!

Furnace Adjustments After the Glass is Melted

After the glass is melted, and if you are not working the glass, you want the glass to "soak," or remain molten but cool. There are a number of important reasons for this: it saves in gas costs, there is less wear on the furnace and tank, and you will get better glass quality (with high temperatures the glass continues to dissolve the furnace refractories and cause impurities). To soak the furnace you simply close the door, cover the air intake ("closed" marking on the blower), and cut the gas back as much as possible.

Adjustments Prior to Working. Turn the furnace up several hours before you want to start working. Open the door about 1", turn the gas up about three-fourths, open the air full, then turn the gas back until you get 1" or so of flame out of the door. Check back in 15 minutes, and periodically after that. Most likely you will have to turn the gas back slightly or open the door to adjust the exhaust flame.

Adjustments While Working. When working you should make adjustments as needed. Only open the door enough for easy entry. If you leave the door wide open for any length of time you will cool the furnace too rapidly and make working uncomfortable and possibly dangerous. Plan ahead. If you have a large piece you should open the door wider before attempting to use the furnace. It is usually easier to get a firm piece into the furnace than to get a soft one out without catching it on the door.

In general, you do not want 6" of flame coming out of the furnace into your face. Because the gas valve is hard to adjust with one hand, you may find it easier to make adjustments by moving the door. A chief fault with many beginners is a reluctance to open and close the furnace door when required.

The settings I have described are for a rather "hot" furnace, and you may find that a cooler furnace is more to your liking. These are preferences you will develop after working with your own equipment.

Cleaning the Furnace

When the glass is in a homogeneous, fined state it is ready to be worked in the manner described in Chapters 5 and 6. When you have finished using the glass in the furnace, or for some other reason want to turn off the furnace, you should clean out as much remaining glass as possible.

The photographs show the method I use to clean out the furnace. This would be done before you added a new color glass as well as when preparing to turn off the furnace. Cleaning out most of a first batch is an excellent idea because 5% or 10% of the finished glass mixed with fresh glass batch serves very well as a catalyst for new melts.

It is important to get as much glass out of the tank as possible before turning off the furnace because the contraction of the cooling glass can literally pull your glass tank apart by breaking off pieces of the tank liner. I use a heavy gathering iron, shears, and cold water for cleaning the tank, but there are other tools that some craftsmen prefer.

1. Fill at least two buckets with cold water and set them near the furnace. Place a metal stand near one of the buckets to rest your gathering iron on. Also have a pair of shears nearby. Heat the end of a heavy-duty gathering iron. Then take the iron and rotate it in the molten glass.

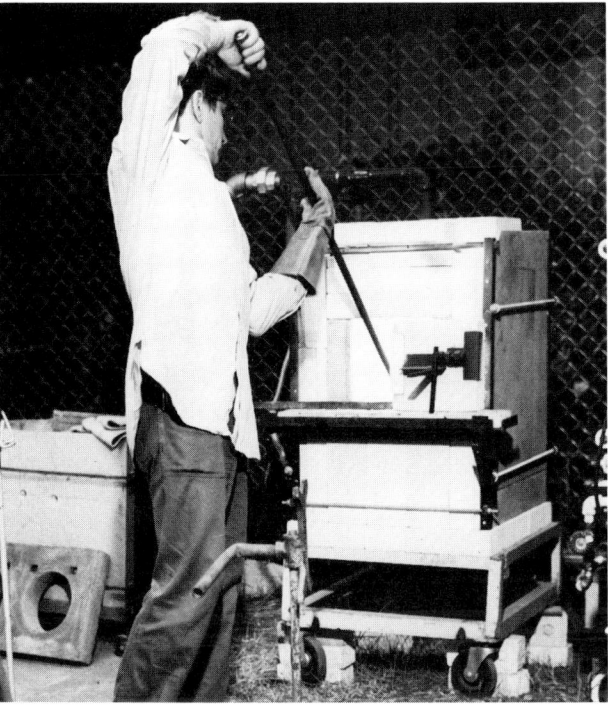

2. Try to gather (pick up) as much molten glass as possible. Rotate the pipe to keep the glass on the iron and remove the glass from the furnace.

3. Place the iron on the stand and hold the molten glass over the first bucket. Use the shears to help force the glass off the iron and into the bucket.

4. This is a close-up of the shears pushing the glass off the end of the rod. Periodically dip the shears (they will get hot and begin to stick to the glass) in the second bucket of water to cool them. When most of the glass is off (or is too stiff to move) cut the remaining thread. Repeat these steps as many times as needed to get the glass out of the furnace.

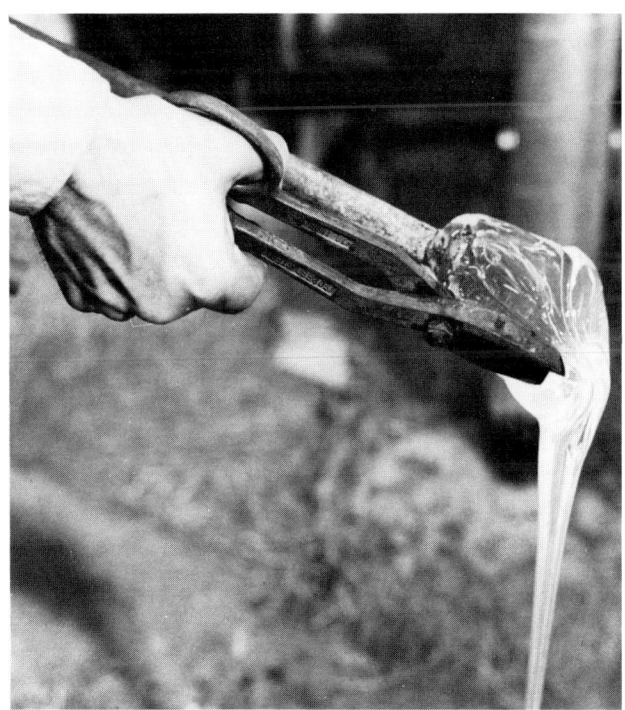

FIRING, MELTING, AND ANNEALING 79

Annealing Glass

Chapter 1 described annealing glass, however a brief review is in order. Annealing is needed to produce a uniform temperature distribution and remove excessive strains as the glass vessel cools. The range for annealing glass is often difficult to establish, but generally there is a great deal of leeway. The upper limit is near the softening point of the glass. This softening point is not a fixed temperature (as is the boiling point of water) but rather depends on such variables as weight and thickness variations of the article being annealed. The lower range is normally the same as the temperature at which there is rapid change in the expansion of the glass caused by heat (thermal expansion). It too is dependent on many variables, including those mentioned for the upper range.

Tests and Standards. The The American Society for Testing and Materials has published a six-page *Standard Method of Test for Annealing Point and Strain Point of Glass* (ASTM Designation C336). Although this may be exact and useful for industry, it is almost worthless for our purposes. Any such test is a mere starting point because it only establishes the annealing point for a uniform glass rod. Enlarge the size of the rod, or change the weight, and the annealing point changes. Put thick and thin, heavy and light, overhang and well-supported parts in the *same* vessel and the annealing point again changes (in fact it may become a series of temperatures and times).

Suggestions on Annealing. When you read literature that seems to be giving exact information on glass-annealing you should realize that you are only getting a starting or reference point. There are some things I have found helpful in using this information and may help you to get good results from your annealing.

When you have finished working the vessel on the pontil you can begin the annealing process by reheating in the furnace or glory-hole before removing the piece from the pontil. You have visual control over the piece at this time and can see when it nears the softening point (the upper limits of the annealing range). If you remove the pontil and put the ware in the oven as quickly as is safely possible you have begun successful annealing.

In the annealing oven, allow the ware to soak at approximately the annealing temperature. When you open the oven for more loading, visually check to see that none of the previous work is at the softening point.

"Natural" Annealing. The term "natural" annealing is used by some contemporary glass artists to describe annealing with the combined heat of the glass and of a burner (or electric source). The vessel is put in a closed container for a period long enough to bring the ware slowly through the annealing range.

This method of annealing generally can be made to work with ovens that are well insulated with standard insulating materials. It does not work well with "super" insulating blankets that take in and hold little heat, or in ovens where air currents can circulate among the glass pieces. In the first case, elaborate methods of slowly lowering the temperature are required (either manually or with the use of expensive control devices). In the second instance, holes can often be found and plugged. It would be possible to systematically turn back the flame and close the damper on the oven you have built, however from my own experience the oven works without these actions.

The Oven Burner

Although the oven is never fired as hot as the furnace, it is actually more dangerous to both fire and use. There are several reasons for this:

First, because the interior of the oven never gets red hot, there is no "built-in" safety pilot. It is likely that a sudden wind might blow out the burner. I use a small piece of insulating brick in front of the burner to help guard against such a problem. When red hot it acts like a pilot and relights the burner.

Second, you have to relight the oven burner for almost every work session. Since lighting the burner is the most accident-prone time, obviously the more often done the more likely an accident. The only suggestion I can make is to treat the flame with respect—but not with fear. The only person who is more dangerous around fire than one who is not afraid is the person who *is* afraid. Making a step-by-step checklist may help you to remember everything of importance. Do each step in a sequential way for each firing.

Third, the flame in the oven is so small that it is almost invisible and may not be noticed if blown out, it is so cool that there is little chance of noticing the absence of radiant heat near the oven, and it is so silent (with no motor or blower) that there is no "roar" to contrast with sudden silence should the oven stop working.

Fourth, you never put your hands or arms inside the furnace, but you may need to do this when placing the ware in the oven.

Safety Devices. None of this is offered to frighten or scare you—only to point up your responsibilities when using the equipment. Some glass craftsmen feel the need of a pilot or other safety devices on the oven. Although I have used my oven without these devices, this is a valid place for such equipment—certainly far more valid than on the furnace.

If you should decide to use a pilot, I feel a gas pilot is better than a one-end grounded, high-voltage, electronic spark device. You will be working very close to the burner and might touch it. Ten thousand volts will certainly do you no good.

Heat rods used as indicators are not

particularly dependable because flame and air currents vary so greatly when fired as low as is needed in this burner. They are not as much of a safety hazard as the spark pilot, but they often cause more trouble than they are worth.

Infrared scanners are cumbersome and delicate, but you may find them useful. I have seen artists have a great deal of trouble with these when they are slightly out of adjustment or get dirt on the scanning lens. In general they are expensive, not particularly dependable, and tricky to operate.

Heat Controls and Measuring Devices. Unlike on the furnace, the burner on the oven is easy to reach. A match or piece of burning paper can be used to light the burner. You should mark the handle with tape to use the more sensitive valve effectively. You can then count the number of turns (or fractions of turns) needed to adjust the burner flame.

The thermocouple on my oven is located 7" from the floor and 9" from the door through the right wall of the oven. The measured wires on the thermocouple have been extended by adding two pieces of 18-gauge electrical wire about 40" long before connecting with the pyrometer. The pyrometer rests on the ground. You can make a more permanent mounting if you so desire.

Neither the thermocouple nor the pyrometer are expensive instruments—in fact they are the cheapest I could find. They do not give a very accurate reading and the extra wire makes them even less accurate. This is not really important as long as you know how the equipment works.

I will make reference to the readings on this device, in the location I have described. It might be a good idea to drill a few extra holes in the oven wall and move the thermocouple from hole to hole during firing. This will help you to understand the differences in temperature in different parts of your oven. You can easily carve or grind plugs for these holes from insulating brick. You could also spend a great deal more money on measuring devices that are more accurate, but I feel the funds could better be spent for other equipment.

LIGHTING THE OVEN BURNER

Remove the plugs from both the back and top exhaust vents on the oven, remove the plumbing fittings from the side and bottom of the burner, and open the door about ½". Adjust the piece of insulating brick so the flame will be hitting it near the tip of the burner. Hold a lit piece of paper, carefully, in front of the burner in the firebox, then turn the gas valve on until the fuel ignites. Turn the gas valve up to two full turns.

Let the oven fire with these settings until it reaches a little over 540°C. (1000°F.) on the pyrometer (this assumes you are using a soda/lime glass given in this book—it would be higher for most cullet scraps or fiberglass marbles and less for softer glasses, etc.). Plug the back exhaust hole on the oven with the piece of insulating firebrick (half of a brick), put the pipe fitting plug in the side hole on the burner, turn the gas valve back 1½ turns (or less), and cover some of the burner port with insulating brick cut to fit around the burner.

Controlling the Oven Temperature. Little or no adjustment is needed when the exhaust hole in the roof is left wide open, the primary air opening in the bottom of the burner is left wide open, and most of the secondary air at the burner port is covered with insulating brick. With these as constants, three factors control the temperature in the oven: the amount of gas going into the burner (if the pyrometer goes to 580°C. (1100°F.) or higher, turn the valve back an inch or so), the number of times the door is opened wide for loading, and the amount of ware in the furnace (the temperature when put in the oven, the size, etc.). In general, most of your control will be with gas valve modifications.

1. Place a small piece of insulating brick in the firebox near the end of the burner. This piece should be high enough to be touched by the burner flame, yet small enough so it does not block the flame from entering the oven.

2. Remove the vent plugs and plumbing fittings, open the door about ½", and light a piece of paper. Hold the paper in front of the burner in the firebox and turn the gas valve on until the gas lights. Remove the paper and extinguish the flame. Turn the gas up two full turns from the closed position.

3. When the temperature of the oven reaches the annealing range, put the plug in the back exhaust hole, screw in the pipe fitting plug in the side of the burner, turn the gas valve back until it is about ½ turn open, and place a fitted piece of insulating brick on the burner to partially cover the burner port.

Using the Oven

This oven makes no claim to great sophistication, but it works. It is basically an insulated box that aids in annealing by holding the heat of the ware around the ware. The burner helps also—first by heating the insulated box before the glass is put in, and second by helping to hold the temperature as the door is opened and closed.

Because the burner is an open burner and burns directly into the chamber, there are hot "drafts" in the oven. And because the door is large there may be cool drafts. Consequently, the point in front of the burner is hotter than the rest of the oven, and the space at the door is (at least when the door is open wide) the coolest. With common sense and practice you can learn to work with these faults and use the oven effectively. Certainly do not put ware in the firebox. When the oven is nearly full you can open and close the door rapidly to prevent cooling the ware near the door.

Added Roof Insulation. If there are leaks in the oven other than those already mentioned, they are most likely in the roof. Some craftsmen have found ovens like mine work more efficiently with extra insulation on the roof. A fairly cheap mixture that seals the space between the roof bricks and also adds insulation is to combine, by volume, one part cement, two parts sand, six parts vermiculite (or other loose home insulating material), plus enough water to make a thick paste. Grease the top of the roof well, then cover the roof with about a 3″ thick coat of the mixture. You could also use commercial insulating materials for sealing and insulating.

Loading the Ware. Start loading the ware in the oven at the back right hand corner and continue across the back of the oven to the left-hand corner. Be sure to load as much and as tightly as possible in the back row because you will not be able to add after you start the second row. You are in no rush when placing the ware in the back of the furnace since there is little chance of thermal shock that far from the door opening.

If you need to use metal tongs when loading the back of the oven, be sure to heat the tips of the tongs to warm any part that makes contact with the ware. I find that using pieces of worn-out asbestos glove over the jaws of the tongs prevents the metal from touching the glass. No tongs work as well as your hands protected by insulated asbestos gloves, but you need long arms to reach to the back of the oven.

As the loading comes closer to the door you should keep the door open for shorter periods of time. This should cause no problem since placement becomes easier when you are no longer stretching deep into the oven. Avoid knocking the vessels together, and try to stand each piece upright. An inch or so of vermiculite or asbestos fiber on the floor helps with uneven vessels or those with large amounts of pontil glass attached.

Turning Off the Oven

When you have completed work for the day, close the oven door tightly and fire until the pyrometer is at least on 540°C. Plug the bottom hole on the burner with a pipe fitting. This will change the flame to a long yellow flame that may appear at the roof exhaust. Next plug this exhaust with a fitted insulation brick plug. All the exhaust plugs should fit tightly. Next remove the brick from around the burner. The flame will be backing up and burning out of the port around the burner. Have a thin piece of metal ready to force between the burner tip and the oven wall. Turn off the gas, and put the metal in place to tightly close the hole in the oven.

If you have a tight-fitting door, well-fitted exhaust plugs, a good, tight burner-port cover, no leaks in the oven walls or roof, have made sure each piece was well heated before being placed in the oven, and have not left the door open for long periods of time toward the end of the loading—you can leave the oven to cool and be fairly sure your glass will be properly annealed.

Close the door of the oven tightly and fire to the annealing range. Plug the bottom hole in the burner with a pipe fitting plug, and plug the exhaust in the roof of the oven with an insulation brick plug. Remove the fitted brick from around the burner. Turn off the gas and force a thin piece of metal in front of the burner tip so the metal blocks the burner entry (to prevent cold air from entering the furnace).

4/Glass

It Rained in Bloomington by Joel Philip Myer. White opal glass (with color additions), 12" x 7¾". A sculptural form produced at the furnace using a variety of colored and clear glasses. It is an excellent illustration of the plastic, moving qualities in glass that seem suddenly frozen in place.

Glass is a rather unique material. It is not a "solid," but instead is a very cold liquid. It is a mixture of various inorganic compounds that on cooling forms a random pattern rather than a set crystalline structure. Glass has no structure or shape of its own, so can adjust to what you want to make it. Glass does not have a true freezing or melting point as does metal or other solid materials. Instead, as a glass cools, the movement of its compounds slow down gradually until they are locked in a random pattern. This movement continues—very slowly—even after the glass is cool. It remains in a liquid condition when below its "freezing" point and stays in that condition indefinitely.

Natural Glasses

There are two types of glasses that occur in nature: those that have been cooled quickly, thereby preventing crystallization, and those called fulgurites and tektites. Examples of the first type are found in erupted rock formations. The chemical composition of all of these natural glasses is nearly the same as the composition of the surrounding rock. Under other cooling conditions these glasses would also have formed into "solid" rock rather than super-cooled "liquid."

Fulgurites are formed by lightning striking sand. Tektites are found worldwide, but are not easily explained. Some speculations are that the tektites are actually aerial fulgurites resulting from dust melting in the air being hit by lightning, or that they are of meteoric origin, or result from meteors striking sand, "splashing" the natural glass in a large circle.

Although these glasses produced by nature are interesting, they are of no value as commercial glasses—their compositions require enormous amounts of heat to melt, and their rapid cooling is impractical for any normal application. Their real interest is that they are "curiosities," since the rule in nature is for long cooling periods to form rocks (and mountains) rather than glasses. Glass is essentially a "man-made" material.

Commercial Glasses

Some requirements for commercial glasses are that they be fluid at temperatures possible with industrial heating equipment, that they be viscous ("sticky") enough to be worked and to prevent devitrification (changing to a crystalline solid) on cooling, and that they have the properties suitable for the purposes intended by the melter/worker. Your purposes as an artist/craftsman include: a wide range of working temperatures so you will have time to carry out your ideas, clarity, good color-producing possibilities, ability to melt at fairly low temperatures, freedom from obvious and dangerous defects, and finally, that the glass be subject to modifications you deem helpful.

Glass Qualities

There are unique qualities in glass that make it a desirable medium for the craftsman—it has depth, brilliant color, durability, remarkable plasticity, ease of working, and yet it need not have any of these—for above all, glass is versatile. It can be a heat conductor or insulator; an electric conductor or insulator; as hard as precious stones or as soft as cotton; more destructive than a torch cutting steel or as easily destroyed as an eggshell; a corrosive dissolver of bricks or a light and delicate tree ornament. Glass is so versatile, in fact, that for our considerations we must limit ourselves to glasses suitable for the purpose of freeblown work.

Kinds of Glasses

It is general practice when naming glasses to refer to the principle glass-forming oxides in the glass and the principle modifying oxides. Thus we find reference to "sand-soda-lime," however there is no rule to follow since we find as many references to "soda-lime," or "lead-potash" (it is generally understood that the principle glass former—sand—makes up the major part of such compositions). Although I will use such classifications, please keep in mind that the variety possible is so great that, as in industrial glass melting, it soon becomes necessary to resort to a numbering classification system.

As starting points for discussion, the following divisions or classifications are of interest: lead/potash, borosilicates, opals, and the most common, soda/lime. The large majority of glasses, however, overlap these divisions.

Some publications note that up until about 100 years ago, glassworkers had only two or three glasses. All the "new" glasses (Corning melts at least 200 "new" glasses every week) being the product of modern man. Although there have been some remarkable new glasses developed, the large majority are not all that "new" because only recently have accurate methods of measurement been available. Some impurities in the materials used to make glass have a pronounced effect on both glassworking qualities and on the finished glass. The glassworkers on two sides of the river in a medieval town may have thought they were making the same glass when they used the same number of shovels of sand, but the impurities in the sand could make, by modern standards, a new or at least different glass.

Today we have very pure materials for our glasses, and we add trace amounts of materials (in the case of arsenic as little as 1/10 of one percent) that have pronounced effects on the glass. At what point this produces "new" glass is open to debate. There can be no debate, however, in the fact that all through history, man has worked with many different compositions of glass—knowingly or unknowingly.

Potash/Lead Glass

Silica is the glass-forming oxide in these glasses, potash is the fluxing (melting) oxide, and lead the stabilizing oxide. Most potash/lead glasses have a wide working range, produce effective strong colors, have low melting points, and have other characteristics that make them popular with offhand workers. They cannot be melted in a furnace where the flame is in direct contact with the glass, however, because of the reduction of the lead oxide to metallic lead (showing as a dirty gray film on the glass surface). The interesting refractory qualities of the lead glasses have been used by the glass artist to produce "cut crystal." Lead glasses are also easily scratched because they are "soft." I have included several potash/lead glass formulas in this book. In general, the proportion is about 60 silica to 25 lead to 15 potash. Surface melting temperatures are in the range of 2500°F. or lower.

Boro-silicate Glass

Boro-silicate glasses are commonly referred to as "Pyrex," and their compositions vary. These glasses substitute boric oxide (B_2O_3) for some of the silica. They are used for applications that require rapid changes in temperature without cracking caused by thermal shock. Although some craftsmen have used these glasses for hand work, you will find they are difficult to melt and require high temperatures. One "Pyrex" type glass has proportions of 80 silica to 13 boric oxide to 4 sodium oxide to 2 aluminum oxide. Surface melting temperatures are in excess of 3000°F.

Group #10, Toadstools by Andre Billeci. Uranium glass. 46" x 66" x 32". This is a detail of a large group of glass figures freely worked while hot at the furnace. The sculpture is dramatically lit from below so that each figure reflects and transmits the light. The overall effect is a marvelous magic miniature world or environment created from molten elastic glass.

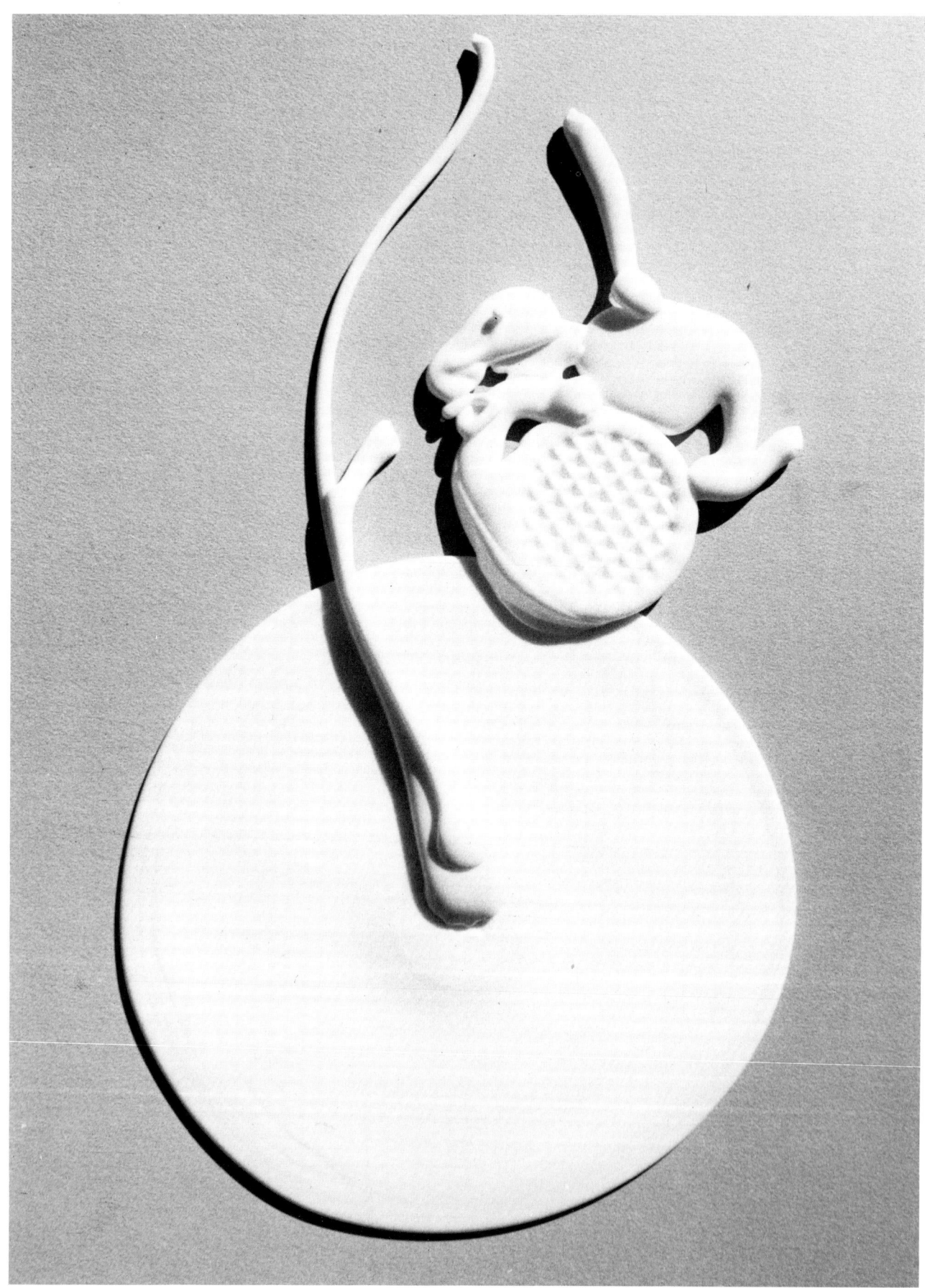

Opal or Opaque Glass

There are two types of opal (or opaque) glasses commonly used in off-hand work—phosphate and fluoride. These can vary from barely cloudy glass to completely opaque material. The opaque glasses usually have tin oxide added to the composition.

Phosphate Glass. These opal glasses are called emulsion or bone ash opals. Actually they are two separate glasses—one a silica base and the other a phosphate base glass—that separate from one another on cooling with the phosphate forming milky droplets in the silica glass. Not only does the relationship of the amount of calcium phosphate (bone ash) to the silica glass influence the opal formation, but the heat treatment during working is also important. These opals are rather safe to melt and work, and are no more corrosive to the furnace than the base glass. In figuring formulas for phosphate opals I have found that between 5 and 10 parts of phosphorous oxide (P_2O_5) to 90–95 parts base glass produces progressively stronger opals.

Fluorine Opals. Fluorine and aluminum compounds produce opal glasses by a controlled fault—devitrification. As with the phosphate opals, there must be a drop in the temperature of the glass to make it "strike" or change color. The material that precipitates out of the glass to make it opal is a complicated alumina/silica/fluorine compound. The fluorine opals are dangerous to work because fluorine gas is given off by the glass in the furnace and while being worked, and these fumes are highly corrosive. The glasses are also very destructive to the furnace refractories. Some glassworkers have noted that the fluorine "burns" (dissipates) out after a time and the glass no longer strikes opal. In general I discourage the use of these fluorine glasses because of the safety problems involved.

Wall Plate by Vernon Brejcha. White glass wall sculpture, 18" × 11". The white glass was formed while hot. The artist used the "plastic" qualities of molten glass for controlled pouring, dripping, and trailing, as well as for impressing textural designs with a variety of tools.

Sand/Soda/Lime Glass

By far the largest percentage of glass melted today is referred to as sand, soda, and lime or soda/lime. The silica is the glass former, the soda the flux (melter), and the calcium the stabilizer. There are great differences in the working properties of these glasses, and in the finished glass. This is because the proportion of the oxides are changed, and because soda/lime glasses are seldom melted without the addition of other materials. Some of these glasses set-up (harden) very fast with a temperature drop of only a few degrees. These fast-setting glasses are developed to use with fast machine production—such as bottle-making machines. Others have a slow setting-up time, making them "easy" or "long-working" glasses suitable for hand processes. The latter groups are those we are interested in. Most soda/lime glasses have proportions of about 70 silica to 15 soda to 15 lime. The surface melting temperature for such glasses is about 2700°F., however changing the proportions and adding other oxides can lower the melting temperatures.

Silica/Soda/Lime Relationship. The relationship of these three oxides is important to understand. Silica is the base melting material, however its high melting temperature makes it impractical to melt singly without some help from other chemicals. The sodium oxide lowers the melting point, however the resulting glass is water soluble. Calcium oxide stabilizes the glass. The variation in the amounts of these oxides decides whether the glass is hard or easy to melt, hard or easy to work, etc. The glass becomes less and less soluble as the calcium increases and the sodium decreases—not only in water but in stronger chemicals. As the calcium increases the glass becomes harder to melt, its working range becomes shorter and shorter, and it develops a tendency to "devitrify." As you can see from this "triangle" of oxides we have a compromise or "trade-off." This trade-off is common with glasses but proportions vary according to usage; obviously the characteristics desired by the machine bottle manufacturer are not the trade-offs you are interested in.

Batch Melts

The revived interest in freeblown and handworked glass over the past 10 years unfortunately involves an "Achilles Heel." This weak spot is the craftsman's lack of understanding of what glass is, and the resulting use of scrap glass, "cullet," or second melts. Although there are advantages to remelting someone else's glass (particularly to a business and certainly to the ecology) I do not feel the glass artist should have to make compromises before he even starts work! It is just as important for the glass artist to understand his material as it is to manipulate his tools. To have to accept a substitute glass because you cannot mix your own is not justifiable. Why postpone the excitement of seeing your own powdered chemicals change into glass literally before your eyes? As with tools and equipment, I want to urge you to "make your own" from scratch rather than starting with discarded bottles, marbles, or discarded factory glass (remember it has been discarded for a reason!).

After melting your own glasses, controlling your color, learning what glass is and how *you* control making it, you can always change to second melts. But what you will have learned from your own glass melts cannot help but increase your confidence and understanding—and the sooner this happens to the beginner the better! I say this even if it costs more for gas for melting, chemicals for mixing, and equipment for weighing and mixing. I use a gram scale for small amounts of chemicals, a bathroom scale for larger amounts; my mixing machine I built myself.

The temperatures for batch melting are not above those you can get using standard refractories and burners. The information is available if you search it out; however, unless otherwise noted, I have personally melted all the formulas in this book. In this chapter I will use a simple soda/lime glass and illustrate some changes that can be made to improve it along with figures, calculations, reasons, etc. I will then start you off on a more complex (but much better glass) recipe and let you carry it through to the finish. You can apply this information to your own formulas if you follow these step-by-step.

MATERIALS

When a glass recipe is described by the percentage of oxide in the composition, it is often possible to maintain the oxide content while varying the materials by which the oxides are introduced. This change of materials may be required for reasons of economics or availability, or may produce desired results in melting or qualities in the finished glass. In order to illustrate this I will include several variations on the materials used to produce the batch.

Purity and Errors in Weight. In these calculations you are dealing with theory, since actuality is impractical. For example, we can use potters flint to introduce silica dioxide (SiO_2) into the glass formula. We figure this to be pure (100%) SiO_2, but in reality there are always impurities. To try to figure minute amounts of impurities would make our calculations endless and would serve little or no purpose in our glass. Accepting the theory that potters flint contains 100% SiO_2 is therefore very practical and sensible. The same is true with the other materials (to a greater or lesser degree).

We carry our calculations to three places (although rounding off final amounts) despite the fact that information on our weighing devices and purity of chemicals often would not justify such precision. The above facts are pointed out not to discredit working out the formulas, but to help you to honestly understand the processes involved.

After seeing so many glassworkers working at tool manipulation (calling it "form discovery") with little or no idea of what the materials they work really are, I feel that a little hard-headed thinking and mathematical accuracy is justified for the glass artist trying to control and understand the results that come from his furnace. In a time of "easy outs" and whims of "fate, furnace, and flocking" work with the basic materials is more than justified. So stick with it through a couple of glasses (formulas that is) before you decide it's too complicated and throw in the coke bottles. If your math is bad (and even if it is not), make the job easier for yourself with a calculator.

Two-Pattie, Three-Footed Glass Cup Forms by Ruth Tamura. Smoky gray glass, 2½" x 7". A "fun" set of cups with added handles. Each has three feet consisting of two glass patties.

Conversion Factors

We are interested in oxides of materials for most of our glass mixing, however it is often impractical or impossible to use the pure oxide form. We must then find out how much of the needed oxide (or oxides) there is in the material we will use. As one common example, consider soda ash, or sodium carbonate (Na_2CO_3), which contains 58.5% sodium oxide (Na_2O). The rest of the weight of carbonate is mostly carbon dioxide gas (CO_2) that is vaporized and driven off by the furnace heat.

To simplify calculations, conversion factors (C.F.) have been worked out for most of the common chemicals used in glass (see the Appendix). If you have a batch formula (a list of materials used to melt into a glass) and have to change it to an oxide formula, look up the C.F. "Material to Oxide" (0.585) and multiply it by the amount of the material (let us say 30.8) to arrive at the amount of oxide in the batch (18).

Conversely, if you have a percentage oxide formula (which is mainly what we will work with) and want to find out how much material to use, look up the C.F. "Oxide to Material" for sodium carbonate (1.710) and multiply this times the amount called for (18) to arrive at 30.8. The conversion of a glass composition into batch composition or vice-versa is a simple arithmetical process, at times admittedly tedious, but none the less valid.

The most common mistake (other than arithmetical) is to use the wrong C.F. Before doing any calculations be sure to ask yourself whether you are working with materials and want to know how much oxide they contain (Material to Oxide C.F.), or if you are working with a theoretical percentage formula and want to know how much material to use (Oxide to Material C.F.).

"Growth No. 2" by Sheldon Carey. Soda/lime glass, 23" tall. A molten glass construction formed on the blow pipe at the furnace. It shows how molten glass can seem "frozen" in place, almost defying gravity.

Developing Your Own Formula

Grossly simplified, what you will be doing now is changing the basic soda/lime formula previously discussed. There are three ways you will do this: (1) you will change the oxide relationship (as you have already seen in the discussion of the silica/soda/lime triangle), (2) you will change the oxides used in the formula (by substituting all or part of the called for oxide with another), and (3) you will change the form (chemical) by which the oxide is introduced into the glass.

Changing the Oxide Relationship

The previously mentioned soda/lime recipe had the proportions of 70-15-15 for the silica-sodium-calcium oxides. In order to make this a longer-working, lower-melting glass for freeblowing, change your proportion to 71.5-18-10.5 as a starter.

You can melt this recipe, however except for its simplicity, it is far from an ideal glass for the novice. Let us use it then with the thought that it is simple and will become more complex. As the new and different materials are added, you will be introduced to more glass materials and oxides, and you will have a chance to work with the appropriate conversion factors.

Changing the Chemicals Used to Introduce Oxides

You will work a material formula for this oxide formula using sodium oxide, which can be supplied by several materials, but the carbonate "soda ash" (Na_2CO_3), is the most common. Nitrate, "Chile saltpeter" or "soda niter" (Na_2NO_3), is also beneficial in small amounts. You will use sodium carbonate and a mixture of sodium carbonate and sodium nitrate. Calcium oxide can be introduced by use of hydrated lime ($CaO \cdot H_2O$), or the carbonate "whiting" ($CaCO_3$). You will work the formula with both of these chemicals. Silica dioxide is generally introduced by potters flint (silica flour, amorphous silica, glass sand, etc.). In more complicated formulas the oxide may be introduced partially from feldspars.

Hydrated Lime (CaO·H₂O). This is a cheap, easily obtained source of calcium oxide. 75.7% of the weight of the lime is the oxide, and the remaining weight is primarily water. The Oxide to Material C.F. is 1.321. To get the 10.5% of calcium oxide needed, multiply the C.F. (1.321) times the amount needed (10.5) to find that your formula requires 13.9 (this could be pounds, grams, kilograms, etc., as long as you are consistent).

Calcium Carbonate, "Whiting," or "Limestone" (CaCO₃). This is another source commonly used for calcium oxide. It is generally purer than lime and somewhat more expensive. The oxide is 56.0% of the weight of limestone, with the remaining weight primarily carbon dioxide (CO_2). The Oxide to Material C.F. is 1.785. To find the amount of whiting needed, multiply the C.F. (1.785) times the amount needed (10.5) to find that our recipe needs 18.7.

Sodium Carbonate or "Soda Ash" (Na₂CO₃). Soda ash is the most common source for sodium oxide used in glassmelting. The oxide is 58.5% of the weight of the material, and the remaining is primarily carbon dioxide (CO_2). The Oxide to Material C.F. is 1.710, so multiply the needed amount (18) by the C.F. (1.710) to arrive at 30.8.

Sodium Nitrate, "Chile Saltpeter," or "Soda-niter" (Na₂NO₃). Another source of sodium oxide is sodium nitrate. The material is more expensive than the carbonate and contains less of the oxide (36.5%). It has some important advantages when used for a portion of the oxide required in the recipe. Part of the remaining weight of the material (which will be driven off by the heat of the furnace) is free oxygen, therefore this nitrate is a strong oxidizing agent. This helps in "burning up" organic impurities in the batch chemicals. The gases given off supply a bubbling action that helps mix the chemicals during the melting process.

An important disadvantage with the use of the nitrate is that it helps in melting not only the chemicals in the batch, but also in the furnace tank. It literally dissolves the refractories of the tank. About 1% or 2% of the needed oxide can be supplied by the nitrate (with an improvement in melting of the glass and improvement of the glass quality), but using more than 3% is rough on the furnace and also begins to introduce inpurities (parts of the furnace!) into your glass.

The C.F. Material to Oxide is 0.365, and the Oxide to Material is 2.743. A short cut to help you easily substitute some sodium nitrate for sodium carbonate in almost any formula calling for sodium oxide is to remember that one part sodium carbonate supplies as much sodium oxide as 1.61 parts of sodium nitrate (conversely one part of sodium nitrate supplies as much oxide as 0.62 parts soda ash). You will find using these figures simpler and faster than using the double computation required with the C.F. Note: sodium nitrate is an oxidizing agent, so should not be used in glasses that should be reduced in the melting—such as cadmium/selenium rubies, etc.!

Silica Dioxide, Sand, Silica, or Flint (SiO₂). Potters flints and silica flour are the most common forms used to introduce silica dioxide into the glass. From now on I will mainly refer to this as "sand," however the material you use should have a fine and even grain. Anything as coarse as ungraded beach sand will add hours to your melting time and increase your fuel costs above any saving in material cost. Also anything but white silica sand will contain so many impurities that the glass quality will be adversely affected.

The oxide makes up the full weight of the material (100%) so the C.F. either way is 1.000. Multiply the amount of oxide needed (71.5) by the C.F. (1.000) to arrive at 71.5 parts sand.

RECIPES FOR SODA/LIME GLASS

Thus far you have developed several ways to arrive at the 71.5-18.0-10.5-sand/soda/lime glass. Some of these are:

Sand	71.5
Soda Ash	30.8
Lime (Hydrate)	13.9

and

Sand	71.5
Soda Ash	30.8
Limestone	18.7

and (suggested but not worked out):

Sand	71.5
Soda Ash	25.7
Lime (Hydrate)	13.9
(or limestone)	18.7
Sodium Nitrate	8.2

(three parts of the oxide has been supplied by the nitrate—you try working it out!)

CHANGING THE OXIDES

A change you can make in the percentage oxide formula *and* the material used that improves the working and melting properties of your formula (but increases the cost) is to use dolomite (CaO·Mg·2CO₃) for the calcium oxide. The C.F. for the calcium oxide to material in dolomite is 3.290. The C.F. for magnesium oxide in dolomite is 4.574. In many ways magnesium oxide and calcium oxide function similarly in the glass, but together they have a more beneficial effect on both the melting and the finished glass than either does alone. The C.F. Oxide to Material for both oxides in dolomite is 1.912. To use dolomite instead of a straight calcium source, multiply the C.F. (1.912) times the amount needed (10.5) to arrive at 20.1.

Converting a Batch Composition into a Theoretical Oxide Recipe

An effective way to check any of your computations of percentage formula to batch recipe is to reverse the process and see if you come out to 100% (or close, since rounding off has been done). The percentage of different oxides supplied by each batch material is calculated and the result expressed as a percentage of the total weight of the different oxides in the batch. To do this, use the Material to Oxide C.F. (listed in the Appendix) and the batch amounts:

Try checking your figures on the recipe using the limestone. Now try reconverting the formula using dolomite and sodium nitrate.

Material	Amount		C.F.		Amount	Oxide
SiO_2	71.5	x	1.000	—	71.5000	SiO_2
Na_2CO_3	30.8	x	0.585	=	18.0180	NA_2O
$CaO.H_2O$	13.9	x	0.757	=	10.5223	CaO
					100.0403 or 100%	

Other Ingredients

In glass calculations (unlike many ceramic glaze calculations) it is often minor oxide and material changes that are important in the glass. Most of these will show in the theoretical percentage oxide formula, but there are some exceptions. For example, the colorants added to the glass are generally not figured in the percentage formula. As a result if you add 2% of a colorant to the batch you end up with about 102%. This is not very effective mathematics, but it is generally understood and accepted.

Other materials that may be used are very minute amounts of colorants added to decolorize the glass. They disguise a color and make the glass seem colorless. These will vary depending on the purity of the materials you use and your esthetic standards. A really clear glass is not the easiest

Globe by Michael Boylen. Freeblown glass with internal divisions, 6" x 6". The artist has been working on controlled interior form techniques for years. The success of his work is illustrated by the large number of similar designs that have appeared recently in the production of well-known European factories. Collection of the Corning Museum of Glass.

thing to produce, and unfortunately when you get it, not everyone (particularly beginners in glass) appreciates the results.

Two other ingredients that are very important but are used in very small amounts (and generally do not appear in the oxide formula) are the oxides of arsenic (As_2O_3) and antimony (Sb_2O_3). Both of these are poisonous. They are fining and decolorizing agents and rarely used in amounts more than 1/10 of 1 percent. The amount used of either arsenic or antimony oxide (or a combination of the two—something I have found very effective although there seems to be no basis in the literature for using both in the same glass) depends on the purity of your materials, type of furnace, kind of fuel, refractories, desired result in the glass, etc. This is usually determined after the melter gains a knowledge of his materials and equipment. I mention this because I recommend both in amounts of about 0.1 of one percent. In general you can work *down* from that figure.

Also, when these ingredients are added, there is a noticeable difference in clarity in the finished glass and advantage in the melting time and heat needed to produce a "seed-free" (bubble-free) glass. Try adding them to the formula we have thus far worked out:

Sand	71.5
Soda Ash	25.7
Dolomite	20.1
Sodium Nitrate	8.2

A "Better" Glass

The following glass is more complicated and uses more ingredients. I will start you off—much as I did in the soda/lime—and then let you use the reference tables in the back of the book and do your own figuring. Here is the theoretical oxide formula:

Silica Dioxide	SiO_2	68.0
Sodium Oxide	Na_2O	15.0
Potassium Oxide	K_2O	5.0
Calcium Oxide	CaO	3.0
Boric Oxide	B_2O_3	2.5
Zinc Oxide	ZnO	2.5
Aluminum Oxide	Al_2O_3	2.0
Magnesium Oxide	MgO	1.0
Barium Oxide	BaO	1.0

The materials will be increased to include:

Potassium Nitrate	K_2NO_3
Potassium Carbonate	K_2CO_3
Zinc Oxide	ZnO
Barium Carbonate	$BaCO_3$
Borax	$Na_2B_4O_7 \cdot 10H_2O$
Potash Feldspar (theoretical)	$K_2O \cdot Al_2O_3 \cdot 6SiO_2$

This formula should acquaint you with many of the commonly used materials in glass and take you through a fairly complicated recipe. In practice you can decide what will be used, and after going through this recipe you will know why. This glass has little or no tendency toward devitrification, melts easily, has a long working range, and has good color-producing qualities. With trace amounts of arsenic and antimony oxide it has excellent clarity. This glass does not fit into one of the common categories of glass types but, as with many good glasses, overlaps categories since it is a mixed alkali (flux), mixed earth alkali (stabilizer).

Suggestions

Since certain materials supply more than one oxide to the melt, and conversely since several materials often supply the same oxide, you should start with the most complicated material and work to the simplest. If a material that is the only source of an oxide supplies other oxides as well, start with this material (or materials). Feldspars (work the conversion factor from analysis or from manufacturers specifications if possible), borax, and dolomite are the most common materials in this category.

Next figure the different materials that supply the same oxides (such as potassium carbonate and potassium nitrate, or sodium carbonate and sodium nitrate, etc.). Lastly figure the easy materials—those that are the only source of the entire needed amount of any oxide (zinc oxide, barium carbonate, etc.).

Your computations will seldom go line by line, so can be worked any number of ways. Conversely, when figuring the oxide percentage from the batch, it is usually possible to do a line-by-line calculation with a final summing up of the oxides in like groups.

Errors. There are several "errors" in these calculations that are common to such work. They are pointed out so the reader will be aware of their existence even if they do not appear in the calculations. Most of these are impurities: alumina, for example, appears in all sand and some lime products; water is picked up (or lost) by some chemicals, thereby changing the weight of the material (calcined potassium carbonate will pick up large amounts of water if improperly stored and borax will lose water for the same reason); alumina is picked up by the melting glass from the furnace refractories; oxides are lost from the melt by vaporization (sodium oxide, boric oxide, etc.); dissolved gases from combustion (carbon dioxide, sulfer oxides, etc.), etc.

Feldspar. The material that is most complicated in this new glass, and that also supplies all the required amount of one oxide (aluminum oxide), is feldspar. There are different types of feldspar, so be sure you are using the figures appropriate for the material available to you. The feldspar used in the following is Kingman potash spar and has the following approximate composition (see Appendix of materials): SiO_2 66.2; Al_2O_3 18.4; K_2O 12.0.

Aluminum Oxide or Alumina (Al_2O_3). In small amounts (about 1% to 3%), alumina is a very beneficial material to use in a glass. It lowers the amount a glass expands and contracts when heated and cooled, it reduces devitrification, it increases the "toughness" and durability of the finished ware, and also imparts other important qualities that are listed in the Appendix.

To figure the amount of feldspar you need to use for the 2% alumina, multiply the amount (2) by the C.F. Oxide to Material (5.434) to establish the needed amount of feldspar (10.868). Feldspar also supplies significant amounts of silica dioxide (SiO_2) and potassium oxide (K_2O). These should be established because there is no way to add the alumina from the feldspar without also adding the other oxides!

Silica Dioxide or Sand (SiO_2). To establish the amount of silica that has been put into the glass by the feldspar, multiply the amount of feldspar (10.868) times the C.F. Material to Oxide (0.662). You have added 7.1946% to the glass. You need 68%, so subtract the 7.2 from the 68. You still must add 60.8% silica to the batch by adding sand. Multiply the percent needed (60.8) by the C.F. Oxide to Material (1.000) to establish that 60.8 parts of sand are needed.

Potassium Oxide (K_2O). The feldspar has added another desirable oxide to your melt—potassium oxide (K_2O). In general, mixed sodium and potassium glasses are more durable than single alkali glasses. Potassium oxide improves the appearance and brilliance of the glass, decreases the tendency toward devitrification, increases the durability of the glass, and gives other desirable qualities listed in the Appendix.

Establish how much potassium oxide you have added with the feldspar. Multiply the amount of feldspar (10.868) times the C.F. Material to Oxide (0.120) to find there is 1.3042% from the feldspar.

Subtract this 1.3% from the amount needed in the formula (5%). This leaves 3.7% potassium oxide still needed. Potassium nitrate (K_2NO_3) will be used to supply 1% of this amount.

Potassium Nitrate, "Saltpeter," or "Nitre" (K_2NO_3). Like nitrate of sodium, this is a strong oxidizing agent in the early stages of melting. It is an excellent flux that helps start the melting of other materials in the glass. It is rarely used in amounts over 2% or 3% because it is also very hard on the furnace refractories.

Multiply the needed 1% by the C.F. Oxide to Material (2.147) for 2.1 parts of potassium nitrate. Thus far 1.3% potassium oxide has been supplied by the feldspar (10.9) and 1% by the potassium nitrate (2.1). If we subtract this total (2.3) from the needed amount of potassium oxide (5) we find we still need 2.7% to be supplied from another source.

Keep in mind that it would not be practical to use our feldspar for more of the potassium oxide because the amount of alumina would become a hindrance rather than a help (you cannot add the "potash" part of the feldspar without also adding the "alumina" part!). Also, to increase the amount of the "saltpeter" (added to sodium nitrate you will add later in your calculations) would be rough on the furnace refractories.

Potassium Carbonate or ("Potash") (K_2CO_3). We can add the oxide needed by using potassium carbonate. To figure the amount multiply the percentage needed (2.7) by the C.F. Oxide to Material (1.467) which equals 3.9609 or 4 parts of potassium carbonate.

Summing Up the Feldspar Oxides. Thus far it has been established that 68.0% silica dioxide will be supplied by 10.9 parts of feldspar (7.2%) and by 60.8 parts sand (60.8%). Your 5% potassium oxide is supplied by 10.9 parts of feldspar (1.3%), 2.1 parts of potassium nitrate (1.0%) and 4 parts of potassium carbonate (2.7%). The needed 2.0% aluminum oxide is of course supplied by the 10.9 parts of feldspar.

From the above it is evident that a line-by-line computation is impractical and it also shows why it is difficult to give a hard and fast rule on the order of computing materials. Now that feldspar and the oxides contained in feldspar have been completed, the next most complicated material—sodium biborate (borax) can be computed.

Sodium Biborate or Borax ($Na_2B_4O_7 \cdot 10 H_2O$). This material will be used to supply the needed boric oxide (B_2O_3). Boric oxide helps in melting the batch, increases the brilliance of the glass, produces better color, improves the chemical resistance of the glass, and imparts other desirable qualities. Using the correct figures and formula, from this point on you should do the needed calculations. Remember that borax supplies more than boric oxide to the glass.

Sodium Oxide. When computing the sodium oxide, add 1% with sodium nitrate. Do not forget the sodium oxide you have already added from other materials and complete the amount needed with soda ash.

Bottle with Hollow Handle by Carol Lynne Osmun. Potash/lead glass, 3″ x 6″. An excellent example of a "hollow" handle (the liquid in the vessel also is in the handle). The vessel has a second colored glass dipped at the bottom and pulled to the lip along the outside of the handle.

Calcium and Magnesium Oxides. We have already discussed the advantages of using dolomite (a double carbonate of magnesium and calcium) rather than calcium oxide alone. The relationship of calcium to magnesium in dolomite is about 3 to 2. The near ideal relationship of these oxides—that adds to the glass quality, melts fastest, and in general improves all aspects of the melting process—is 3 to 1. To obtain this (which is what the formula calls for) you will use dolomite and another source of calcium (such as hydrated lime). Check and use the appropriate C.F. for these materials.

Barium Oxide. Small amounts of barium oxide have a very beneficial effect on most glasses. Barium lowers the melting point of the glass, decreases the tendency toward devitrification, imparts higher density and higher refraction, has a beneficial effect on most colors, etc. Use barium carbonate ($BaCO_3$) to supply the needed barium oxide. Remember, however, that barium is toxic.

Zinc Oxide. In small amounts zinc oxide is beneficial to almost any glass. It increases the brilliance of the glass, helps the color, extends the working range, reduces devitrification, etc. Use the correct C.F. when figuring the zinc oxide. Note: zinc is poisonous.

***Bud Vase** by Monona Rossol, "Soft" borosilicate glass, 3″ x 8″. Here an applied design of colored glass has been added to the clear vase shape from a pontil. The colored glass echoes the basic shape of the vessel in a "variations on a theme."*

Second Melts (Cullet)

Second-melt or cullet is glass that has already been melted and cooled and is then put back in the furnace for remelting. A certain amount of cullet (10%-25% approximately) in "first" or batch melts will help melt the batch chemicals. What I am referring to now, however, is the use of *all*-cullet (raw cullet) glass.

There are safety and economic advantages to using of second melts. Some glass chemicals are poisonous, and all dusts can cause lung diseases (such as silicosis). The use of explosive materials in the melt is sometimes mentioned as a hazard, but generally speaking this is unfounded.

Economics is a different matter. There are savings in fuel, in time, and in furnace life when using some cullets. If we add to that a *free* supply of glass (discarded bottles, broken window glass, etc.) second melts become very important to a business, although I still have some reservations about their use by the artist.

Disadvantages. The first, and I feel most important disadvantage of using cullet (particularly for the beginner) is denying oneself the experience of seeing powdered chemicals change into this sort of magic stuff we call glass. I find it hard to believe that the person who goes through that experience will not become "hooked" on glass to some degree. Equally important, he learns what glass is in the most direct, responsive way possible. No one reading about glass can possibly "know" the material in the same way.

The economics of cullet can also become illusionary if you begin spending large amounts of money for a glass that is not really designed for hand work. A glass that was designed and melted *specifically* for the making of fiberglass insulation is not designed for hand work. With a material as versatile as glass, for you to make such a compromise just does not stand the test of objective judgement. If we add to that the large sums of money charged for transporting such cullet, most of the economic advantages no longer exist. You should also seriously question using discard glass from hand factories (often this is "bottom glass" with at least the potential of faults).

Scrap Cullet. Most scrap bottle or window glass has a composition that has been adjusted to the speed and kind of machine on which it was originally produced. These formulas can vary. You are in a good position if you have a fairly consistent source of the same glass (but there is no way for you to be certain a company may not alter a glass formula without sending notice to offhand workers using their scrap!). It might be possible to obtain a formula analysis for a sample and to modify it if need be by increasing the flux (usually soda ash). Indeed, many small handworking glass factories in the United States and Mexico rely entirely on discard clear glass for their main supply. Their furnaces are large, and in this case the larger the furnace tank the better the chance the over-all composition will "even out."

"What" You are Working With. Although you can establish a rule of thumb that works for adding soda (or borax, etc.) to a scrap glass, in general I feel it is not worth the effort to find out what you are really melting. To work the formulas I have given you with scrap glass (that probably has a variety of different compositions mixed in), using the "easy" way of adding so many pounds to so many pounds, changes the percentage of every oxide in the glass! Such computations are simply not worth the Herculean task involved.

If the above comments seem to be designed to convince you to formulate and melt *your own glass*—good. They are presented with just that aim in mind.

5/Working Freeblown Glass

Two-Piece Vase by Dominic Labino. Freeblown and joined glass, 5" x 5". A very interesting piece from my collection done in a yellow glass. These are two vessels (one for the hollow base the other for the bowl) joined foot to base. Final forming was done on the top "vessel" after the pieces were joined.

In this chapter I will show you how to work the glass on the blow pipe and the pontil. As with most processes, this is one way of working, but not the only way. Any method the artist chooses is fine as long as the desired results are obtained.

Materials and Organization

Molten glass in a furnace and a blow pipe are essential items for freeblown glass. Jacks, blocks, pontil, shears, and an annealing oven (or substitutes) are also needed for most work. A marver, a glassblower's bench, and a gloryhole round out the useful equipment.

Working with glass—unlike working with many other materials—is a continuous, uninterrupted process. The "pace of the glass" does not allow for easy stopping and starting, fumbling for tools, and the like. It is important for the glassworker to have his tools in the right place at the right time. Starting with the very first work session, try to always plan one step ahead. Place the tool needed for the next operation close at hand *before* starting the next step.

Although most artists decide on a layout of tools that works best for their own needs, I have included a suggested arrangement for you. The jacks are close to you, the shears come next, and at the end of the bench is a file for "cracking off" from the pipe. Nails on the front edge of the bench hold other tools that may be needed.

On the right-hand side of the photograph is a pail with *one* block in it. This bucket is where you keep the wooden tool to be used next. More blocks are within your reach in another bucket, and other wooden tools are in yet another bucket behind the bench. The metal container on the floor under the bench is to catch scrap glass cut of the piece, etc. Note that the buckets have been raised on brick or cement blocks so they are within easy reach.

The Pace of Glass

When the glass is first gathered from the furnace it is very liquid and you must watch its flow very carefully. You must rotate the pipe steadily to keep the glass on the pipe and "on center." Let gravity work for you by turning the pipe just enough to keep the soft glass from dripping off onto the floor. If you rotate the pipe too fast (a common mistake for beginners) the centrifugal force of the rotation will tend to force any off-center glass further away from the pipe, or even off the pipe. The glass moves more and more slowly as it cools so rotation should be slowed accordingly. In the steps that follow, remember that the pipe is being rotated all the time you are working.

Keeping the Glass and Pipe Hot

It is important to keep the glass on the pipe hot. This is done not only to facilitate forming, but also to prevent thermal strains from breaking the vessel. Use your furnace as a glory-hole for such periodic reheatings. The type of glass, the thickness of the walls (thin-walled pieces need to be heated more often than thick-walled), and the amount of contact the glass has with cold tools all determine how often to reheat. There is no minute-by-minute rule to use, so this is something you must develop a feel for by trial and error. Some of the commercial glasses (fiberglass marbles, scrap plate glass, etc.) require a great deal more reheating than most batch glasses because they have a shorter working range.

It is also important to keep the tip of the pipe hot while working the glass or the vessel will crack off the pipe and be destroyed. Usually when you reheat the vessel you take care of reheating the pipe tip as well, but when adding a new gather this may not be so. The hot glass added over the bubble keeps the vessel hot, but not the pipe. To avoid this you should go back to the furnace to heat both the vessel and pipe. Then you block the vessel to chill the glass, and the pipe tip stays hot. Note that only the tip of the pipe should be hot—keep the rest of the pipe as cool as possible to prevent burning your hands. This cooling can be done by splashing or dripping cold water on the pipe.

(Above) A view of the bench ready for use. On the bench are jacks, shears, and a file. Hanging in front are tools that may be needed for a specific job. Blocks and other wooden tools are in pails around the bench, with the right-forward pail always containing the next tool you will need.

(Right) A water container can be used to drip water on the pipe to cool it. It is important to rotate the pipe so it is cooled evenly on all sides. The sudden cooling of a part of the pipe may cause warping.

The Glassblowing Procedure

The ordinary procedure for working freeblown glass is presented here to give the beginner an overall view of the sequence of actions and the relationship of the equipment to the process. Later in the chapter each step will be examined in detail.

1. Molten glass is gathered from the furnace on a heated blow pipe.

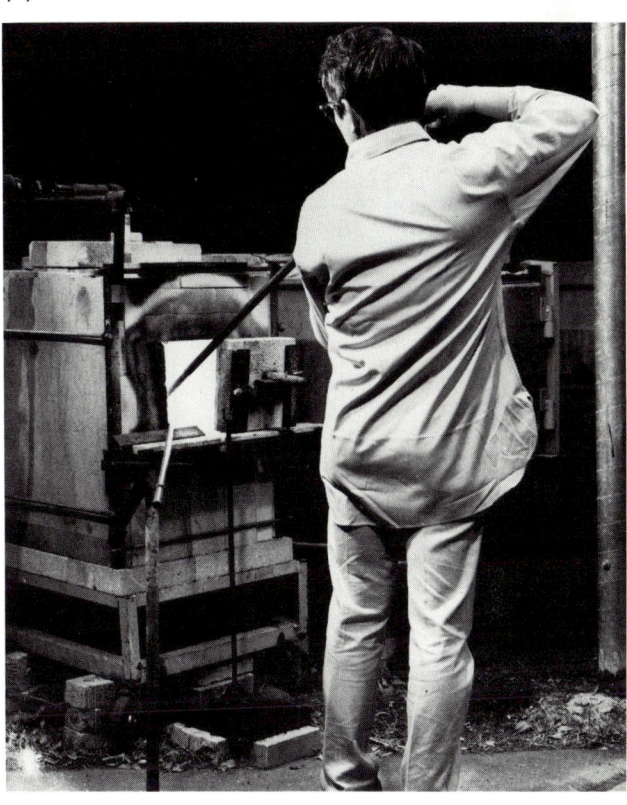

2. The gather is rolled (chilled and centered) on the marver.

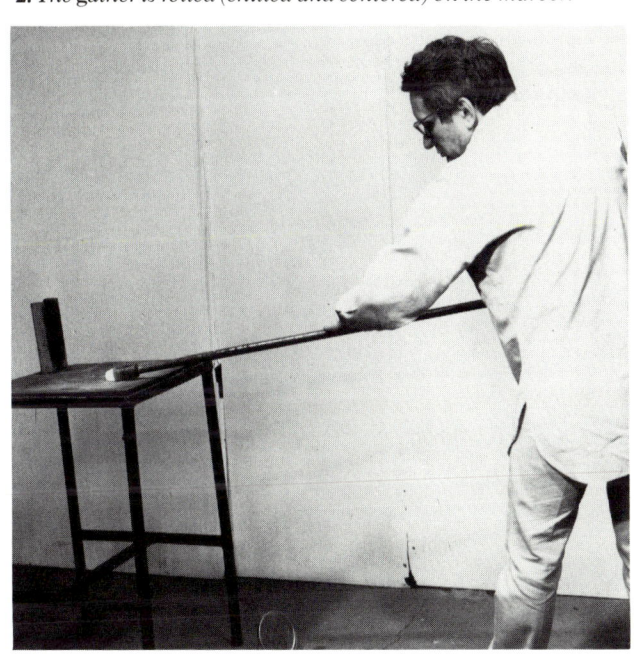

3. After marvering the gather a bubble is blown (note the placement of mirror).

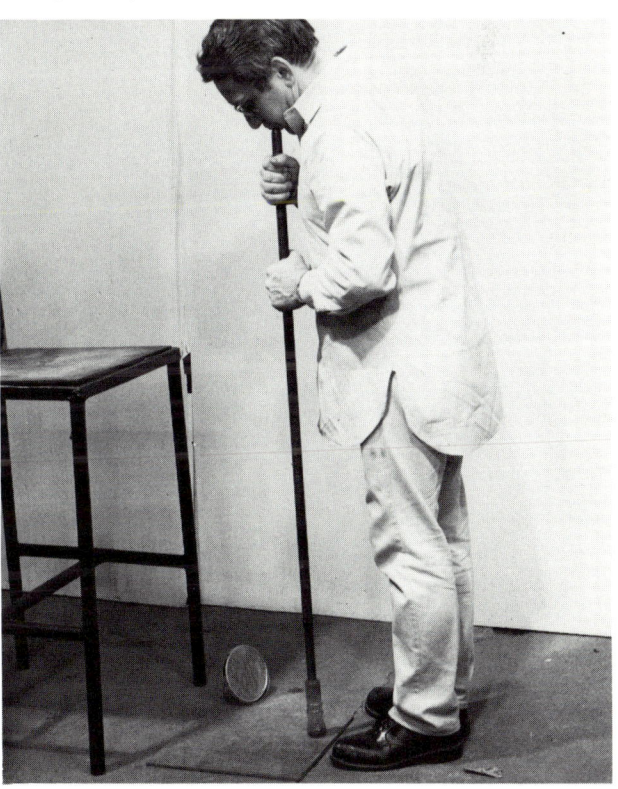

WORKING FREEBLOWN GLASS 103

4. *The bubble is necked on the bench using forming tools.*

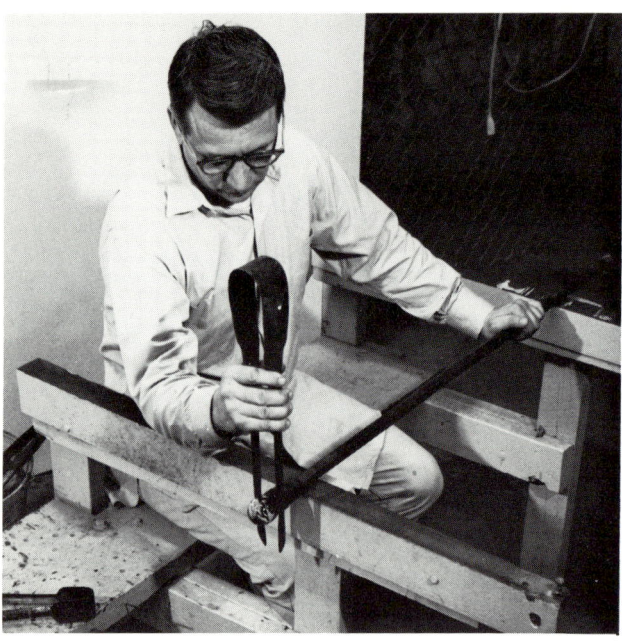

5. *Additional gathers of glass are made over the first gather.*

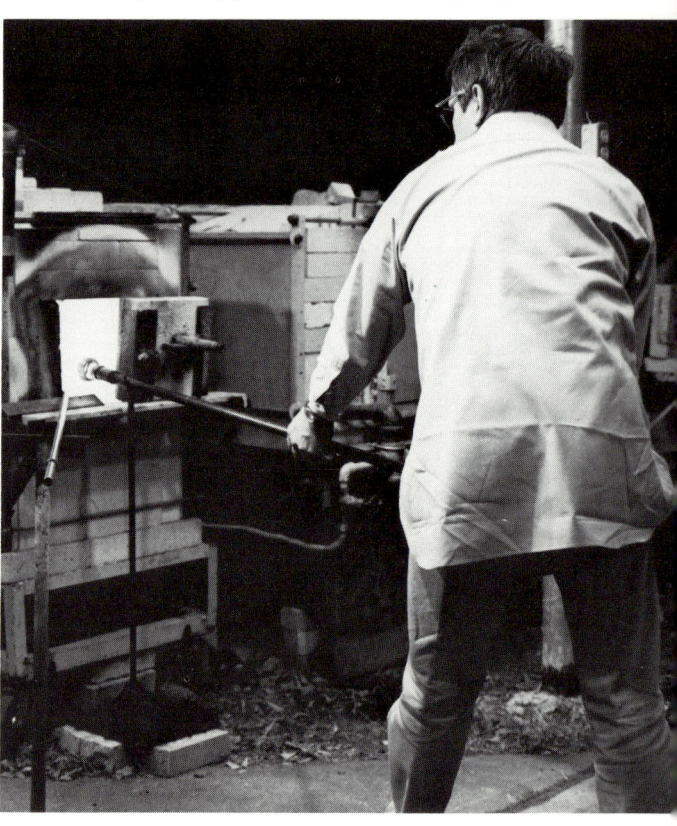

8. *The bottom of the vessel is flattened with a paddle.*

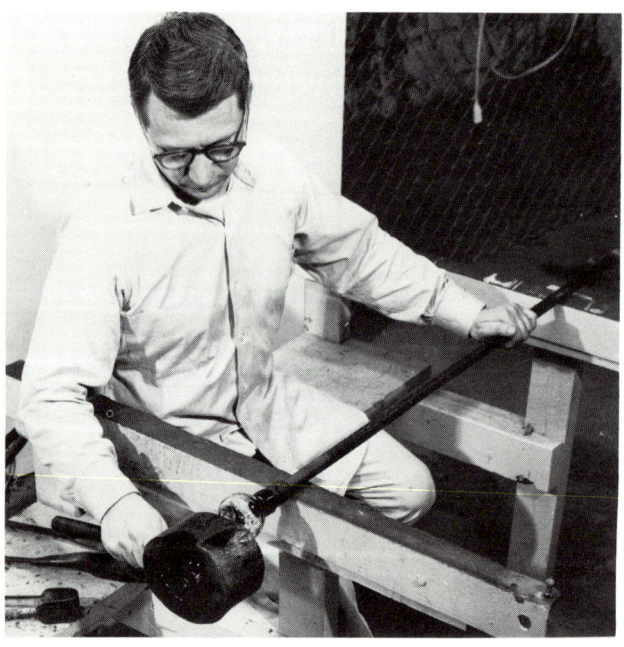

9. *The glass vessel is attached to the pontil.*

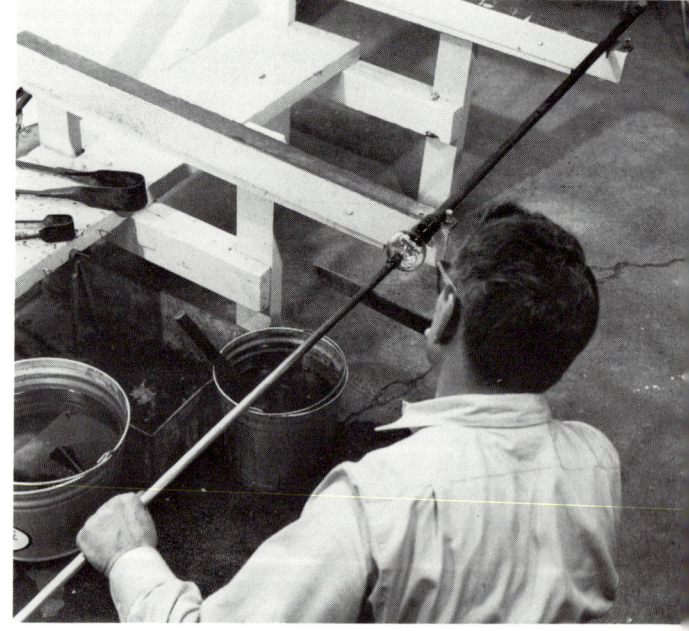

6. The glass is chilled and formed in a blocking tool.

7. The glass is reblown (enlarged).

10. The vessel is cracked from the pipe.

11. The vessel is reheated.

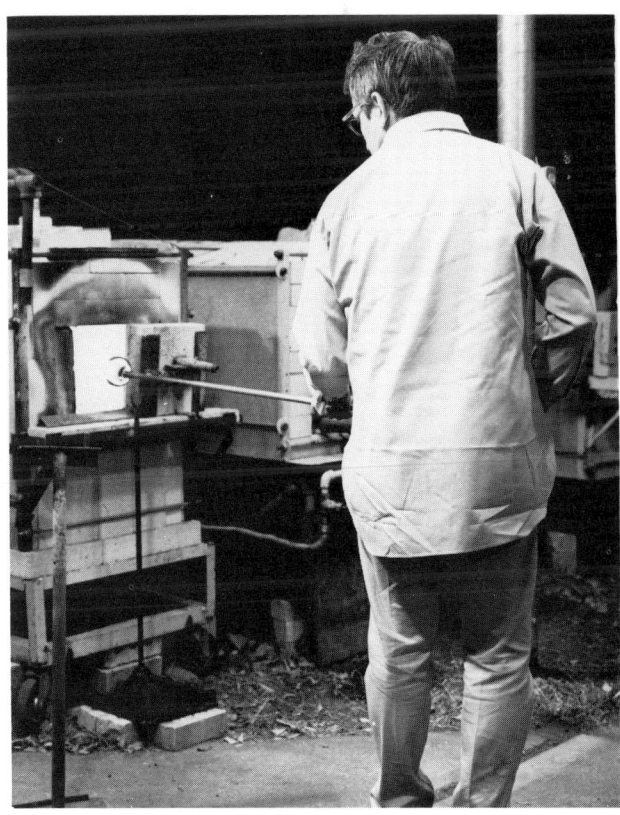

12. It is then worked with wood or metal tools.

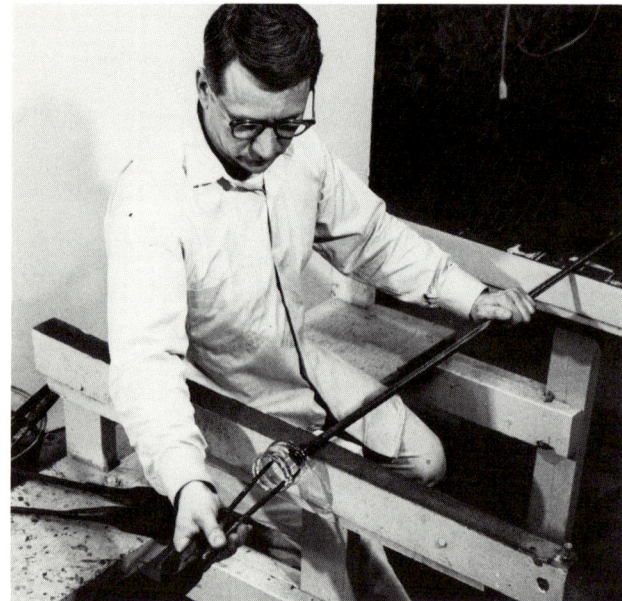

13. When the vessel is complete, it is removed from the pontil.

14. It is finally placed in the annealing oven to be cooled slowly.

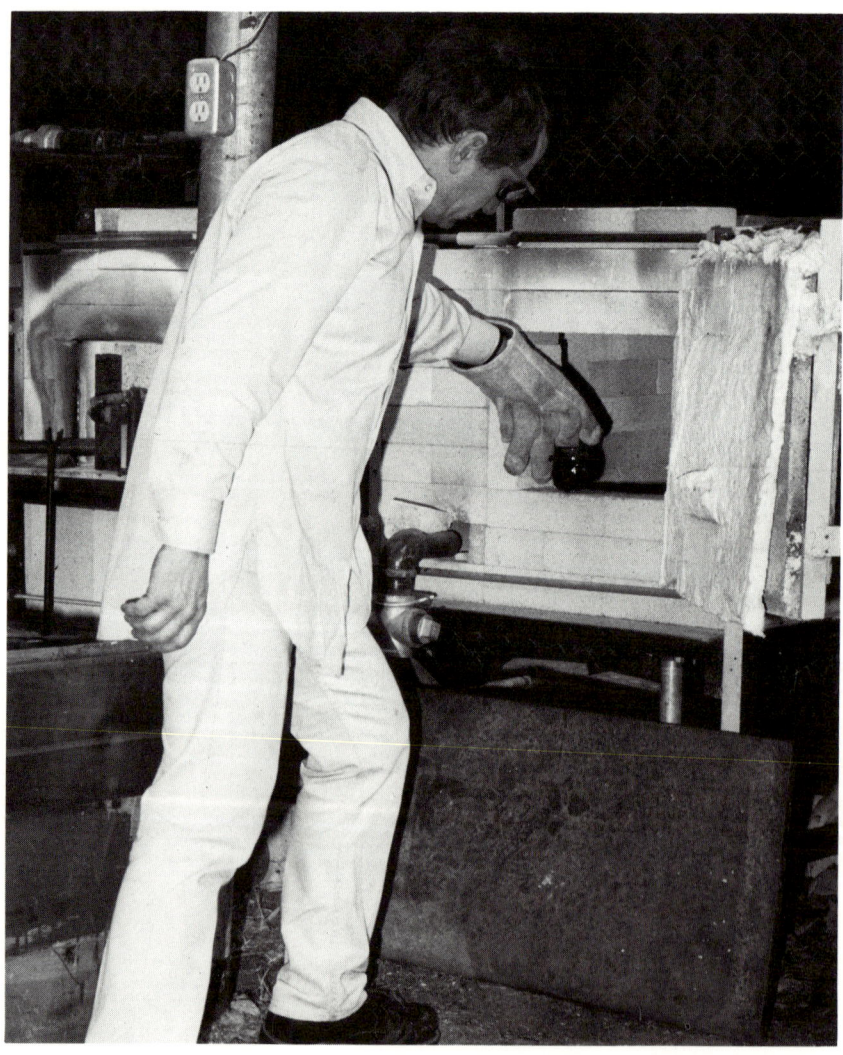

Gathering Glass

Gather the molten glass from the furnace on a blow pipe (or blowing iron). Heat the tip of the pipe to a dull red before gathering or the glass will not adhere. Do not plunge the pipe into the molten glass, but rather drag it across the surface of the glass toward the door while slowly rotating the pipe. When this is done properly, not only does it keep molten glass from getting into the pipe, but a small bubble may already form at the tip of the pipe. Some artists find that it helps to hold one finger over the mouthpiece to trap air in the pipe. Lift the pipe off the glass surface by using the metal edge of the furnace as a fulcrum. Continue rotating the pipe in the furnace until the thread of molten glass breaks off. Remember to keep rotating the pipe as you take it out of the furnace as well. With molten glass gathered on the head of the pipe you can blow into the pipe to enlarge the vessel; swing the pipe to elongate the piece; and roll the pipe on the glassworker's bench to form the vessel. These processes are the basic ones used to form any type of vessel. Always handle the pipe carefully. Allowing the pipe to roll off the bench, or beating the pipe to remove glass, are practices that are certain to bend the pipe's shaft. Attempting to form a round piece with a bent pipe is comparable to trying to throw a pot on a wheel with a bad set of bearings—it might be done, but only with needless difficulty.

1. Bring about 1½" of the heated head of the revolving pipe into contact with the molten glas surface in the furnace. Rotate the pipe as you drag the tip along the top of the glass surface toward you to make the gather.

2. Raise the pipe above the molten glass surface using the metal support at the front of the furnace as a fulcrum, and rotate until the glass thread falls back into the tank. Keep the gather on center by rotating the pipe as you remove it from the furnace.

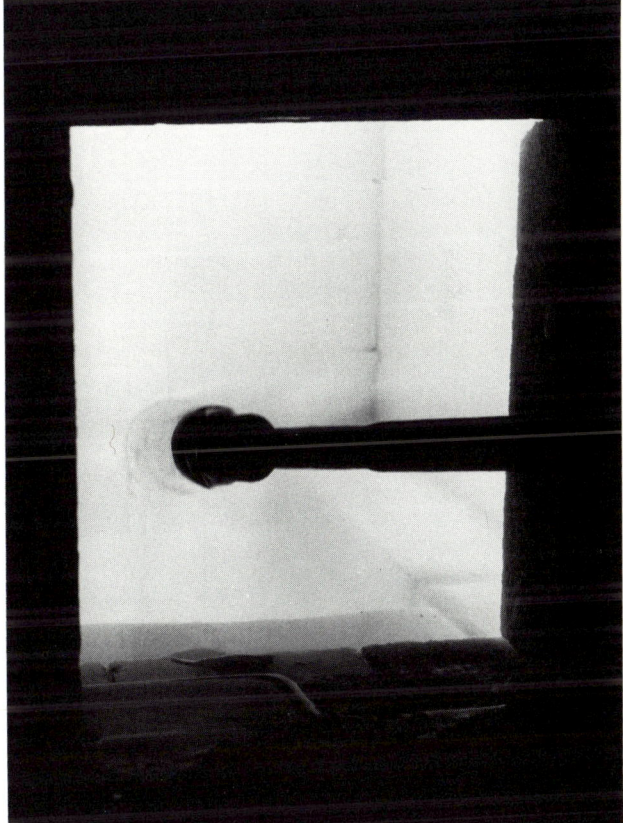

Marvering and Blowing the Bubble

Roll the first gather of glass on the marver to center and chill it before you blow the first bubble. A wet wooden paddle is sometimes used in place of the marver for work on the first gather.

To blow the first bubble, hold the pipe either horizontally or down toward the floor. The practice of pointing the blow pipe straight up into the air, although showy, is not safe—hot, loose fire scale in the pipe might fall back into your mouth. A mirror placed on the floor is useful for watching the bubble while you are blowing. Stop the bubble before its bottom becomes too thin.

1. Roll the gather on the marver to chill the glass and center it.

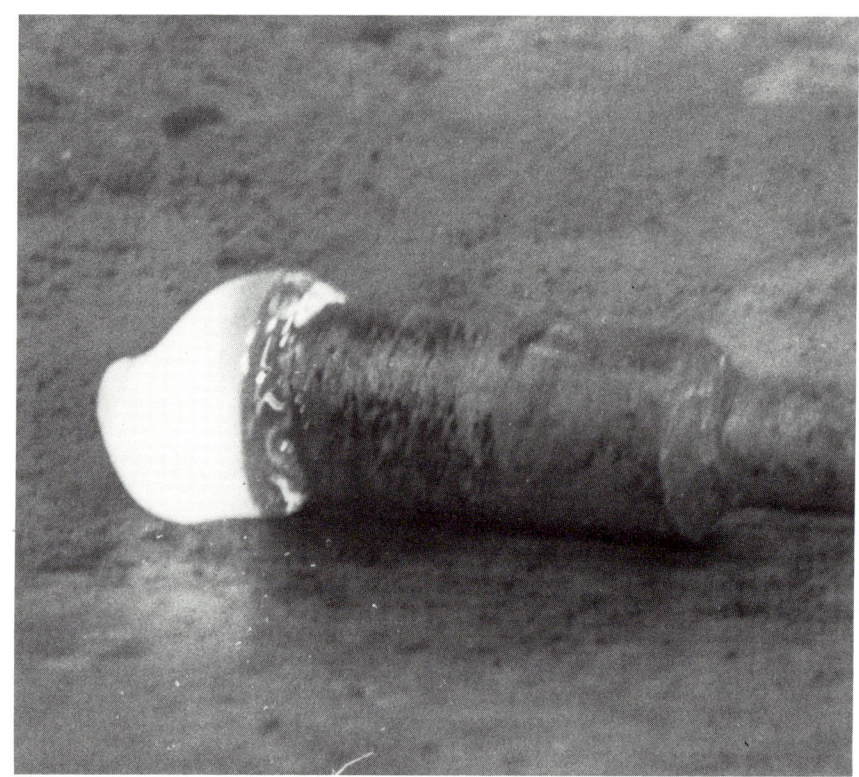

2. Blow the first bubble into the gather.

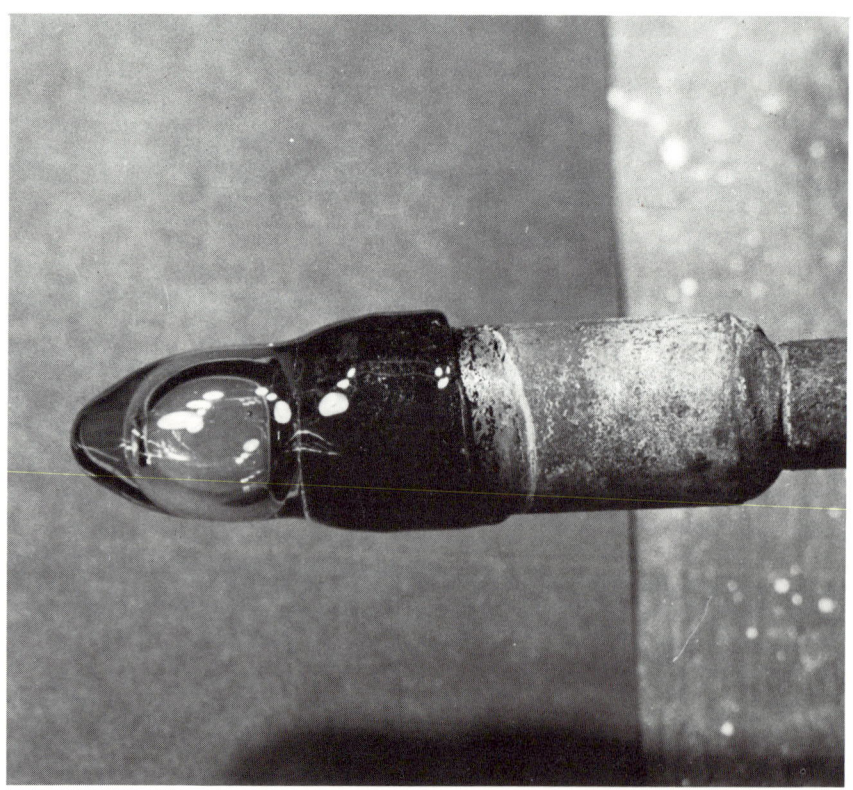

108 GLASSBLOWING

Necking the Bubble

While rolling the pipe on the glassblower's bench, use jacks to indent a shallow groove on the bubble just beyond the head of the pipe. This groove will facilitate later removal of the vessel from the pipe.

1. Apply pressure with the jacks just beyond the end of the rotating pipe to make a groove in the bubble.

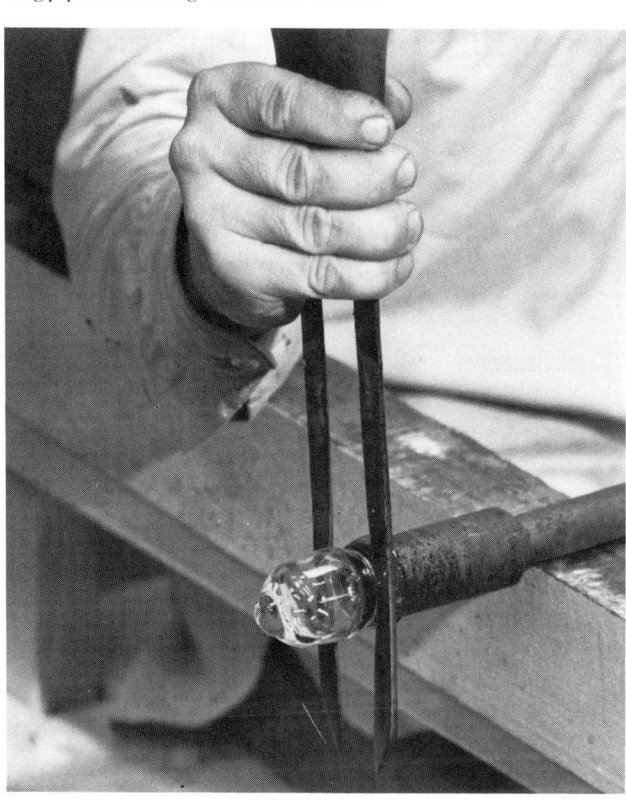

2. Or use the edge of the bench rail in place of the jacks.

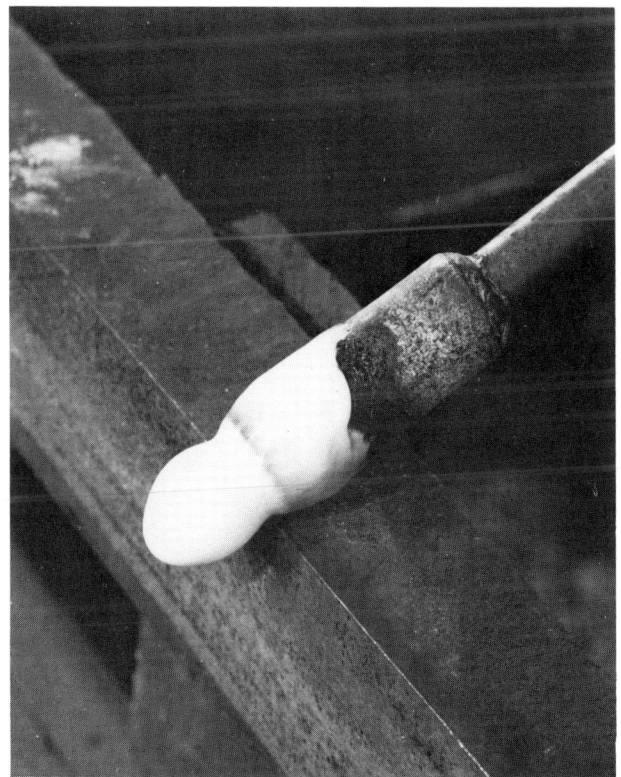

3. Or a wooden tool may be used to form the groove.

WORKING FREEBLOWN GLASS 109

Blocking and Additional Gathers

Make the second gather after the color that indicates heat in the bubble has disappeared. Push the bubble under the surface of the molten glass almost to the neckline and rotate it once. If the molten glass goes over the neckline by accident, the vessel can be renecked. Continue to rotate the pipe, and using the metal fulcrum at the front of the furnace, lift the gather out of the tank and rotate until the tail of glass melts off.

Remove the gather from the furnace and take it to the bench. Roll the gather in a forming block to remove irregularities and to chill the glass. This "skin" of chilled glass helps prevent you from blowing through the bubble. Blocking centers the gather much as the potter's hands center clay on the wheel. The pipe should be in motion before contact is made with the tool. The movement of the pipe on the bench is steady and controlled. Do not exert too much prssure on the block, particularly if the glass is not rotating, or you may force the gather off center. If more glass is needed, you can make successive gathers, etc., until the vessel is the desired size. Forming, at this point, is determined by the shape you plan to make.

1. Make the second gather over the bubble, follow the procedure used for the first gather.

2. Rotate the second and successive gathers in the wet block to center and chill the glass and produce a "skin" to blow against.

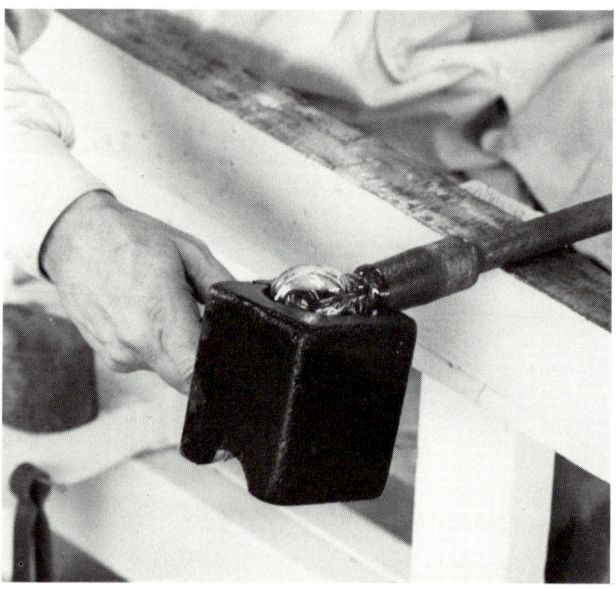

3. The gathering process can be repeated using larger blocks.

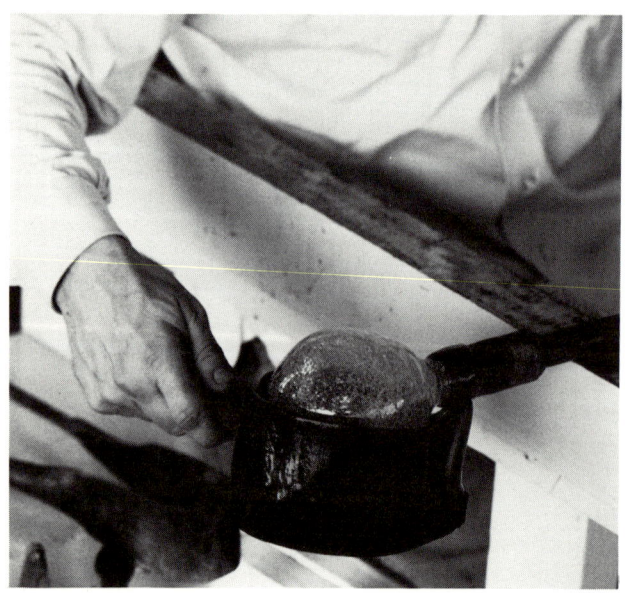

4. An open ended blocking tool can be used for cylinder-shaped vessels.

Forming on the Blow Pipe

The vessel can be shaped in a number of ways while still on the blow pipe. The glass can be formed in various blocks, worked on the marver, shaped with paddles, squeezed with jacks, or cut with shears. Swinging the pipe will elongate the vessel. Care is obviously needed here, since vigorous, careless swinging endangers everyone in the shop. Unfortunately, some artists use this swinging process as a display of virtuosity—and this has been copied by beginners with dangerous results.

1. The jacks can be used, as shown here, to straighten and form the vessel on the pipe.

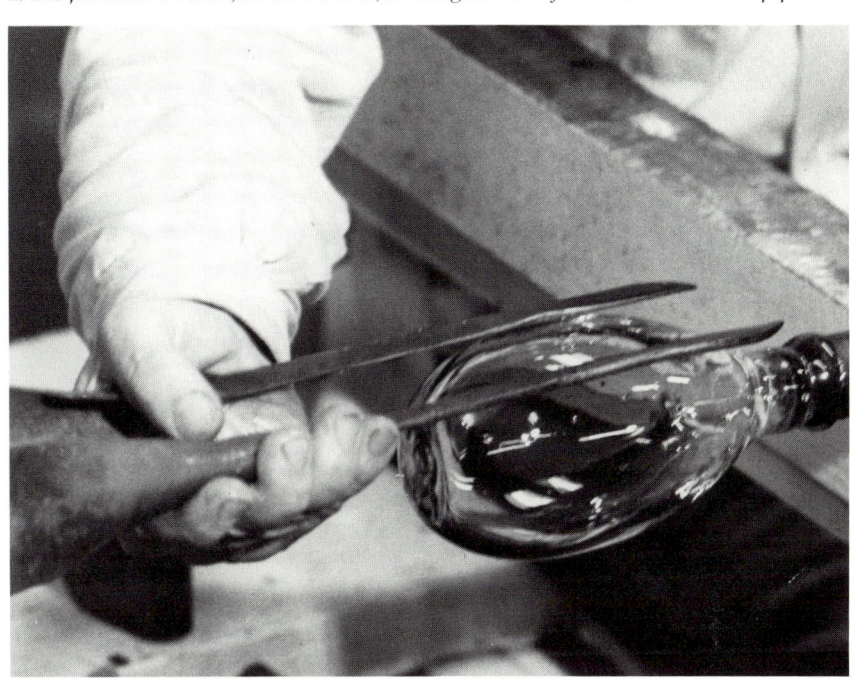

2. If you plan to do a closed form, it helps to start forming while the vessel is still on the pipe. These wooden jacks begin to form the neck near the lip of the vessel. Pressure with the jacks continues to the desired point at the shoulder of the vessel.

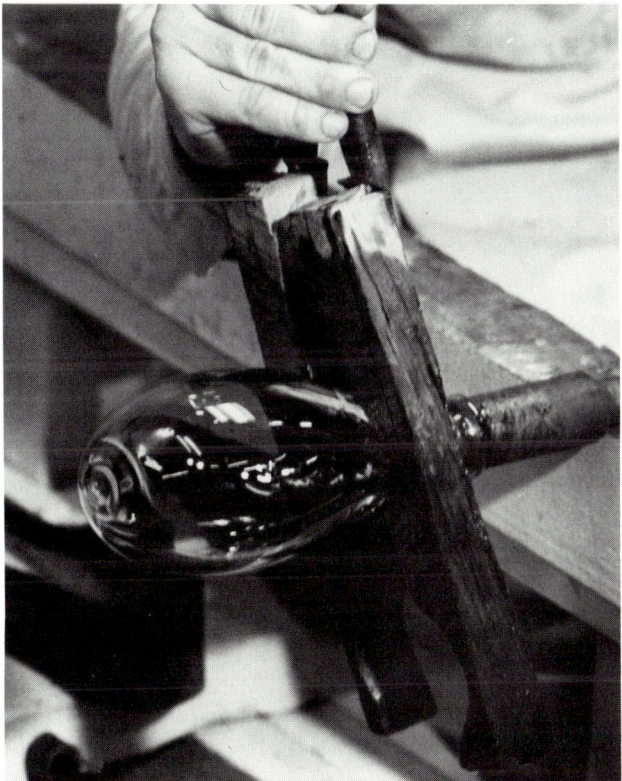

3. Here a bent pipe, filled with running water, is used in place of the jacks. I took this photograph at the Hoya Glass Co. in Tokyo, Japan.

Attaching the Pontil

When the vessel is the size and shape desired, you will attach it to the pontil and then remove the blow pipe. To do this, first flatten the bottom of the vessel with jacks, a paddle, or against a metal plate. Make a small gather of glass on a hot pontil (you can also attach the vessel to a very hot pontil without an extra gather of glass, but this may be more difficult for the beginner). The glass bond should stick to the vessel strongly enough to complete forming work, yet should be weak enough to break cleanly, without damage to the vessel when you are finished. There are several methods to help produce this imperfect bond: you can dip the bond glass in sand, press it against scored metal, score it with a file, or press it against wood (to coat it with ash). Following any of these operations, the pontil is again marvered.

Hold the pontil in the left hand and rest the front (just behind the molten glass) on a file. Guide the pontil to the center of the bottom of the piece (which is on the bench) and attach it by pressing. There should be glass between the pontil tip and the bottom of the vessel. Drip water off a file or off the blades of the jacks into the neck groove on the vessel as the pipe rotates. Next vibrate the blow pipe by hitting it with a file or against the bench. this breaks the glass at the neck mark. Hitting the pipe against the bench can only be done with a helper (pontil-boy).

After removing the vessel from the blow pipe ("cracking off"), the lip should be reheated immediately to prevent thermal strains from breaking the glass.

1. Chill the bottom of the vessel and flatten it with a paddle, the back of the jacks, the bottom of a block, a metal plate, or a concrete floor. Hold the pipe in the left hand with the vessel down while you prepare the pontil.

4. Water, either on a file or on the blades of the jacks, is scored around the neckline indentation near the pipe.

2. Now make a small gather of glass on a heated pontil and roll the gather on the marver to center and chill it. Dip the glass in sand (or use one of the other methods discussed earlier) to make the bond imperfect. Then marver the pontil again.

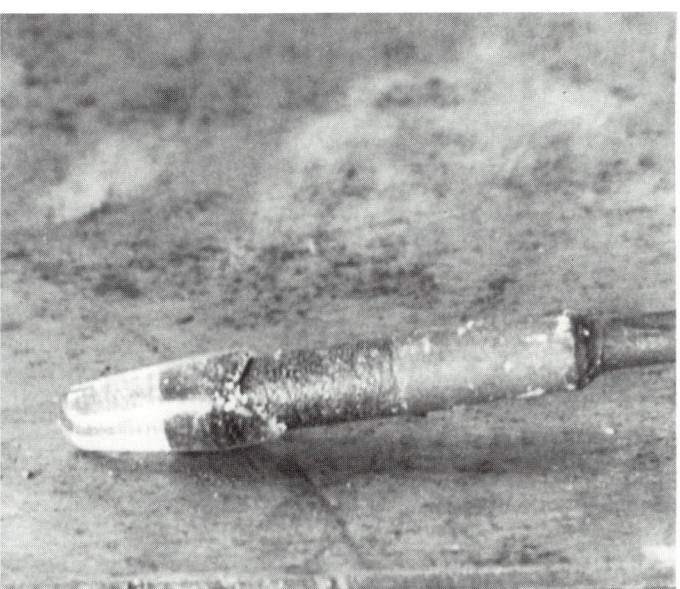

3. Lay the pipe on the bench. Use a file to guide the pontil to the venter of the base of the vessel and press it in place. Pull on the pontil to make sure it is firmly attached to the vessel.

5. Hit the pipe with the file (or the pipe can be hit against the bench if a pontil-boy is used) to break the glass at the score line.

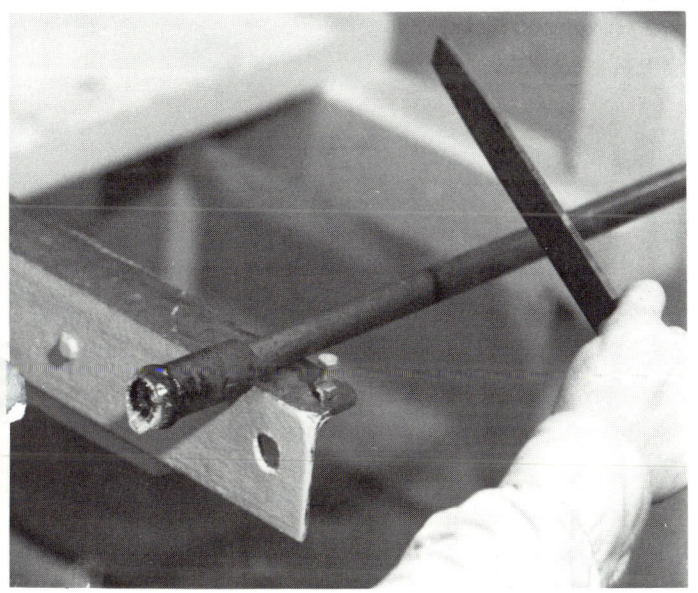

6. Immediately heat the vessel lip to prepare for forming and to remove the strains caused by the water used to crack the glass.

MAKING CLOSED SHAPES

To make closed or bottle-shaped forms, most of your work with forming tools will be done on the outside surface of the vessel. The jacks are used to pinch in the vessel and to pull the form. You can use centrifugal force (spinning the pontil) to widen the form somewhat. If you want to enlarge a closed shape, the vessel can be blown out with compressed air or with steam from a wet stick held tightly in the mouth of the vessel. Special tools for blowing the forms with mouth pressure should be avoided—they are dangerous and clumsy to use.

1. The jacks begin to close the neck of a vessel by applying pressure at the shoulder of the vessel.

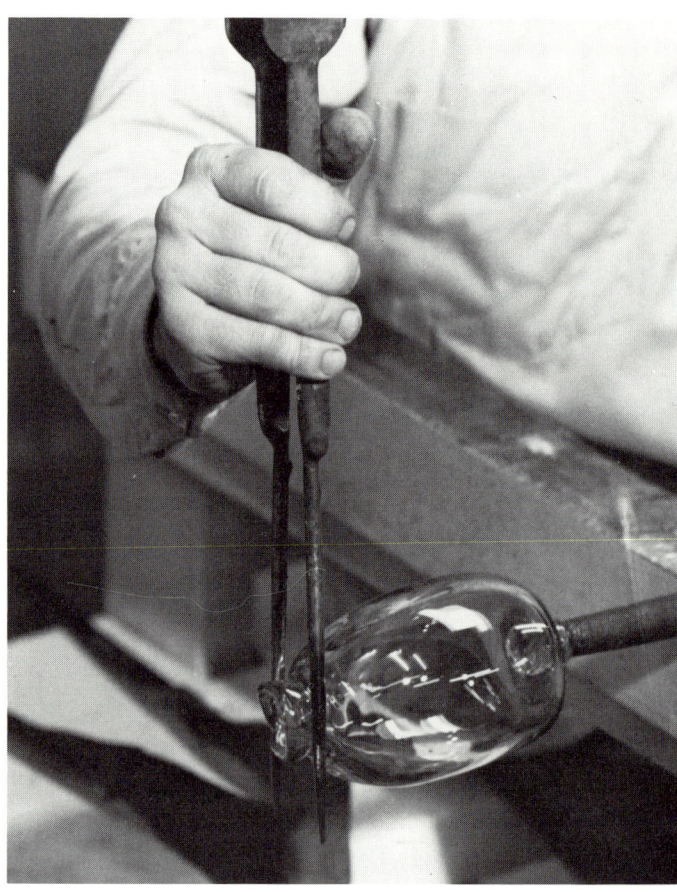

3. The lip may be flared out with the points of the jacks.

2. *The pressure continues using the jacks to the desired point at the base of the lip.*

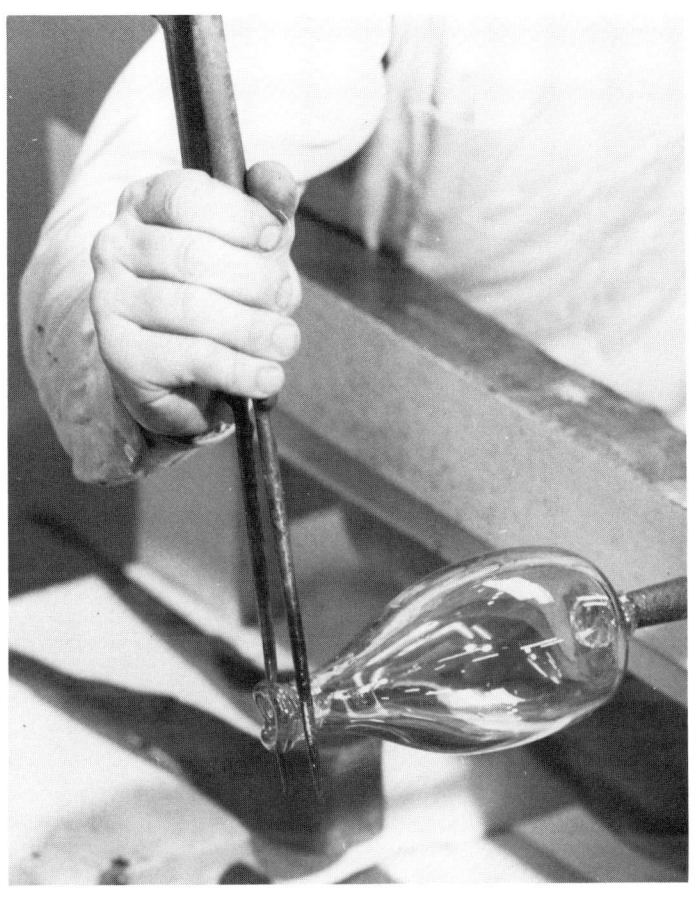

4. *It can then be straightened (or flattened) by using the back of the jacks as shown.*

5. *The jacks are used to round the neck with inside pressure. These steps can be repeated until the desired shape is produced.*

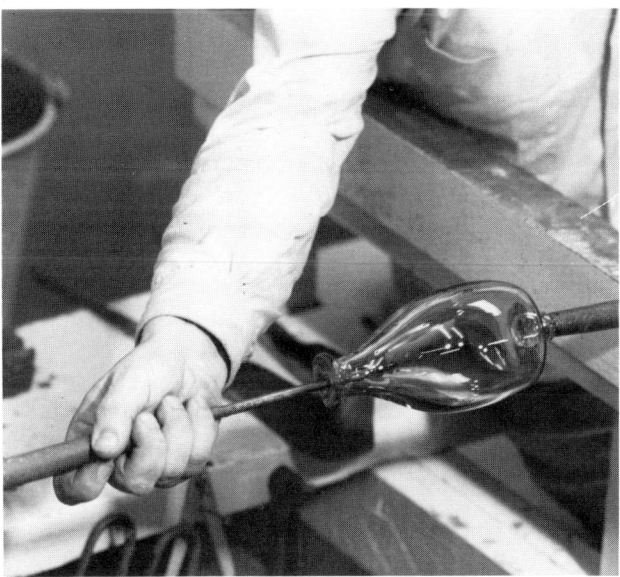

WORKING FREEBLOWN GLASS 115

Making Open Shapes

Tools are worked primarily on the inside surface of a vessel to open the form (for bowls, jars, etc.). Jacks can be pressed closed and placed inside the heated lips of the revolving vessel. As the pressure on the jacks is released, the arms expand and push the lips open. Further opening and forming can be done with the edge of the jacks, wooden paddles, or sticks. By spinning the vessel on the pontil you can make plates or other flat forms.

1. To make an open shape, the tips of the jacks (pressed together) are placed inside the softened lips of the vessel.

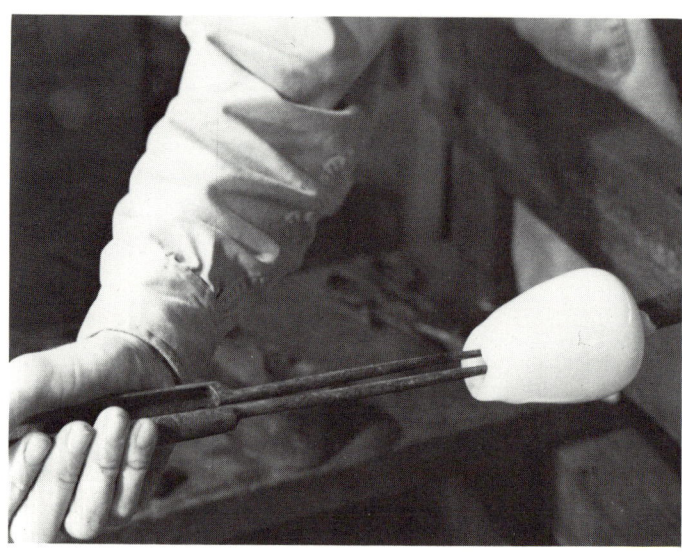

3. If the lip of the vessel is uneven, you can cut the molten glass with shears to even up the bowl.

2. *The tips of the jacks are allowed to expand as the vessel is continuously rotated.*

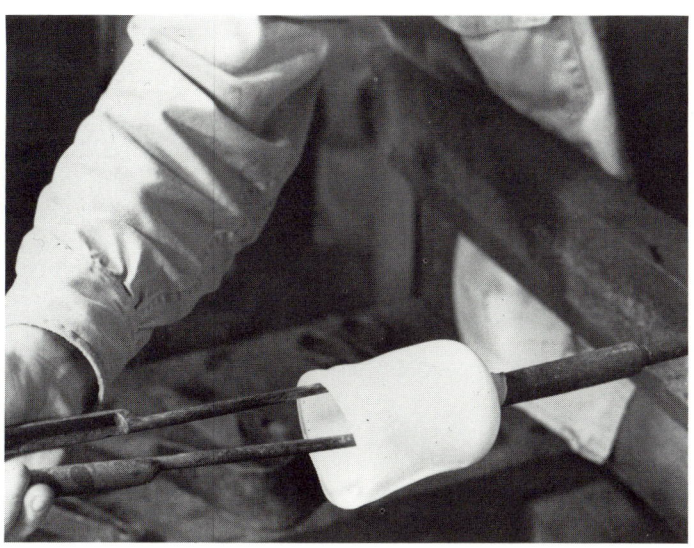

4. *After the jacks completely open, the vessel is further opened with the sides of the jacks until the desired shape is produced.*

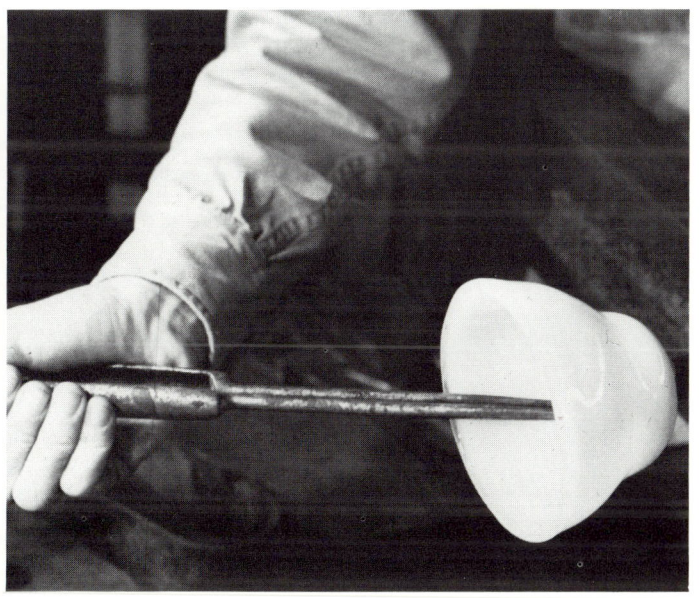

5. *Alternately, a wooden paddle may be used to open a vessel.*

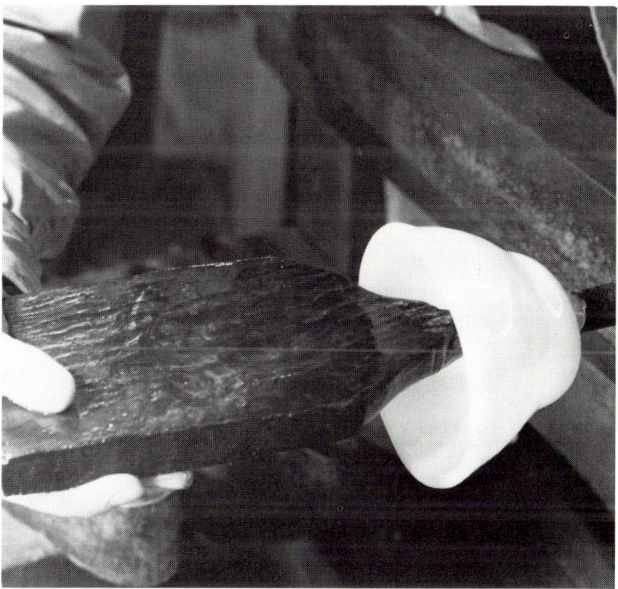

Removing the Pontil and Annealing

When the desired shape is complete, remove the vessel from the pontil by hitting the juncture between the glass bond and the vessel bottom with a knife or the sharp end of a file. This will begin to break the bond. Then give the pontil a glancing blow with the file to vibrate the pontil and completely break the bond. The vessel can either be broken off directly into the oven or broken off on a soft, fireproof surface and then placed in the annealing oven using heavy asbestos gloves. Various metal forks or hooks (covered with asbestos cloth) are used commercially to place ware in the oven. If you put your arms into the oven when you are placing the ware, be sure that they are covered with *densely woven* cotton or wool—not synthetic material that can melt and cause burns. Glass is very fragile in the early stages of annealing, and rough handling can show up as cracks in the finished piece. Annealing temperature and time will depend on the type of glass used and the thickness and evenness of the ware. The glass must be brought through the annealing range slowly (see Chapter 3) to prevent strains and breaking. When removed from the oven, various cold glass processes can be used (see Chapters 6 and 7) to enhance the artistic product.

1. Loosen the completed vessel from the pontil by hitting the glass bond and the pontil with a knife or the sharp point of the file.

3. The vessel is put into the annealing oven. Be sure to wear insulated asbestos gloves.

2. Then hit the pontil with the file (or other tool) to remove the vessel. This should be done on a soft, fireproof surface.

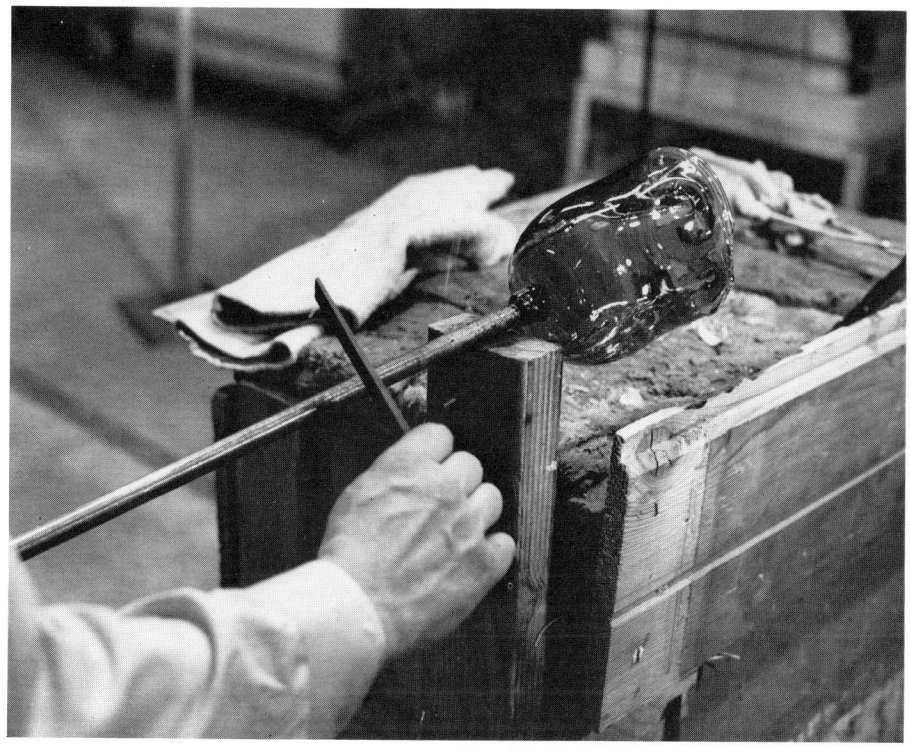

4. Or the vessel can be placed in the annealing oven while still attached to the pontil and broken off by hitting the pontil.

SOME WORDS OF ADVICE

I want to end this chapter with a word of advice. There is a temptation for the beginner to accept anything that happens at the furnace as desirable. Unfortunately, the art world today enforces this by its acceptance of almost anything. Only *you* know how much progress you are making, because only you know for certain what you are trying to do. Do not fool yourself.

Size of the product is one of the criteria mistakenly used in evaluating art, but it is not a valid criterion for you at this stage. A more important, meaningful developmental experience is to produce many small items in a session at the furnace. Struggling to produce one or two "large" things, and possibly picking up a great many bad habits in the process, can only be detrimental. In making small things, you go through all the steps until you can afford to stop thinking about how to hold the pipe, file, etc., and can use the tools rather than having the tools use you. Despite the present state of art and critical awareness, it is still a basic truth that the large ugly pot is uglier than the small ugly pot.

6/Stems, Handles, and Other Additions

Bottle by Frank Kulasiewicz. Soda/lime glass, 8″ x 7½″. A small bottle that illustrates several useful forming techniques. Between gathers, the bubble on the pipe was pressed against metal forms so the successive gathers formed bubbles (an "Ariel" pattern) in the wall. The vessel wall was cut with shears and reblown to form the "wings" on the side. A section was heated strongly and then pushed in with a tool to form a "bridge" or "angel swing" inside.

Once you have mastered the basics of making freeblown glass shapes, there are a variety of decorations and additions you can make using the techniques shown in this chapter. These often involve the addition of molten glass to the basic vessel at some point in its creation. This, in turn, may call for help from another person to bring the glass to you at the proper time and in the proper form. With ingenuity, however, you can usually "go it alone" for most of the things you want to accomplish.

I will discuss a variety of these techniques, and will show at least one method for each process. Please keep in mind that craftsmen have all developed varied ways of accomplishing these tasks. If they work, then they are "correct" for that artist—and perhaps for you. What I present are only ways that have worked for me. Also keep in mind that these are not the only techniques possible. You can, for example, crack hot glass by plunging it in hot water, spin "bull's-eyes," pull cane for lampworking, etc. Do not be afraid to experiment with these and other processes. There is no real limit to what you can do with glass except your own imagination.

Casing

The term "casing" can be used to describe almost any gathering of molten glass over somewhat firmer gathers. Technically, however, glassblowers use the term when referring to gathering one color over another where the separation between layers remains distinctly visible. Related terms are "flashed" (a thin coat of color over a clear vessel) and "sandwiched" (a colored glass between two clear or lighter-colored glasses).

The successive layers of glass repeat the form of the vessel and thus establish interesting design relationships. There are many possible variations when you use several colors. You can do partial casings with or without partial overlap of one color on another, or flatten the early gathers to form three-sided or square shapes that can be cased in round vessels.

The use of opaque glass further increases casing possibilities. All the variations already mentioned are possible when opaque is used under transparent glass. When opaque is used over transparent, or opaque over opaque, more effects are possible by removing sections of the outer casing after the glass is cool.

STEMWARE

Work your glass on the pipe in the usual fashion until the bubble is about the size you want for the stemware vessel. Add more glass to the bottom of the bubble by dipping or by adding with a gathering iron. Excess glass can be cut away with shears. The molten glass is formed into a conical shape, gradually tapering away from the bubble. Forming can be done in a number of ways, including using the back of the jacks, a paddle, or wet newspapers cupped in the hand. This shape is then pulled out with the jacks to form the stem. Gravity or swinging the pipe can also be used to elongate the stem. These forming operations are continued until you achieve the desired shape, thickness, and length of the stem.

Another gather of glass is then added to the end of the stem to make the pedestal. Preliminary forming, such as flattening the gather, can be done with the jacks, wooden paddles, or cupped wet newspapers.

Various special tools made of steel, wood, or graphite can be used at this point. A very simple tool of this type would be two pieces of wood (about

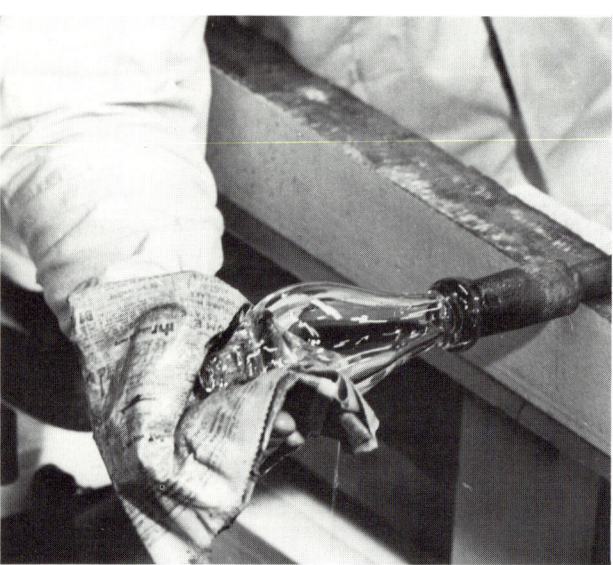

1. Molten glass is added to the bottom of the bubble on the pipe (either with an iron or by dipping) and formed into a conical shape with wet newspaper cupped in the hand (or a paddle or wooden jacks).

2. Forming can continue using the back of the jacks (or other tools).

5. Preliminary forming is done with paddle (or jacks or newspaper).

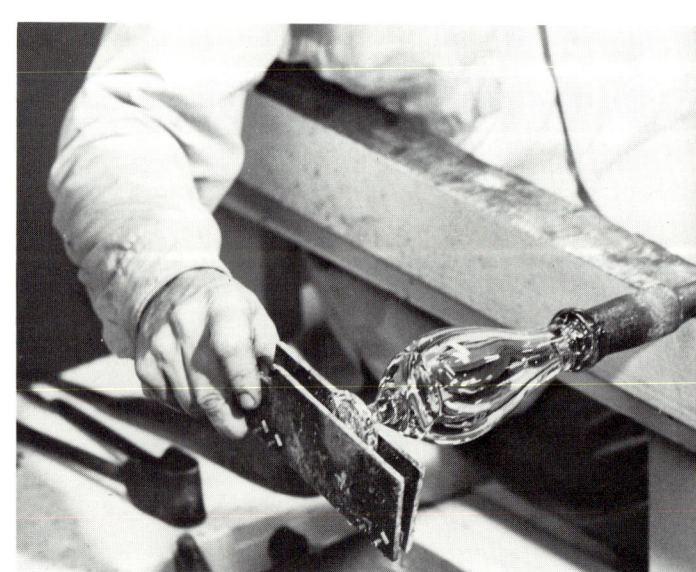

6. A special hinged tool (made of wood, metal, or graphite) is brought in contact with the rotating molten glass. Pressure is applied to flatten and form the pedestal.

122 GLASSBLOWING

4" square by ½" thick) held between the thumb and fingers of the hand. A more elaborate, more easily controlled tool would be one that is hinged or mounted in a spring tool similar to jacks. These tools can have a series of notches along the top edge of the paddles, or arms that can be used to both form the stem and act as a measure of the stem's thickness.

The purpose of this type of tool is to form the last gather of glass on the end of the stem into the base or pedestal. The molten glass is pressed between the two paddles of the tool as the glass is rotated on the pipe. Pressure on the tool thins and flattens the glass to form the base. Further forming and straightening is done with the jacks.

At this point the vessel is attached to the pontil and the lip is finished in the same way as with any other type of vessel. Another possibility (used often in commercial production) is to break the vessel off the pipe and place it directly in the oven. After annealing, the vessel is cut below the lip. This new lip is then polished to complete the piece.

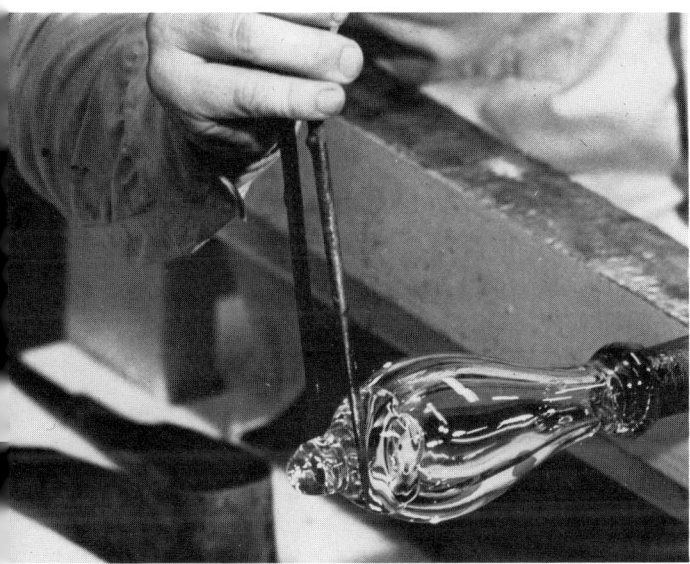

3. Jacks begin to stretch and form the stem. The pipe is rotated as pressure continues until the desired shape is produced.

4. More glass is added to the stem from an iron or by dipping.

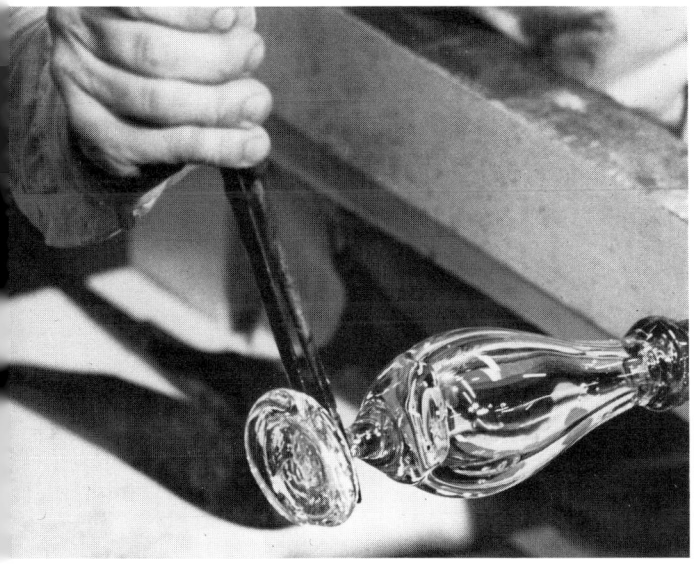

7. Further forming and straightening can be done with jacks (if needed).

8. The pedestal is trued to the lip with jacks (or paddle). Now the vessel can either be broken off the pipe and annealed or attached to the pontil and the lip finished.

Hollow Stemware

It is possible to produce a "hollow" pedestal and stem on a vessel without the addition of glass. First blow a fairly cylindrical form on the blow pipe. Heat the vessel in a strong flame about a third of the distance from the base. Using jacks (or some type of pulling tool), neck in the vessel walls and "stretch" a tapered stem towards the base. Flatten the base (pedestal) if the forming operations have tended to round it. Attach a pontil and complete the rest of the forming.

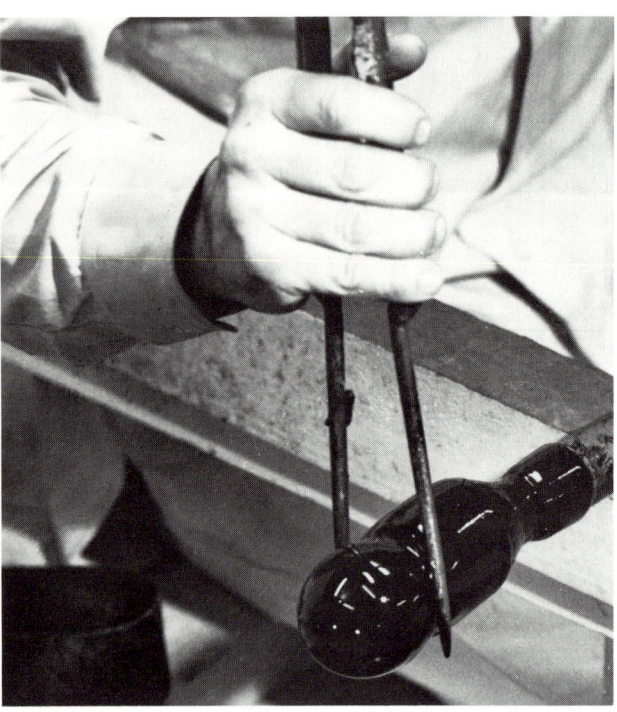

1. A cylindrical shape is formed on the marver (or with other forming tools). After heating the bottom third of the cylinder, jacks are used to begin forming the stem and base.

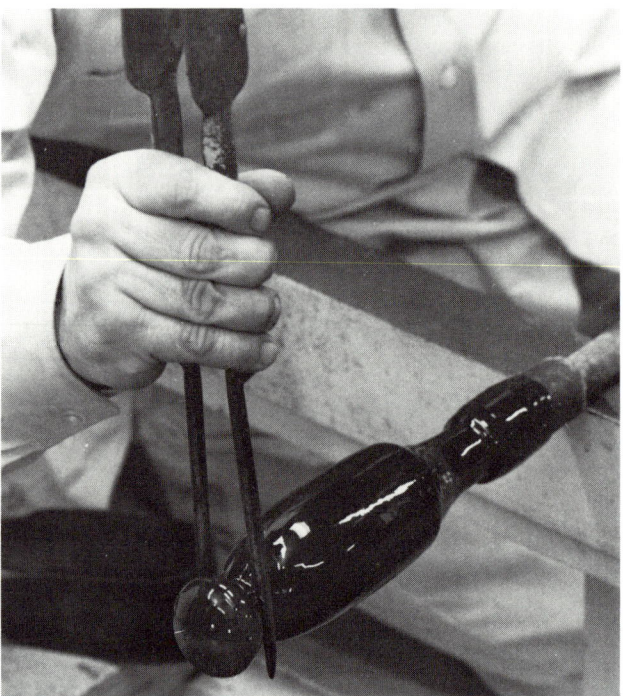

2. The hollow stem is stretched out and completed (these exterior forming operations can also be coupled with blowing).

3. The base is flattened (it can be left hollow or pushed until the walls join to make a near solid base or pedestal). Forming is then completed in the usual fashion on the pontil.

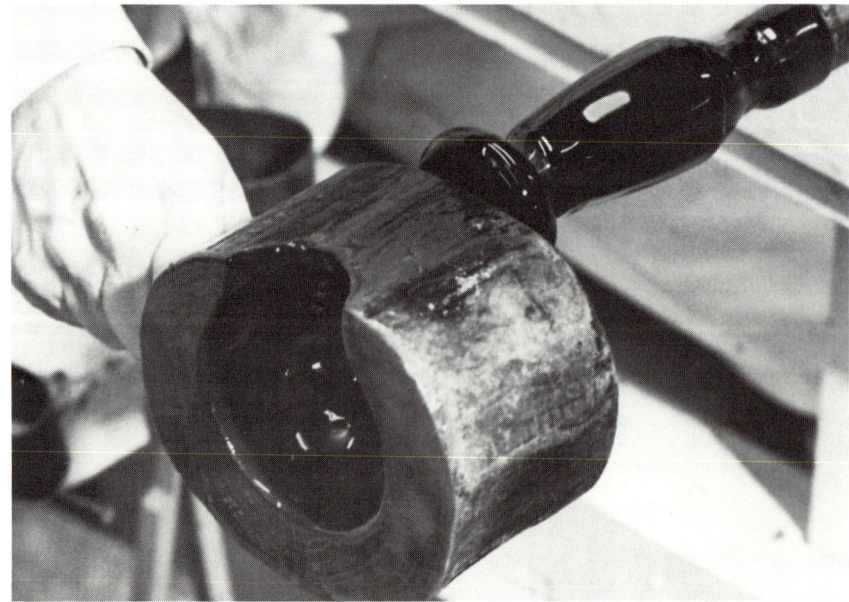

Handles

Handles can be added at various stages in the production of a vessel, however they are most easily attached when the vessel is being worked on the pontil. Applying the handle is usually one of the last forming operations. If you do much more forming after attaching the handle, centrifugal force will tend to distort the vessel shape because the weight of the handle makes it "side-heavy."

After the vessel has been blown, transferred to the pontil, and most of the forming operations performed, a gather is made on an iron and marvered into a cylinder about 2" long. This gathering of glass and bringing it to the vessel is commonly done by a helper in factory situations. For very complicated pieces, using a helper (commonly called a "pontil boy") is effective, however most contemporary glass artists work out ways to do many of these operations on their own.

In the demonstration I show how to add a handle doing all the forming and gathering operations without a helper. The gather of glass is brought into contact with the vessel on the bench, and the amount of glass needed for the handle is cut off. If both ends of the handle are to be attached, tweezers can be used to hold the handle in position to check visual placement, shape, etc. If you feel the need to lengthen or thin the handle, spin the pontil and centrifugal force will lengthen the soft, hot glass. When ready to attach the loose end, the freshly heated glass is pressed firmly in place on the vessel.

To be functional, the handle is *usually* formed in a vertical straight line and balanced. Decorative handles need not be functional but they should be visually and tactually pleasing.

You can alter the length of the handle, as well as its relation to the vessel size, curvature, distance from the body of the vessel, etc. A simple forming tool for this is a wooden stick or bar of metal put under the handle. Remember that work on the handle also tends to modify the vessel. Before putting the vessel into the annealing oven, any undesirable distortions should be corrected (the vessel may be pulled so far off center it will no longer stand, etc.). Make sure the handle glass is firm and the oven temperature well controlled so the handle does not melt or distort.

In most handworking factories a helper or "pontil boy" is used to assist the artist when producing complicated pieces that require additions of hot glass. This photograph shows me bringing hot glass to the bench where Erwin Eisch, noted European glass artist, is placing the glass in position for a handle. For safety it is important for the artist at the bench to have complete control of the hot iron and molten glass, and to have the helper bring the glass to the artist from the proper angle (usually right and back of the bench). Photo by Bob Florian.

1. *A gather is made on an iron and marvered into a cylinder shape about 3" or 4" long. This gather is brought to the vessel on the pontil and firmly attached.*

2. *The correct amount of glass for the handle is cut off.*

3. *The vessel is rotated to thin and lengthen the handle.*

4. *The loose end of the handle is attached.*

5. *The handle is formed with a stick (or jacks). Then the vessel is removed from the pontil and put into the oven.*

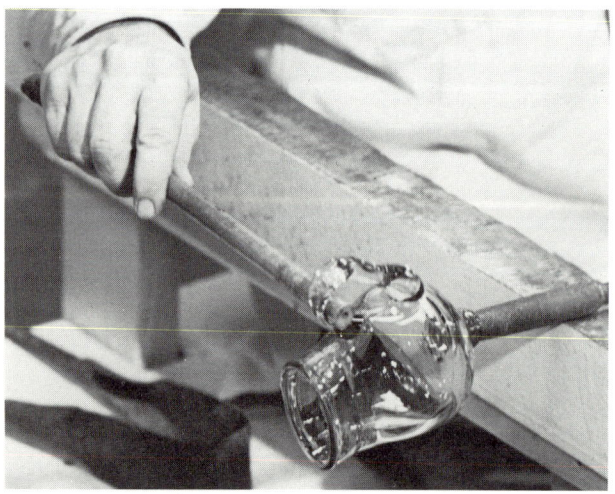

Hollow Handles

It is possible to form handles by developing the handle from the vessel itself. A hollow handle for example, is effective for light-colored or transparent glasses. In this type of vessel the liquid level is visible through the handle as well as through the vessel wall.

An effective way to make the hollow handle is to do all the forming while the vessel is still on the blow pipe. First make the vessel on the blow pipe, then flatten it so two walls are brought close together. Heat these walls strongly and punch (using the special hole punch) through both walls. This will also join the walls together. Heat the vessel strongly to melt the rough, sharp edges around the hole, and then use a pair of jacks to begin to enlarge the hole to form the handle. A stick or piece of pipe may be used to further enlarge the hole. Continue forming operations until the desired size and shape is produced. Blowing may be required as part of these forming operations.

The above steps are repeated until the size, shape, and esthetic effects desired are produced. Care should be taken in all these forming operations to prevent the hollow handles from melting closed. This can happen because of too much heat on the handle or from too much vigorous tool manipulation. The bottom of the vessel is flattened, the pontil attached, and forming completed with the vessel on the pontil.

1. Blow the desired shape on the pipe and flatten the walls slightly. Heat the walls to be joined and punch the hole. Heat the hole to remove strains in the glass and to soften the sharp edges.

2. Use jacks to enlarge the hole and begin forming operations.

3. Reheating as needed, enlarge the hole in the handle and shape it using various tools. There a piece of pipe is being used for forming operations.

4. The vessel is blown to keep the handle from closing on itself and to correct any distortions that may have occurred. Steps 3 and 4 may be repeated as needed until the desired shape is produced. The vessel is then transferred to the pontil for completion.

Angel Swings or Bridges

It has been noted by both historians and estheticians that all too often glass form has been influenced by earlier ceramic form. To a degree this is true today as many ceramic artists turn their attention to glass.

There are qualities in glass that are so unique they literally make it impossible for glass to mimic other materials. One such design potential—inner forms—results from the combination of fluidity and transparency. In this group are the form modifications known as "angel swings" or "bridges."

Angel swings are literally swings of glass inside the vessel from one part to another. One way to produce these swings is to heat the vessel wall until molten and use a tool to push the wall "inside" the vessel. Or, as I will demonstrate, you can gather a prunt and allow the heat from the molten glass to soften the vessel wall, and then use a tool to push the wall into the vessel until it sticks to the opposite wall. In both instances, the vessel is usually blown again to return it to its previous contours.

1. A vessel is blown on the pipe and a prunt dipped on to one side. Let the hot glass soften the wall, then take a tool (jacks, ice pick, pointed file, graphite rod, wooden stick, etc.) and begin to push the tool into the soft glass.

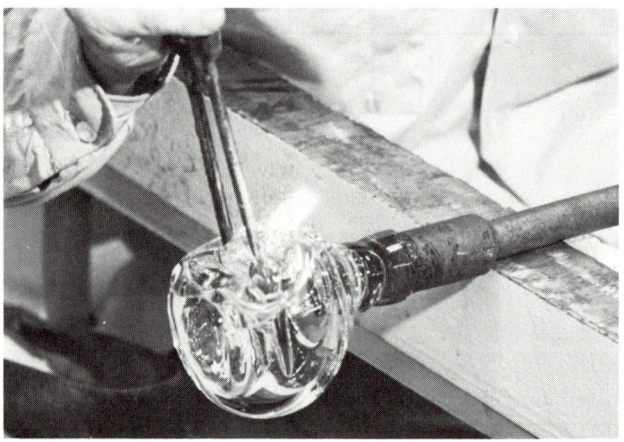

2. Push the wall in until it makes contact with the opposite wall. The flames visible here are caused by wax on the tool burning. If you use the metal tool and keep it in contact with the glass for any period of time it may heat up and stick to the glass. To prevent this, either work fairly fast or chill the tool by dipping in cold water.

3. The vessel has probably been distorted somewhat by the pressure of the tool, but you can blow the form out again to restore the shape. Care should be taken to prevent the prunt glass (which is probably still quite soft) from blowing too thin. Then the bottom can be flattened, the pontil attached, and the vessel completed.

Wings

"Wings" can be added to the vessel either on the pontil or on the blow pipe. After the basic shape is produced, an iron is used to gather molten glass. The glass is placed in position on the vessel and the required amount cut. This molten glass addition is then formed with tweezers, tongs, pucellas, or pliers, depending on the textural effect desired. This can complete the design, and the vessel is then worked in the normal way. "Wings" can also be heated strongly and then cut with shears before attaching the pontil and completing the vessel.

1. After forming the vessel on the pipe, gather molten glass on an iron and put this in place on the bubble.

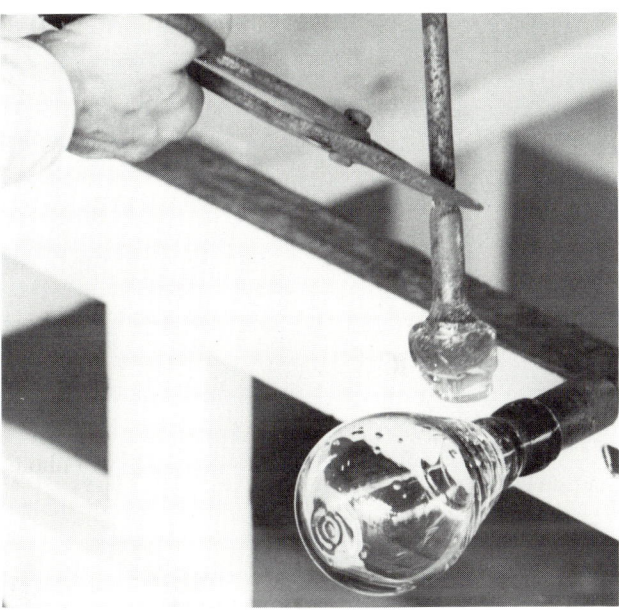

2. The required amount of glass is cut off with shears.

3. After reheating (if necessary) use tweezers to pull and form the wings. If desired, decoration can be completed with the tweezers and then forming done on the pontil.

4. Or you can heat the added glass and cut the wings with shears. Again heat after cutting to "fire-polish" (smooth out the sharp, thin edges left by the shears).

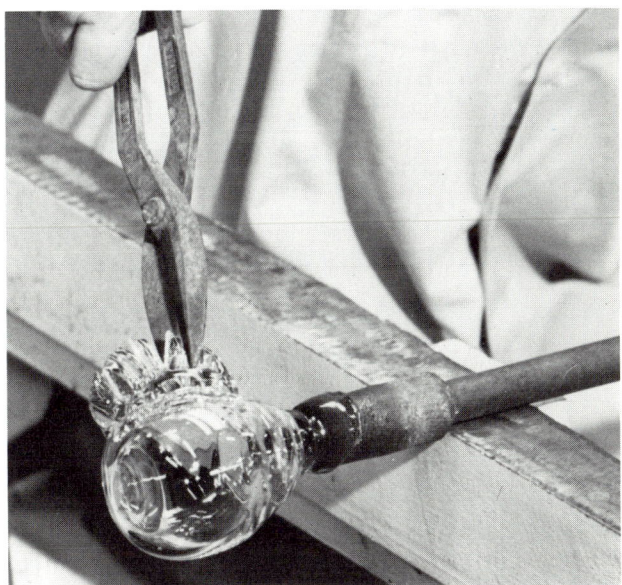

Trailed Glass

Because of its fluid qualities, hot glass lends itself to rather spontaneous dripping of molten glass from a gathering iron to the vessel. This is usually referred to as "trailed" or "threaded" glass.

Trailed decorations can vary from free designs "drawn" on the vessel to very controlled additions of thin threads of molten glass. They can be of a variety of colors, can be left on the surface or cased over, or the raised surface decoration can be "pushed" into the glass surface on the marver to give an inlay effect. As with many simple techniques, what you do with this trailing technique is limited only by your imagination.

1. A vessel is blown on the pipe and a gather of glass made on an iron. The pipe is placed on the bench and a thread pulled from the molten gather. The large glob of glass at the start of the thread is cut off with shears.

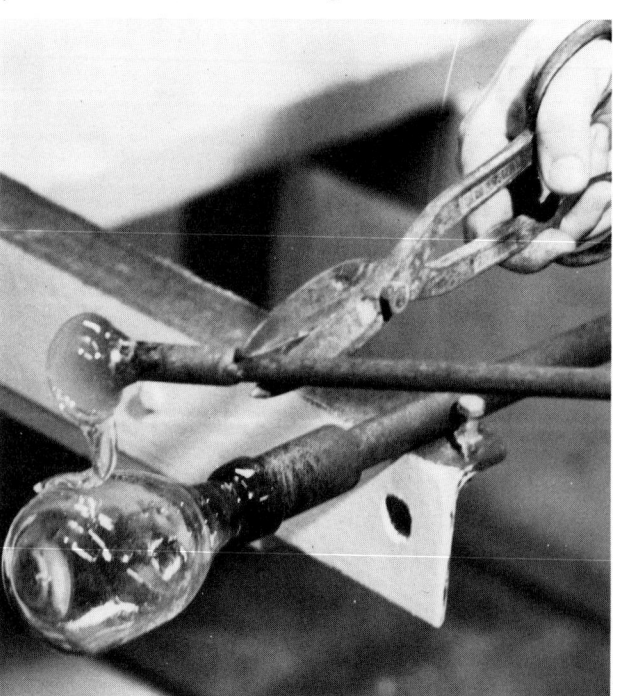

2. Shears help guide the iron with the glass thread to the right place on the vessel, and the molten glass is attached.

3. The vessel is rolled (push with your body up the bench) and the thread is wrapped around the rotating vessel. The thread is cut with shears when the design is complete. Then the vessel is heated to make sure the thread is attached firmly.

Multi-Chambered Vessels

Because of the fluidity of molten glass on the pipe (and pontil) it is possible to cut glass with shears. You can make multi-chambered pieces on the pipe by pressing the walls together with the shears and sealing them (indeed this pressing together is enough to form multi-chambered vessels of a slightly different character). Cutting usually destroys the firm base, and it is likely that an added glass gather may be required to form a foot or pedestal.

1. Form a rather long vessel on the pipe in the usual manner. Heat the vessel strongly and cut with long shears as deep as desired. The amount of separation and the number of chambers depends on your design. Here the cut is about half the chamber.

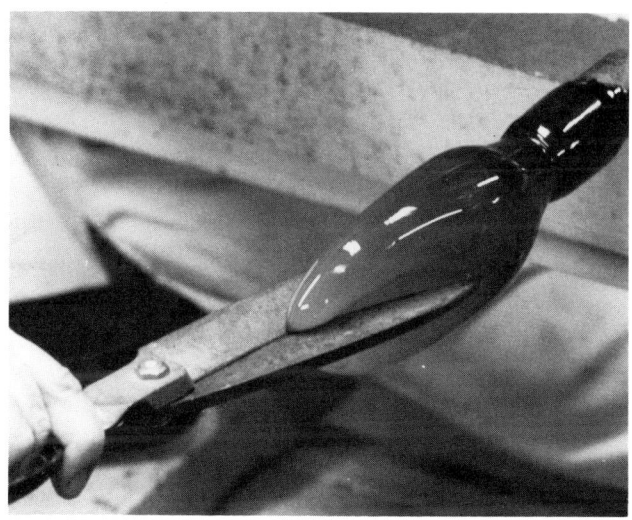

2. The two sections of the vessel are detached from each other to the length of the cut. They may remain apart to be formed, but in this piece I reform them (with the paddle) so they again make contact.

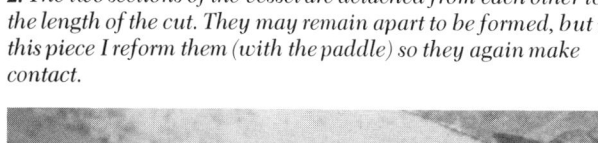

3. A gather is made over the bottom of the vessel to form the foot. Wet newspaper is used to start forming the molten glass.

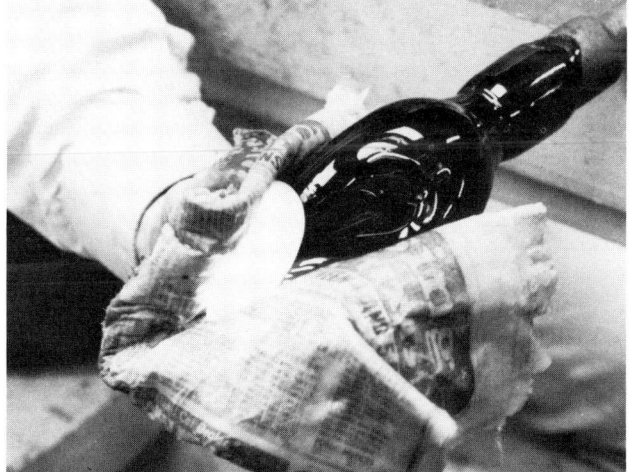

4. The foot is formed using appropriate tools, transferred to the pontil, and completed according to your desired intent.

STEMS, HANDLES, AND OTHER ADDITIONS

Cold Glass Additions

The addition of various forms of solid pieces of glass to to the molten vessel offers a large range of effects to the glass artist. The number of colors is not limited to the number of color furnaces (or color pots) available at any one time, because pieces of glass from any melt can be kept for later use. The time needed to arrange patterns or designs is not dependent on the pace of the glass since such arranging can be done leisurely with cold glass. There are, in fact, small hand factories that work with only one furnace of clear glass and chips of colored glass. These chips are picked up by the hot, clear glass, then heated and cased before being formed into objects.

The "cold" glass can be in the form of rods, lumps, powders, or combinations of any of these. In reality, this glass is not always "cold." It is advisable to heat the colored glass to prevent or cut down on spattering. The method of working can vary from simply picking up chips on the marver with the hot bubble on the pipe to picking up complicated patterns out of molds. Any of these can have a place in freeblown glass.

Some splattering is anticipated when hot glass is brought in contact with cold. This spattering and crackling does not necessarily indicate incompatibility if the glass is of the same composition (or has the same expansion and contraction rate). As a rule, the more the added pieces are heated the less likely strains will form in the finished vessel if it is properly annealed.

When the vessel is worked only slightly, the added pieces will keep their original shape. If much forming is performed after incorporating the colored pieces, these shapes will be modified by changes in the vessel shape. Very planned patterns find their greatest use in paperweights where little or no form modification takes place after incorporating the colored glass. The degree of variety possible is limited only by the inventiveness of the craftsman—particularly when these effects are combined with other techniques. A great many of the special "glasses" made by Carder for Steuben have proved to be ingeneous combinations of impressed textures and powdered colored glass.

1. The bubble is formed on the pipe and heated until fluid. This is marvered on pieces of colored glass (or powdered metal, metal foil, thin wires, powdered colorants, chemicals to form bubbles, etc.) until the glass on the pipe picks them up. The vessel is then heated strongly to melt the pieces into the vessel wall.

2. The molten glass on the pipe is again marvered to help anchor the pieces to the bubble. While the glass is still very molten, pull it up with some tool (tongs, pliers, or picked up. Further gathering (casing over the chips of colored glass) and forming is continued until the vessel on the pontil is complete.

Impressed Decorations

It is difficult to draw a line between impressions on the glass surface and texture. The vessel on the pipe can be rolled against almost any fireproof surface to transfer the impression (texture) to the soft glass. Some of the materials with textures that can be used are metal screens, nails pounded through a board, etc. Selective designs can be added with wooden, clay, graphite, or metal stamps.

Many impressed decorations in the glass surface can be cased over, and if the impression is deep enough a controlled air pattern can be captured in the vessel wall. If this is done early in the forming operations the air patterns (bubbles) can be modified by changes made in the shape of the object as the artist works the glass on the pipe or pontil.

1. Molten glass is added to the bubble on the pipe (or pontil) from a gathering iron (or by dipping the vessel directly in the molten glass). If a gathering iron is used the glass can be cut with shears.

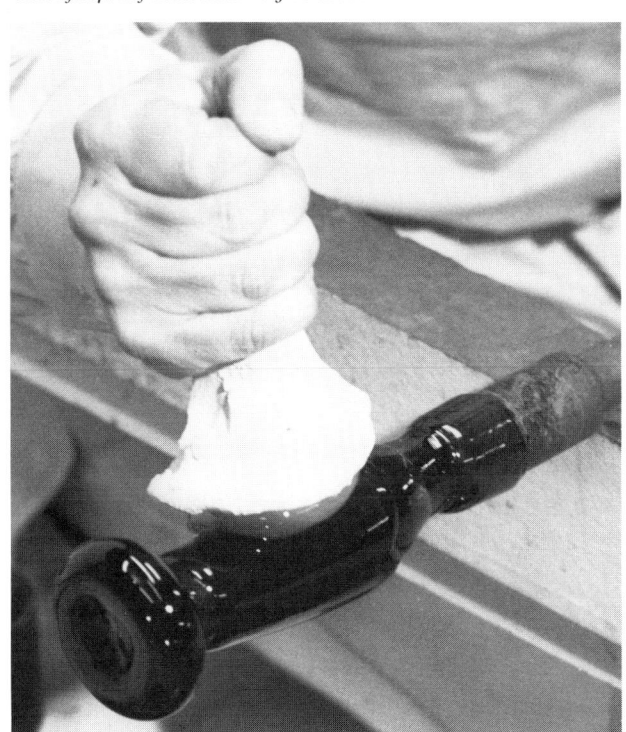

2. A stamp is pressed into the molten glass. Here a clay stamp is used, but metal, wet wood, graphite, mica, or any number of other fireproof materials may be used.

3. The stamp is removed showing the design impression transferred to the vessel.

Lily-Pad Design

The most significant American design contribution to glass has been the lily-pad decoration so common on early American glass products. The lily-pad generally consists of a gather near the bottom of the vessel that is pulled up to form a decoration on the upper half of the piece. Purists (and antique dealers) will argue that the true lily-pad has to be pulled up with a certain tool and in a certain way. I will treat the general procedure and let you decide yourself what tools (fireplace tongs, corn-cob holders, pliers, jacks, tweezers, etc.) you want to use.

1. Form a bubble on the pipe, then make a partial gather below the lower half of the bubble. While the glass is still very molten, pull it up with some tool (tongs, pliers, or related tools can be used for a variety of effects).

2. Repeat this procedure as desired around the base of the vessel. When you arrive at the shape you want, flatten the base, attach the pontil, and proceed to complete your vessel.

Prunts

The term "prunt" refers to partial gathers of molten glass on a vessel usually applied while working the glass on the pipe. "Blown prunts" are such partial gathers blown out and formed. The prunts can be added from a gathering iron or by direct dipping. Direct dipping is not only the easiest method of adding the prunts, but produces a design that relates to the shape of the vessel. The molten glass is level in the furnace, and as the bubble is submerged under the glass the shape of the bubble influences the shape of the prunt. The thickened glass wall of the prunt, if left unworked, produces an optical effect in clear or light glass, a deepening of color in dark glass. It can also be blown to change the shape of the basic vessel. You have already seen how this partial gather or prunt can be pulled to produce "wings" and related forms (including lily-pad decorations) or can be pushed to produce angel-swings and other internal shapes. The variety of other creative modifications is limited only by the ingenuity of the artist. I will demonstrate the basic steps in what can be called a prunt-on-prunt design.

1. Form a vessel on the blow pipe and dip a section of this into molten glass in the furnace. This fresh gather softens the cooler vessel wall beneath.

2. The prunt is blown out. Partial blocking may be necessary if the fresh glass stays fluid enough to collapse on the vessel or if it blows too thin. It may be possible to control the shape by slowly rolling the pipe on the bench, allowing gravity to help in the shape formation.

3. The prunt is now dipped into the molten glass, and this process of melting the earlier prunt wall is repeated.

4. This fresh prunt is blown out. These steps can be repeated until long forms are produced, colored glasses can be used in different prunts, the prunts can be applied to several parts of the vessel, etc. After forming the vessel is transferred to the pontil.

Multiple Forms

Joining molten glass forms to produce multiple vessels is usually done with several craftsmen working together, however many contemporary artists work alone. To do multiple forms you will need to keep two or more pontils and pipes, with glass, hot at the same time. If you work alone you should have several "hangers" prepared before you start. These hangers are hooks or nails arranged to hold the pipe and pontils vertically to free your hands for work on other sections. The method and angle of joining the vessels can vary according to your plan, but I will illustrate a fairly simple two-piece vessel joined vertically lip-to-base to form a hollow stand or pedestal. (A fairly common trick in the old glass factories was to toss a coin into the bottom part of the multiple section piece for a "head or tails" bowl).

To start, heat two pipes and a pontil. Gather on the first pipe and blow a simple form as the base for the piece. Attach this to the pontil and flare the vessel lip slightly. Then hang the pontil to free you for work on the next section in your multiple piece. *Remember*: periodically you will have to hang up your second pipe (and vessel) while reheating the other pontil and vessel to keep it hot. How often this is done will depend on how fast you work, the working range of the glass, the climate (temperature and air circulation) around the hanging piece, etc. I have used a small reheat oven with a burner to help keep the hanging piece hot, but for most situations this is not essential.

Gather glass on the second pipe and blow another form. Be sure to get a good neck groove on this bubble so you can break it easily and cleanly from the pipe. Heat both the vessel on the pontil and the vessel on the pipe with extra heat on the lip of the pontil vessel. Lay the pipe on the bench and guide the vessel on the pontil in place, treating this vessel as you ordinarily would treat the pontil alone. The lip of the first vessel is then attached to the bottom of the second vessel. Make sure the vessels are firmly bonded together. Apply water to the neck of the vessel on the pipe, and *tap* the pipe until it breaks off. Keep a *strong pressure* against the pontil so neither the pontil bond nor the vessel-to-vessel bond breaks. All you want to break off is the neck-to-pipe connection. Heat the lip of the second vessel at once, and also heat the junction line between the vessels to make sure they have melted together. If the junction is weak (or if an added decorative design is wanted) glass can be added with an iron. Finish the lip and neck of the top section and do any other forming operations you feel are needed before "breaking off" and annealing.

1. Heat two pipes and a pontil. Blow a vessel (the base) on the first pipe. Attach a pontil to the base and break loose from the first pipe. Heat the lip strongly and flare it out. After you form the second section, you may have to adjust this lip to the shape and size of the second piece. Meanwhile, hang this piece up out of the way to free your hands for work on the second section. Remember to periodically heat this section to prevent it from cooling to the point that it breaks from "thermal shock."

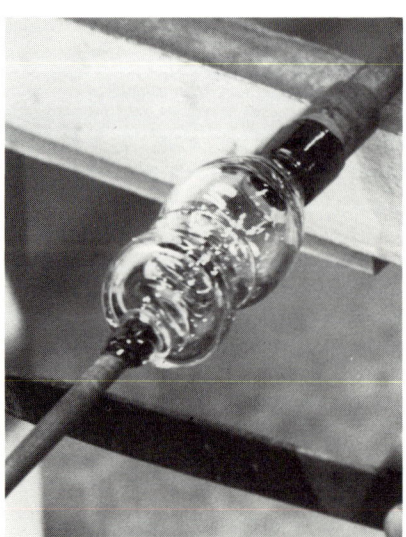

2. On your second pipe, blow and form the upper part of your two-piece vessel. Try to produce a sharp neck line to facilitate easy and quick removal from the pipe. Reheat both vessels, with particular attention to the lip on the pontil vessel. (With practice you can learn to handle both pieces at the same time, but be careful not to stick them together in the furnace during reheat.) Lay the pipe (second vessel) on the bench and guide the pontil (first vessel) into contact with the bottom of the second vessel (treat the pontil vessel as you ordinarily would the pontil alone.)

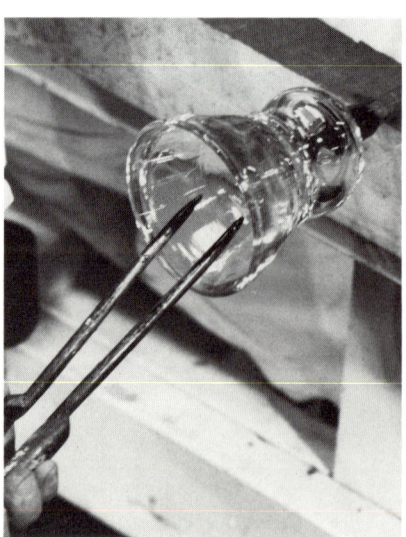

3. Make certain the lip-to-base joint is firm all around the piece, then score with a wet file in the neck line. Tap the pipe to break the vessel free (keep pressure against the pontil to help prevent breaking at either the pontil or connection line). You could also trail molten glass over the connection for strength or decorative effect. Finish the vessel using whatever forming operations you feel are needed, and anneal the two-piece vessel as you would any other freeblown vessel.

Steam Bubble

It is sometimes helpful to blow the vessel after it has been transferred to the pontil. There are special blowing tools that can be used for this, but most are dangerous and clumsy to use and I would advise against them. Tools used with compressed air are safer and more easily controlled, however this equipment is expensive.

A simple and cheap tool for you to use is a wet stick held tightly in the mouth of the vessel on the pontil so the resulting steam pressure enlarges the form. The shapes produced in this way are often very distinct forms from those blown completely on the pipe and as such are a fertile field for your explorations.

1. After the vessel has been blown, formed, and transferred to the pontil, heat it strongly in the glory-hole or furnace. Then hold a wet stick so it acts as a "stopper" in the mouth of the vessel.

2. If held tightly in place, the water on the stick will be vaporized by the heat of the glass and the steam pressure will blow out the vessel walls.

3. This process is continued until the vessel is the desired size and shape. It may be necessary to reheat the vessel or rewet the stick to prevent excessive burning. You may also have difficulty with blowing the walls too thin and pushing the mouth inside the vessel (although the latter can be a desirable decorative effect).

Paperweights

There are a multitude of types and kinds of paperweights that can be produced by the artist at the furnace. In most instances "something" is cased in clear or light glass either on the blow pipe or pontil. This "something" can be bubbles of various shapes and sizes, colored glass formed and shaped, or other materials (such as thin wire, metal leaf, or powdered metals). A simple paperweight is made by blowing a small bubble on the pipe, forming the bubble by cutting with shears, and then casing this central form with layers of clear glass.

1. A small bubble is blown on the pipe and necked with round jacks to close the opening. Cut the bubble with shears (these cut marks will form a bubble pattern when cased).

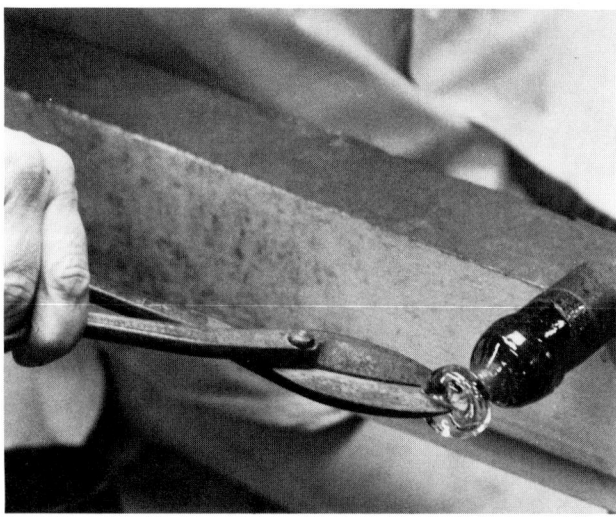

2. Make a gather over the shape on the pipe, then block it in a small forming tool. A thin section should be necked with jacks to facilitate breaking the finished piece off the pipe.

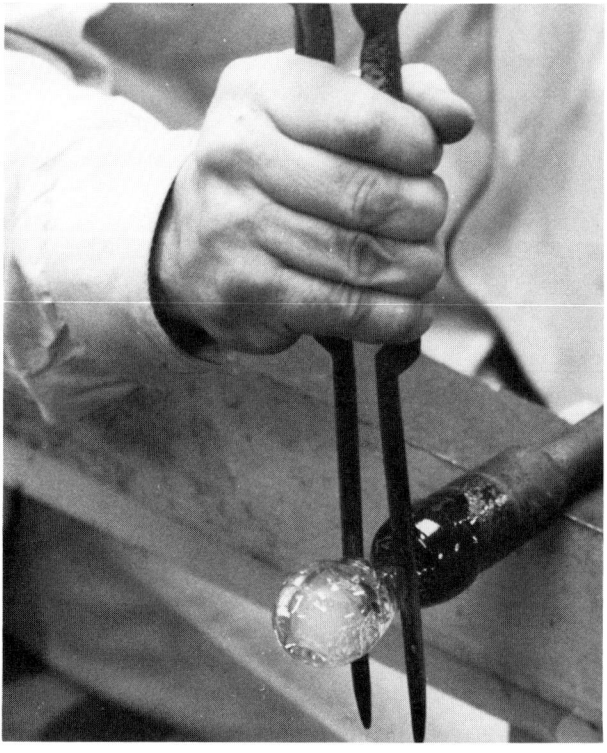

3. More gathers are made and blocked until you have the size and shape paperweight desired.

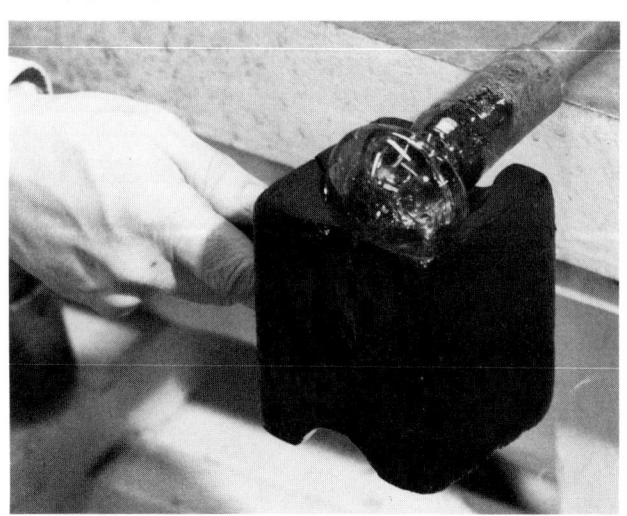

4. The neck line is scored with a wet file, and the piece is broken off and put into the oven.

Simple Molds

Using a mold is a method of duplicating forms in industrial glass production. As an artist you are not interested in mass production (since the machine can do the job so much better and faster) but simple molds can be a good starting point for further form development in your work.

One of the chief difficulties in the use of any mold is the lack of visual control over the glass as it is being blown in the mold. The only way to overcome this is by practice. You need to develop a "feel" for the invisible form being produced. The photographs show the steps in blowing a square form in a square wooden mold. This shape should only be the starting point for further work.

Large-diameter, oiled metal pipe can be used as a mold for cylinders. Wet wooden boxes can be used for square or other geometric forms. For the creative artist, these molds are a start toward a statement in glass, a tool to be used in conjunction with other tools and not an end in themselves.

1. A vessel is blown on the pipe and heated prior to being put into the wet wooden box mold.

2. Blow the bubble into the box until the bottom and sides come in contact with the wood. Steam is generated by the contact of the hot glass on the wet wood, so make sure your mold has escape places for the steam (open spaces in the mold or holes drilled) to prevent pressure from building up under the glass vessel. This pressure could force the vessel and pipe out of the mold with explosive force.

3. The square piece is removed from the mold and forming operations are continued to complete the vessel.

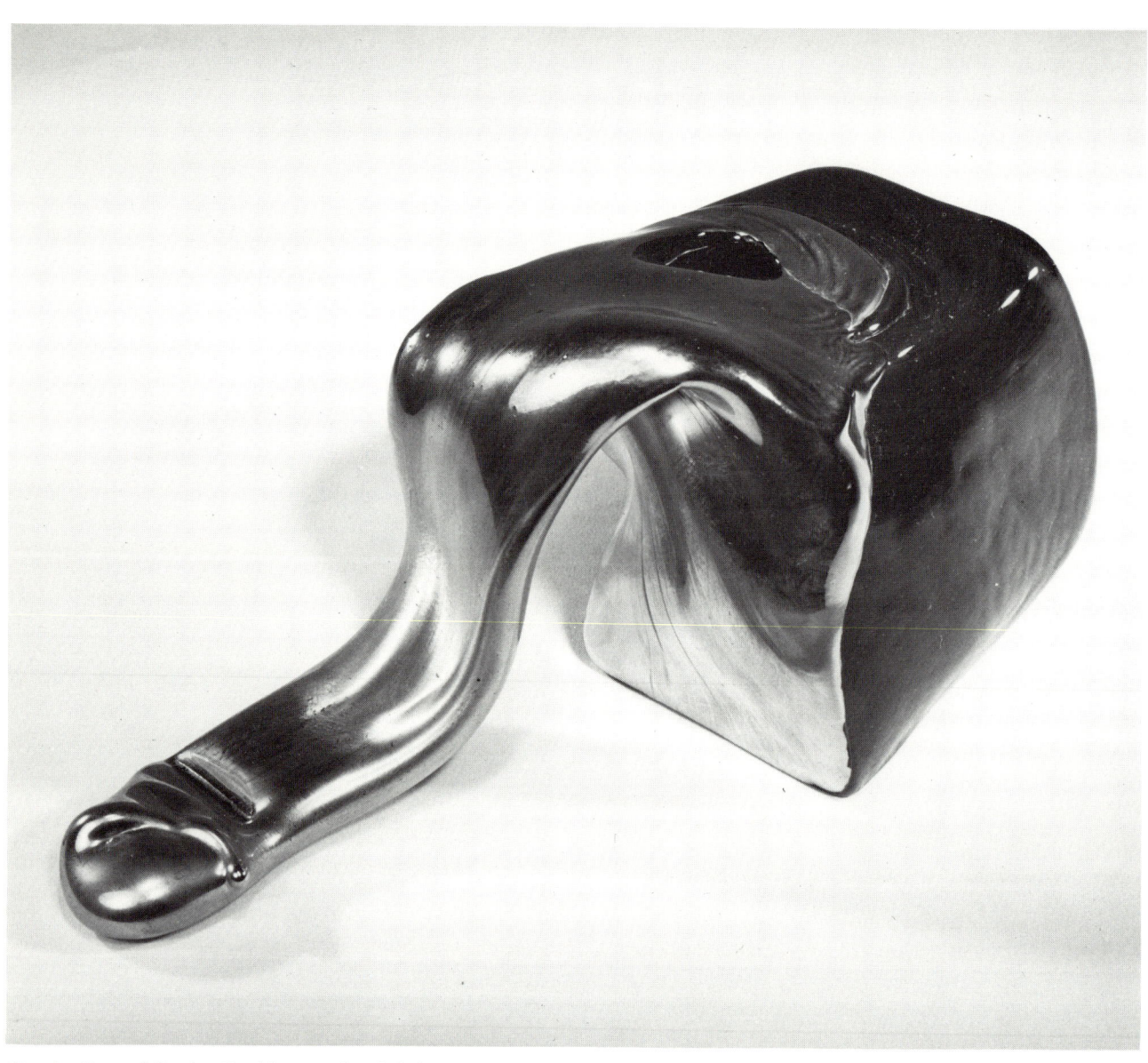

Vase by Howard Kottler. Freeblown and tooled glass, 6" high. A "vase" that was partially blown in a square mold and then modified by the artist into this very fluid sculptural form with its dropping appendage.

7/Color in Glass

Despite the advances made during the last century in the production of pure chemicals, color in glass has suffered. At the turn of the century, Louis Comfort Tiffany wrote that the glass in common preserve jars had a richer, more vibrant color than stained window glass. This, he found, was because impurities were left in the sand used in the jars and removed from the window glass. Some of the more "difficult" colors produced historically were actually dependent on impurities. Adding the right "impurities," however, is often difficult. As modern industry produces larger volumes of glass there is less concern for the nuances that influence subtle color changes. You, as an artist, are not pressed by the demands for large amounts of clean, cheap, but sterile glass.

The addition of color to the glass batch exploits some of the characteristics that make glass a unique material for the artist—transparency, varying light transmission, and luminescence. Related to color changes are additions to the melt that modify the glass to an opaque material. This adds the possibility of combined color and opacity effects.

METHODS OF ADDING COLOR

Although coloring material can be marvered into the vessel on the blow pipe, to obtain a thoroughly mixed colored glass the colorants should be added directly to the melt. Unfortunately, a simple rule covering the chemical properties of colorants is impossible, and those who look for a list of tried and true recipes will be disappointed. Lists of glass formulas and colorants are subject to many variables. For a more thorough discussion of the problems and possibilities involved, I recommend *Coloured Glasses* by Woldemer A. Weyl.

FACTORS THAT INFLUENCE COLOR

Below is a list of some of the factors that can influence the color of the glass:

1. Temperature of the melt.

2. Temperature of reheat during working.

3. Temperature of the lehr (annealing oven).

4. Duration of the melt.

5. Time/temperature relationship at different stages in production.

6. Type of colorant.

7. Concentration of colorant.

8. Composition of the glass.

9. Composition of the colorant within the glass composition. For example, when iron is added to glass, the type of iron oxide formed decides whether the glass will be yellow or blue. Unfortunately both forms of iron oxide are usually present, so an "iron green" is most common.

10. Atmosphere of the furnace.

11. Number of times the same glass is melted (repeated meltings of cullet usually give darker tones).

12. The position the ion assumes in the glass structure. Some of the varying colors of nickel, copper, iron, etc., are due to the different positions in the glass network.

This list is not complete, but it helps to illustrate a few of the problems in coloring glass, and it may also help to clarify some of the "unexplained" effects that occur when working glass. Many of the above factors are beyond the control of all but the most experienced glass craftsman, and then only with the use of equipment that is more likely to be found in the laboratory than the artist's studio. I will treat primarily those factors that can be coped with in the studio.

Furnace Atmosphere

A general rule (not completely accurate, but generally effective) is to reduce the furnace atmosphere when working with dark colored glasses and to oxidize when working with clear glasses. There are a few exceptions to this, and manganese would be one of the most important to consider. Almost all of the other commonly used colorants in reduction produce darker, less brilliant colors.

Composition of Colorant

I have often used carbonates instead of oxides for coloring the glass batch. The carbonates cause a bubbling action (because of carbon dioxide) in the melt that helps in mixing. I have also found that beginners are less likely to confuse the carbonates, which often have a characteristic color (pink for cobalt, green for copper, brown for manganese, etc.), than they are the oxides, which are generally black. The carbonates are less potent colorants pound for pound therefore so the margin for error in weighing the colorant is greater. When heated the carbonate is reduced to the oxide, and it is the oxide that causes the color in the batch. Therefore the comparative price of the carbonates and oxides is also of prime concern in deciding on which colorant to use.

Base Glass

The color obtained from various colorants will change in different base glasses. Copper, for example, produces three different blues when used in potash, soda, or lead-base glasses. The base glass also influences the quality of copper ruby produced. In general, potash glasses produce more varied, brilliant colors than soda glasses, and lead glasses produce more varied, brilliant colors than straight potash glasses. In discussing the colorants I will attempt to point out the differences caused by the base glass.

Oxidizing and Reducing Agents

Pyrolusite (a manganese compound) is a good commercial oxidizing agent, but the most important oxidizers are arsenic and antimony oxides. One of the many possible reducing agents that can be used in the melt is powdered coal. Some of the other oxidizing and reducing compounds were covered in Chapter 4.

Types of Colorants

Among the most common and useful colorants available are: chromium, cobalt, copper, and manganese. Also of interest, although less stable, more difficult to work, more dangerous, or more expensive are: gold, iron, nickel, silver, sulphides of various types, titanium, and uranium. In the first group, we are dealing with fairly consistent color producers. In the second group, special requirements sometimes make them difficult for the beginner to use successfully.

Sequence of Color

When working with only one furnace in your studio, there is a sequence of colorants I would like to suggest. Clear glass should be melted first, then colorants are added as work progresses. You should start with the lightest colors and work to the darkest. The exception already mentioned is manganese, which tends to lighten if reducing conditions are present. The last colorant in the series is usually cobalt or mixtures with cobalt.

The addition of color in this sequence produces mixtures that are dependent on: the amount and kind of colored glass used previously, how well the furnace is cleaned, the amount of mixing and settling that has taken place, and the varying amounts of colorants in relation to the glass used. This system is far from scientific, but it has proved workable for beginning glass artists. Before cadmium-selenium rubies are attempted, your skill, working habits, and understanding of colorants should be considerably advanced.

Chromium

Because this colorant is difficult to dissolve, it is best to use the chromates instead of chromium oxide to help bring the metal into solution. The usual color produced in the glass is a yellow-green that can be modified with small amounts of other colorants, such as the addition of cobalt for an effective blue-green.

In general, strong oxidizing produces chromium yellows, and reducing produces chromium blues. Potash helps in obtaining chromium yellow in the glass. The spectrum of color is increased to oranges and reds by using lead. This may be partially caused by the lower melting temperatures required for the lead glass. In my opinion, the production of any of the colors mentioned, except yellow-greens and blue-greens, is difficult for the beginner.

Chromium and Other Colorants. Chromium combined with manganese produces a black glass because of the decomposition of the chromium compounds oxidizing the manganese. The deep colors of the manganese are stronger in the presence of chromium than they are without the chromium. Combinations of pyrolusite and potassium dichromate can also be used in the production of such glass. I have produced several effective amber colors with combinations of manganese and chromium, as well as a nearly black glass. Some of these are listed in the Appendix.

Cobalt

Cobalt blue is consistent, and it is this consistency coupled with its strong lasting power that makes it a fairly serious problem. Long after the blue is no longer desired in the glass, it appears from the pot, tools, or cullet. There are several methods of controlling the blue produced by cobalt. Earlier glassworkers were forced to introduce the cobalt by means of "smalt," a form of cobalt cullet. "Powdered blue," a commercial compound that is a great deal weaker than the metal oxide, is often used today.

Modifying the Harsh Cobalt Blue Colors. Still another avenue of study is combining other colorants with cobalt. Some combinations are mentioned primarily to produce variations in the non-cobalt colorants (for example, chromium). In ceramic glazes, iron and nickel are often used to modify the brilliance of cobalt. Tin, which produces a more intense blue, is therefore avoided. I suggest that such combinations are a fertile field to explore in glass. It is unfortunate that beginners are so strongly drawn to the predictable results of using cobalt when they could be working toward a more subtle handling of the metal.

Another problem with cobalt centers around its infrared absorption properties. Infrared radiation normally heats the bottom of the tank, but in this case it is absorbed by the blue glass. Experiments have indicated that the working span of cobalt glass is less than other glasses of the same basic composition because the cobalt-containing glass surface cools more quickly. I have noted more stones in dark blue glasses than in lighter colors. A possible explanation is the cooling of lower layers caused by infrared absorption of top layers, thus destroying the lower tank lining.

A "Strike" or "Flash" Color

"Striking" or "flashing" a colored glass usually refers to a chemical reaction in molten glass that leads to the formation of particles of colloidal size precipitating out of the saturated glass. Most of the strike colors cannot easily be diluted as can other colored glasses that do not depend on the saturation of the glass. The striking process is complicated and often depends on special heat treatments to start the crystallization process and special chemicals to reduce the metal out of the melt, or to act as the nuclei for growth. Extensive studies have been done on the various glasses that can be made to "strike," and complicated theories have been published, yet these do not dispel the magic of clear glass suddenly becoming colored. Conversely, there is little consolation when the desired color development does not take place, or continues until the glass is a "livery" mass.

To strike a color requires a knowledge of the glass, the furnaces, and the appropriate time/temperature sequence (without an optical pyrometer in one hand and a stop watch in the other). "Ideal" timing and measuring might exist in the laboratory, but it seldom exists where the craftsman works. Despite all that has been written on the various strike colors, it is still up to the craftsman to get a feel for the process.

Copper

Copper is one of the most versatile colorants used in glasswork. The ancient glassworkers produced effects that are not often used today—these include opaque yellows as well as a variety of transparent and opaque reds. I have seen the same copper glass melt, over a period of several days, change from a transparent alkaline blue with touches of opaque red on thin surface areas, to a dark green, then to a mass of marblized black, brown, yellow, opaque red, and other colors that defy accurate verbal description.

Today copper is used for turquoise blue colors under oxidizing conditions, a "striking" ruby under special reducing conditions, a pink surface "blush" or a thin layer of metallic copper with exposure to a strong reducing flame, and a copper stain that has already been discussed.

Copper Ruby. There is little difficulty with any of these colors except the ruby. As with most rubies this color must be "struck." After its formation the color is very intense—actually black in thick sections of the vessel. To produce a uniform color the ruby is usually sandwiched or "cased" between two layers of clear glass. Otherwise the color may vary from black in thick sections to red at thin edges. Even with casing, the ruby tends to become "livery" or form an opaque "hematinone" glass (at one time a prized color).

Reducing Agents for Ruby. Copper rubies usually require reducing agents in the melt, and these can make a difference in the quality of the color produced. In most instances tin oxide is sufficient as a reducing agent, however a secondary agent is helpful. Among the safest are sodium-potassium tartrate (Rochelle salts) and sodium tartrate (cream of tartar). One of the best reducing agents—sodium cyanide—is a poison (I do not suggest you use it), but it reduces the copper more effectively than other agents. Charcoal is a consistent reducing element in batch melts, but the ruby produced is usually of poor quality with gray-black tones.

Gold

The problems with using gold are the high cost of the salts and the difficulties in controlling the conditions needed to produce the desired color effects. The first problem is beyond the craftsman's control except that he can decide to use another colorant in an attempt to produce the results desired from gold glass—a brilliant ruby. The gold ruby is usually produced in a lead glass with tin present, and in almost all instances it must be cased to produce an effective color. In the Appendix I show some formulas I have used to produce gold rubies, although I feel that the time and money involved could be better spent on copper rubies.

Iron

The most common impurity in many of the chemicals used to make glass is iron. The cost of iron-free ingredients increases the cost of the glass. As a result, the glass producer often resorts to methods of neutralizing the greenish cast caused by iron impurities. A notation from the New England Glass Company, dated 1885, illustrates the attitude held by the producer. The formula for a non-lead iron glass is called "green glass for *junk* bottles."

Iron produces a golden yellow glass in oxidizing conditions if there is no sulphur, carbon, or sodium nitrate present. I have produced an iron yellow in a closed crucible (in an open tank the same mixture has been light green). If sulfur is present browns or olive colors are likely to be produced. It must be noted that iron is one of the slower dissolving colorants.

Manganese

Manganese is an interesting colorant for reasons that relate to its particular sensitivity to oxidation and reduction. This sensitivity causes behavior that is contrary to almost all other colorants.

Manganese used with soda glasses produces a brown-purple under oxidizing conditions, and with potash glasses it produces an effective bluish-purple. Its sensitivity to the furnace atmosphere causes color loss almost as soon as it is added to the pot. Under the average studio conditions (meaning the likelihood of reducing conditions in the furnace) it has been my experience that in the space of several days the glass changes from a bubbling mass of dark purple to a not particularly effective light green. Somewhere between these two extremes is a period when the blue-purple appears.

A vessel made of manganese glass is likely to show random color swirls. This effect may be caused from the mild reduction produced by the contact of the glass with the wooden forming tools. Paradoxically, manganese glass tends to look incompletely mixed the more thoroughly the colorant is suspended in the melt (this suspension comes about after long periods of heating and reducing). The color sensitivity of manganese does not end with oxidizing and reducing variations. The more intense colors (other factors being equal) are formed at low temperatures. Arsenic compounds produce a stabilizing action that helps compensate for both atmospheric and temperature conditions. Manganese, when first introduced into the melt, tends to bubble strongly—be forewarned!

Adding Other Colorants. The addition of a very small amount of cobalt, usually in the form of powdered blue or blue cullet, intensifies the blue of the purple in soda glasses. Black glasses can be made from combinations of manganese and cobalt oxides. Chromium and manganese combinations have already been mentioned for ambers. A mixture of manganese and iron can be used for dark amber colors. I have included some of these formulas in the Appendix.

Goblet by Robert Biniarz. Clear and yellow borosilicate glass, 4″ x 9″. An excellent example of a stemware vessel, this piece shows the artist's success with combining opaque and transparent glass, as well as his strong sense of form. The goblet was colored with silver and then "tin fumed."

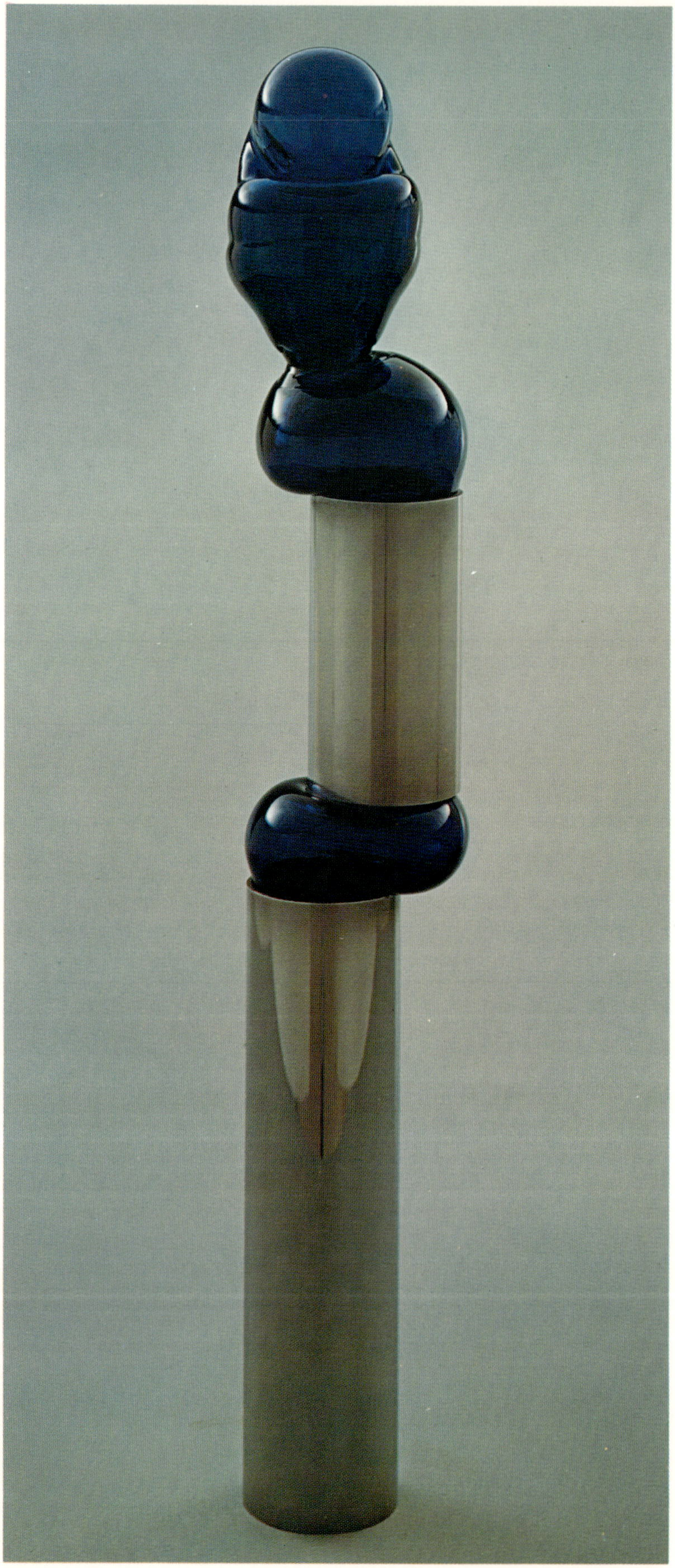

Bottle (Top) by Peter Vanderlaan. Soda/lime glass, 7" x 10". Colored glasses are trailed from the iron while the piece is still on the pipe. A tool then forms the "feather" shape. When on the pontil, the vessel is strongly reduced to bring the metals to the glass surface.

Bottle (Above) by Roger Lang. Freeblown glass with gold luster and sandblasting decoration, about 9" tall. Collection of Ronald Probst.

Untitled (Right) by Donald Hartman. Blown glass and chrome, 28" high. The artist is currently concerned with the integration of geometric configurations of metal with the fluid, organic qualities of glass.

Ruby Bottle (Left) *by Frank Kulasiewicz. Cadmium-selenium in potash/zinc glass, 7" x 7" x 7". The deep red color of this lily-pad design was developed by reheating the glass when adding additional gathers for the stopper and handles. The green color is the same glass, but not reheated.*

Interaction (Below) *by Harvey Littleton. Freeblown glass, 12" x 14" x 10" high. Made essentially from selenium amber, this piece was worked hot. A copper glass strip was placed on the second gather, which was then covered by additional gathers, elongated, and bent. Courtesy of the Lee Nordness Galleries, New York.*

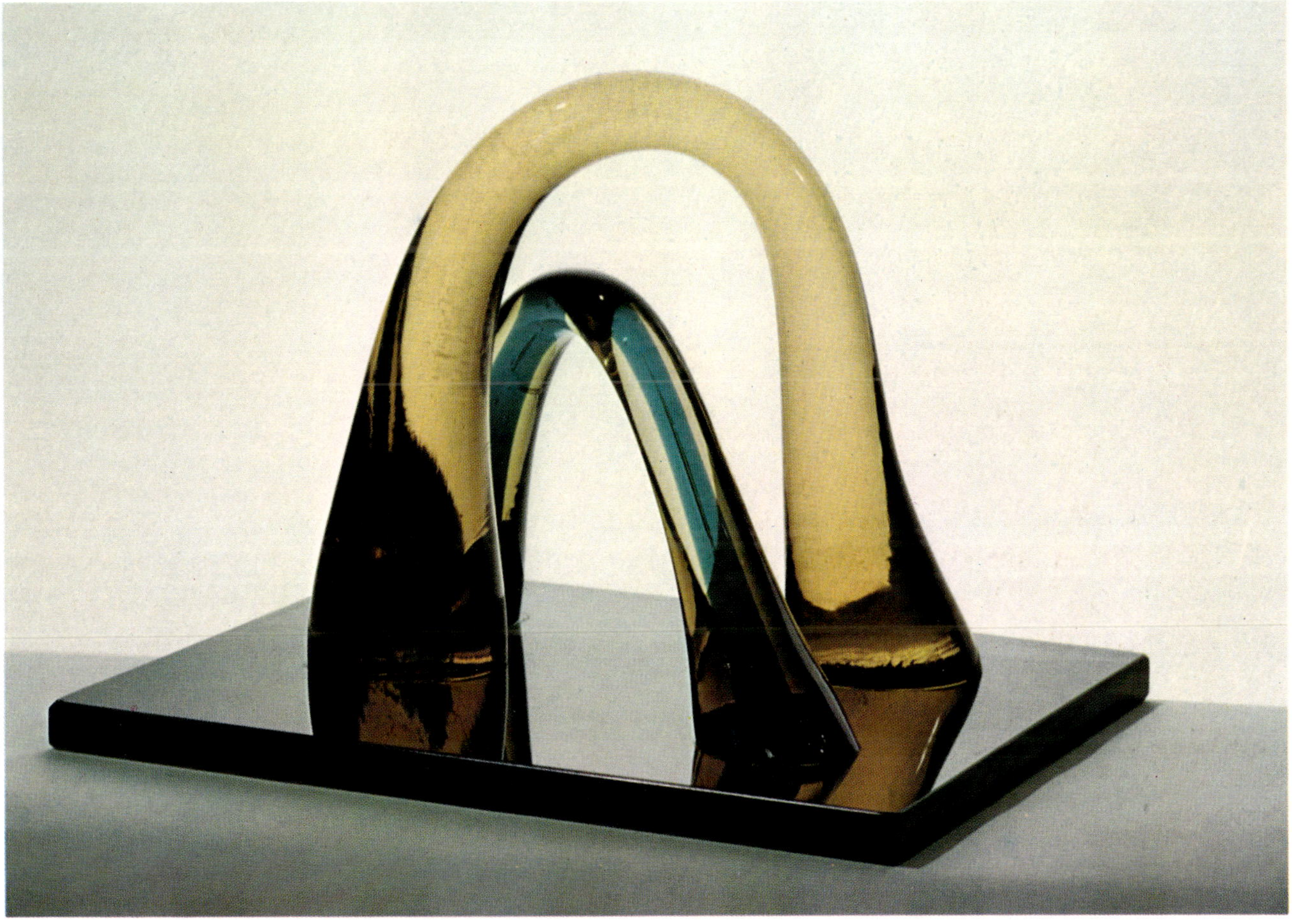

COLOR IN GLASS 147

Blue and Silver Flask (Above) by Quintin Lake. Freeblown cobalt glass 5" x 2½" x 8". "From a round shape attached to the blow pipe, I softened it and laid it on the marver and let it flatten on its own weight. Then I spread some silver nitrate on the marver and laid each flat side into it.... The stoppers I make by gathering and blocking glass into a ball, then using jacks I pull it away from the blow pipe to create a long neck."

Nuutajarvi Suomi Finland Series, Blue, 1971 (Top Right) by Marvin Lipofsky. Blue, red, and turquoise freeblown glass, 14" x 12". According to the artist, this sculptural form has something to do with "... business, political, and love reasons...." Courtesy of Arabia Glass.

Dual (Right) by Frank Kulasiewicz. Glass, brass, and wood, 13" x 12" x 14". The blown forms of this piece are colored with silver and manganese, and the stems are cast bronze. The concept for this sculpture developed from the nature of the glass, and the secondary materials were chosen to complement rather than compete.

Footed Bowl (Above) by Vernon Brejcha. Freeblown glass, 9" x 8" in diameter. A red and orange bowl with silver trim and a clear stem illustrates the artist's statement "... the hands tune themselves to primitive tools to master another golden flowing liquid—molten glass giving off light only for the artist to enjoy before it stiffens into a statement that had to be made."

Candle Holder by Dominic Labino. Freeblown glass, 3" x 9". This is an excellent example of a hollow base tooled from a single vessel. The typical swirls of manganese purple are evident in the thick central section where the vessel has been closed. Collection of Frank Kulasiewicz.

COLOR IN GLASS 149

White Bug House (Right) by Thomas Kekic. Freeblown glass, 5" x 13. One in the "Bug House" series—or, in the artist's words, the "Double Bubble" series. The white glass vessel sets off the bright reds, yellows, and blues on the vessel surface. The handles whimsically repeat the clear glass collar that both joins and separates the body from the sholder of the "house."

Bottle (Far Right), anonymous. Potash/zinc ruby glass, 7" x 10". A vibrant cadmium-selenium ruby bottle that I purchased at a small factory on the island of Majorca. Besides the color, the vessel is interesting because of the "donut" shape. It was first blown, then pressed between two fireproof discs. A gather of glass was added with the iron and the foot formed.

Untitled (Below) by Boris Dudchenko. Freeblown glass, 12" x 18". This is a constructed piece with glass mounted on a base of chromed steel, black formica, and wood. Collection of N. Wayne Taylor.

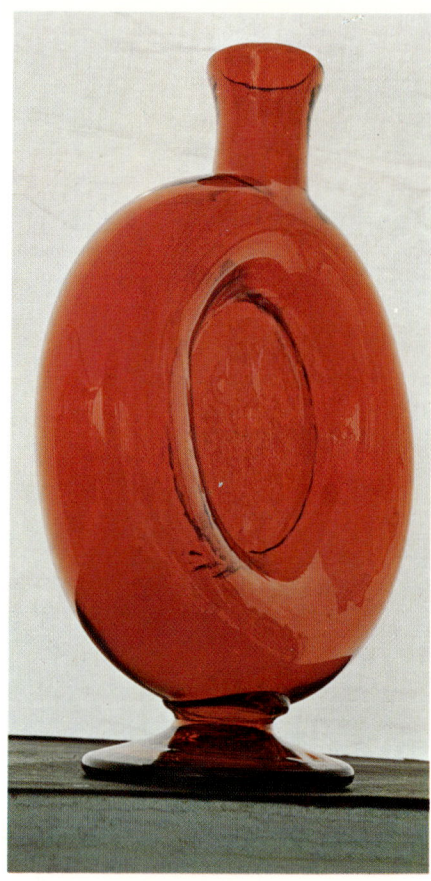

Untitled (Top) by Jammie Carpenter. Opal glasses, mirrors, lights, etc. A complex sculptural statement in glass.

Sculpture (Above) by John M. Bingham. Mirrored clear glass, 7" x 7". No technical information was supplied by the artist on this handsome little sculptured form.

Vase (Left) by Michael Boylen. Yellow and crystal blown glass, 3" x 7". Here a complex internal sculptural configuration is contained in a single, almost classic form.

COLOR IN GLASS 151

NICKEL

In contrast to the wealth of colors possible with nickel in ceramic glazes, its use is limited in glass. In most instances it is used to produce "smoky" gray glasses, as one of a number of "decolorants," or as a modifier of stronger colorants such as cobalt. It is possible to obtain a violet glass when nickel is used in glasses strong in potash, but in soda glasses it tends toward the production of "dirty" amber-brown glasses that are not particularly attractive. I have produced very intense purple colors with nickel in lead batch melts. The color of all nickel glasses, like the color of cobalt glasses, seems independent of oxidizing or reducing conditions. And no matter what the color of the thin walls of a nickel glass vessel, the thicker sections are a deep (almost dirty) red.

SILVER

Although not as expensive, silver has not enjoyed the special attention that gold has historically. Silver can be added to the glass melt to produce colors varying from yellow to brown, however, this use of silver has never gained importance in glass technology. Silver has been used in the form of a surface luster, generally referred to as "silver glass."

Contemporary craftsmen are using silver salts in the melt for a large variety of color and texture effects. Coupled with this is the reducing silver in the furnace flame to produce the expected "mirror" deposit on the vessel. Although other developments may be obtained with this type of experimentation, I question the economic factors involved when using silver compounds. Silver tends to settle out of the melt rather rapidly, and after a time the bottom of the tank or crucible will be covered with undissolved metallic silver droplets.

Rose Gun Bottle (Left) by Kim Newcomb. Milk glass, 4" x 8". This is one of a series that makes use of molds for preliminary forming. The artist's "pop art" sculptures also serve a purpose (vases that are fish, guns that are bottles, etc.).

SULPHIDE

A great variety of specialized colors can be obtained with various sulphides: zinc for white, antimony for red, cadmium for yellow, iron for black, molybdenum for orange-red, and a yellow (that behaves much like cadmium) from a combination of zinc and arsenious oxide. Most of these are "Art Glasses" developed and used by the Bohemian glass factories.

There are two glasses among the sulphide group that will be treated separately because of their historical importance, their beautiful color effects, and their wealth of scientific information on the nature of the glasses. These glasses are the misnamed "carbon ambers" and the cadmium-selenium rubies.

In general, the production of sulphide glasses is beyond beginning work in glass because only the purest materials can be used and exact temperature control must be maintained. The glasses have many faults even at their best. The antimony glass has a strong tendency to turn brown in annealing. Even with stabilizers added, the color can change from exposure to heat and sunlight. These glasses are often brittle, particularly the iron glasses. These factors combine to cause "delayed cracking" because of local strains produced by differences in thermal expansion. The only sulphide glass I have had a real interest in and worked with is the cadmium-selenium ruby, so I can offer little information on these other sulphide colors.

CADMIUM-SELENIUM

I already mentioned using cadmium sulphide to produce brilliant transparent yellow glasses, but the selenium pinks are far more difficult to produce. Both cadmium and selenium are of interest to the glassworker, however, it is the combination that produces the ruby that causes the greatest difficulty as well as the most brilliant results! Obtaining a good cadmium-selenium ruby requires precise control over all factors that affect the melt: heat, atmosphere, working time, ingredients, and striking, but do not let that scare you away! Cadmium-selenium is an interesting glass for study because the red produced is so much more brilliant than the gold and copper rubies, and it further offers clear crystal and yellows from the same tank of glass!

A well-known contemporary glass craftsman offered the following suggestions, partially in jest, for producing the red: the glasses are easy to make if you use the correct formula, the correct flame, do not overheat the glass, melt it in a closed pot (but I find it works in an open tank), and use a compound that has both the selenium and cadmium in it (rather than using two separate compounds).

Difficulties with the Cadmium-Seleniums. I have melted several ruby formulas in open tanks using both elemental selenium and various selenium compounds to produce true, deep, even-toned rubies. With all of these glasses the thermal history is far more important than the formula. Perhaps most exciting of all—they do not have the monotonous consistency of color production that is found with cobalt!

Selenium and cadmium both vaporize well below glass-melting temperatures, so certain points should be remembered. Strong reducing will "boil" out the selenium, and strong oxidizing will vaporize the cadmium. Long soaking periods will diminish the color and produce ambers, while low loading temperatures will vaporize the colorants before they are caught in the melt. The selenium is rather stable, once in the melt, however the cadmium continues to vaporize. It is estimated that even in the most ideal conditions 50% to 60% of the selenium will vaporize in the early part of the melting process, and of the remaining amount 90% will form colorless and brown compounds. The amount left produces the ruby! The final glass must have cadmium, sulfur, and selenium or it will not form a ruby.

Two-Spouted Bottle by Frank Kulasiewicz. Titanium/soda glass, 12" x 12". A yellow/pink and crystal was produced by casing the clear bottle with pink. The vessel was dipped into clear and yellow glasses while still on the pipe. These prunts were cut with shears to form the "wings." On the pontil, the lip was pushed together and then pulled with tweezers.

Ways to Introduce the Cadmium-Selenium. All through history the glassworker has been a very secretive person, always guarding his formulas, materials, etc. Unfortunately, much of this attitude still exists today. If I have any secret it is probably in connection with these illusive ruby glasses. One of my "secrets" is the use of the unscientific, expensive, "shot gun" method. This has no justification for use (since it has the faults already mentioned plus more) except that it works!

Instead of putting in 1% selenium and 1% cadmium sulphide I have gone as far as using ¼% selenium, ¼% selenium dioxide, ¼% sodium selenide, ¼% barium selenide, ¼% zinc selenide, ¾% cadmium sulphide, ¼% cadmium oxide, and 1% sulfur. All of these materials have different melting points, and their essential ingredients "boil" off at different temperatures. It could well be that only one or two ingredients are working—but they *are* working!

Glass Composition for Cadmium-Selenium Rubies. I list several glass compositions in the Appendix. They all seem to work, and they share certain characteristics. They contain zinc oxide, some potash, some borax, and they all are "reducing" formulas (no nitrate, arsenic, or antimony) using chemicals like table salt (sodium chloride) as fining agents. If you use any of these base glasses for colorants that should be oxidized (or for clear glass), be sure to adjust it to oxidize or you will not be particularly happy with some of the results. I have found that some cadmium-selenium cullet from a previous melt is of great help when added to the fresh batch. Once the colorants are in the glass there is a better chance of keeping them there.

Melting and Working Cadmium-Selenium. Before beginning to load the glass, get the empty furnace as hot as you can—use almost any means possible (that is safe!) to push the temperature up. When you start to load, try to shovel the glass as fast as possible—do not stop until you have the batch nearly to the rim of the tank. Close the furnace quickly and keep the heat up. The flame should be slightly more reducing than the one described in the chapter on firing the furnace. This flame is produced by giving the burner full air and increasing the gas until the flame is reducing. Since you cannot use the easy melting nitrates in the reduction batch you need the extra heat; also, the faster you can melt at least the top layer of glass the better your chance to keep the easily vaporized colorants in the glass.

When all the materials have melted, turn the heat back and keep the furnace cooler than usual. Do not just let the glass set in the furnace if you can help it! Remember that all those expensive colorants are vaporizing. Take a test gather and begin to work if the glass is *nearly* seed free and strikes. As the colorants vaporize and as the glass is exposed to longer periods of heating, the color of the ruby will change.

Between work sections keep the heat low and the flame slightly yellow (reducing), but do not get it so cool that you have to heat strongly to work the glass again. If you have a reboil with these glasses, it is likely that selenium and cadmium will be part of the bubbles formed with the usual oxides.

When working the glass itself, in general, the more often you cool and reheat the vessel (the longer you work a vessel) the darker and more opaque the color will become. If you want a stemware piece with a red bowl, yellow stem, and clear foot (from the same tank of glass) you cannot waste any time. The change in the color of the glass in the furnace is generally caused by vaporization that alters the zinc/selenium/cadmium relationship. The variation in the color of the pieces made at the same work session is probably caused by differences in the thermal history of each vessel.

Finally, save all the cullet (even the cordy bottom glass). If it has any colorant (and particularly if it has already struck) it is most helpful when mixed with the next batch of ruby.

Carbon Amber or Sulfur Amber

The other sulphide color that bears mentioning is one that was once very important to the glass industry—the carbon or sulfur amber. The amber color is produced by the reducing action of carbon changing sulphates to sulphides. Many of the technical difficulties mentioned with the ruby colors are also present with this amber, and despite the wealth of technical information on it, you would do well to look to other ambers. The mineral "pyrites"—or the famous "Fool's Gold"—is a form of iron sulphide that can produce an amber. I have already presented an amber produced from manganese and chromium.

Titanium

Although rarely used alone, titanium dioxide intensifies and brightens other glass colorants, and changes the expansion/contraction rate to an often adverse extent. It further changes the colors produced by several other metals. When 10% is added to green iron glasses, deep browns are produced. The oxide turns copper blue glasses to green or even to brown. Cerium-titanium yellows are possible, as are strong amber colors with manganese-titanium. I have produced pinks through ambers using varying mixtures of manganese, cerium, and titanium.

Uranium

Uranium salts are now available to glass programs in schools following a period when government regulation made obtaining the uranium compounds nearly impossible. Although uranium can be used for a number of color effects, it is usually used to produce a brilliant yellow with green fluorescence. In reduction, the color is either black or dull gray. In lead glasses I have produced brilliant yellows without fluorescence. The yellow is intensified and becomes almost orange with the addition of titanium. Although costly, the yellows produced with uranium are brilliant and consistent under oxidizing conditions in potash/zinc glasses and so are well worth your interest.

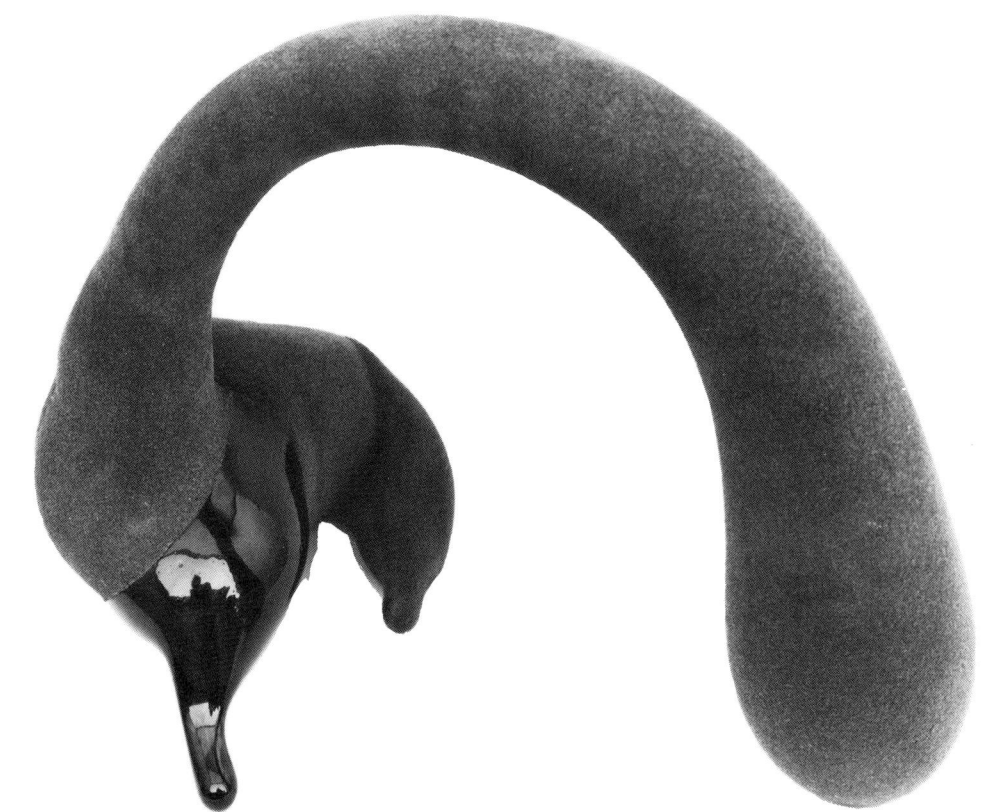

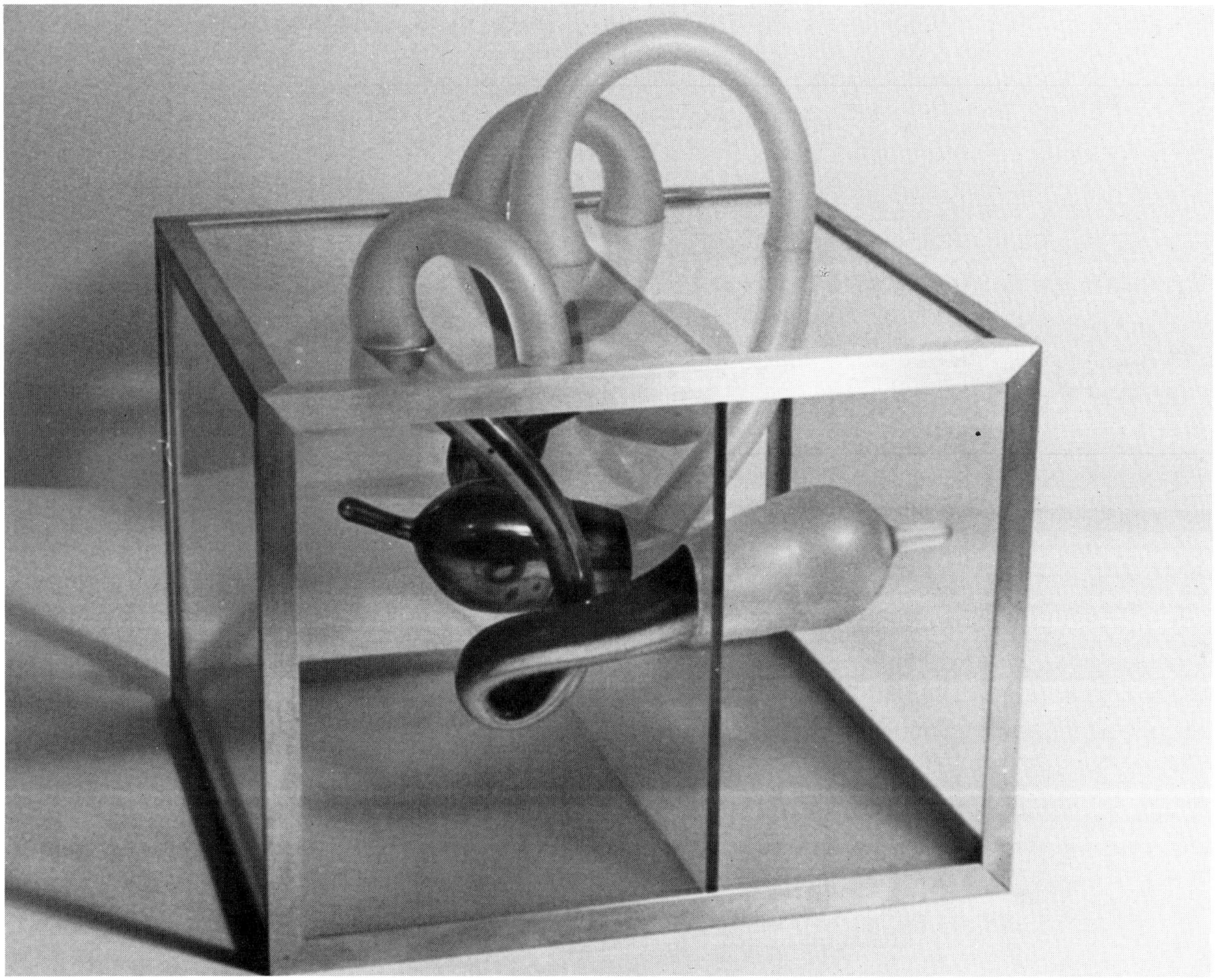

156 GLASSBLOWING

8/Decorating and Finishing

California Loop Series (Above Left) by Marvin Lipofsky. Freeblown dark glass forms, 10″ x 14″. One of a series of glass sculptures done by the artist using the fluid sensual forms possible in glass. Cut and joined, sandblasted and flocked areas contrast the slick glass with a variety of other textures.

Construction 1972 (Left) by Brian McNally. Freeblown glass, 12″ x 12″ x 10″. These forms are part of a "box series" making use of both blown pieces and plate glass. The blown forms are frosted and electroplated, and the boxes are plate glass with aluminum angle. The "organic" blown forms are not contained by the box, but appear to escape and re-enter through the divider and top.

Decorations in glass can take a variety of forms and use a variety of techniques. In this chapter I will be dealing with decorations that are usually done after the shape of the vessel has been established, or often after the glass has cooled. I will also discuss methods of finishing glass (some of the machinery used in decorating can also be used for finishing).

Types of Decorations

I will discuss two general types of decorations. The first adds something to a glass surface—lusters, mirror finish, etc. The applied materials usually form a bond to the glass surface, often because of a heat treatment. The second group of decorative techniques are those that remove a portion of the glass surface—sandblasting, grinding, etching, etc. These decorative techniques will be discussed not only to further your technical knowledge, but also to increase your appreciation of the glass (both historical and modern) that is so much a part of our world.

Esthetic Considerations

Almost all decorative techniques have at one time or another been popular with both the glassworker and the public. Some have not fared well with a change in fashion or taste. To disregard one type of decoration because it has been abused in the past is not justified. There are far too many fascinating possibilities in these areas for you to set any one aside without first exploring its potential for your own creative efforts.

Erwin Eisch once said that "No epoch before ours made a principle that glass must not be decorated. Formerly glasses which were not decorated were regarded as vulgar and cheap...." It might be added that no epoch before ours had so much glass decorated at such low prices by so many fast machines. The success of the glass industry in America makes it clear that the stenciled or silk-screened label on the container has become synonymous with cheapness because it *is* literally cheap.

Safety Considerations

There are potential hazards involved in almost any activity. Some of the procedures described in this chapter make use of poisonous materials, others give off fumes, etc. Techniques that are potentially dangerous should be tried only after you thoroughly understand the dangers and use all the safety equipment, caution, and common sense called for.

When using any power machinery for cutting, grinding, or polishing—particularly those using water as the lubricant—be certain that the machine is properly wired and that a special ground is supplied to protect you from electrical shock. If you have any doubts about the safety of the machine, wrap a wire around a bare (unpainted) screw in the body of the machine and run the other end of the wire to a definite ground (such as a metal water pipe, radiator, etc). Be sure that this end of the wire is also firmly attached to bare (unpainted) metal for maximum protection. Most heavy-duty industrial glass equipment is generally well designed, however when using substitute tools (such as a hand power drill) with water as a lubricant special care must be taken. Besides the above considerations, *never* use any power tool without wearing shoes, when standing on damp floors, without proper eye protection, without long hair secured, or with loose clothing that might get caught in the machine's moving parts.

APPLICATION OF DECORATIONS

Most of the techniques are applicable to all glass production methods, but a few are more easily adopted to a specific way of working. There is a wealth of techniques, so I will not attempt to compile a definitive listing.

Although there are logical divisions, the categories become rather arbitrary when a complex procedure requires parts of the process to be done at different times in the work sequence, or when several processes depend on one another.

"Fired-On" Techniques. Most of these processes are performed after the vessel has been gathered, formed, finished, annealed, and cooled. After the appropriate treatment the vessels are refired, either in ceramic kilns or ovens, to the proper temperatures for the decorative materials used. When you are using "fired-on" decorations, be sure to pay attention to the manufacturer's directions and suggested temperatures.

Vitrifiable Colors. Vitrification refers to the transformation of a mixture of inorganic matters into a hard, glassy nonabsorbent material—in effect—into glass. In general these colors do not have a fixed melting point, but instead depend on a time/temperature relationship to mature. They are low-temperature glasses with overloads of inorganic oxides or pigments. The glasses without pigments are "fluxes." Some of the vitrifiable colors offer little advantage over ordinary paints and enamels, but it is possible to use these colors to bring out the richness of transparent glass.

A great variety of compounds are available on the market for application to the glass surface. Many have been developed for commercial use, so a bit of creative thinking is needed to apply the material for results other than bottle labels.

Metallic Decorating Materials

These materials—usually a metallic salt dissolved in oil of lavender—are fired to a low red heat on the vessel surface. The material is fired high enough to fuse the metal to the glass and burn off the resin, depositing a thin metallic coating on the glass surface.

Bright Metals. The first of this group are the Bright Metals. These are essentially oil solutions of gold, platinum, palladium, and silver. These amber liquids decompose under heat leaving a deposit of metal. This is often barely attached to the glass surface and in the case of gold is easily scratched. To improve adherence of the gold the vessels are sometimes "mudded" with equal parts of copper sulphate and ocher (see the section on copper stain) first and fired at about 475°C. After cooling and washing the bright gold is applied and the vessel refired. Again, following the manufacturer's directions is your best assurance for good results with these metals. The demonstration shows gold luster being painted on the vessel surface and the vessel after firing. This painting method is one of the basic ways to apply vitrifiable colors, lusters, etc., to the glass surface.

Luster Colors. These are also metallic resinates of metals, however they produce a variety of colors—reds, yellows, browns, etc., depending on the metals in the material (copper, manganese, cobalt, uranium, zinc, etc.) and mixtures of these metals. Many of these luster colors have iridescence. Brushing, spraying, and dipping are among the methods used for application. Coats, in general, must be thin. More than one coat can be applied with a firing for each coat.

Work Area. Both the bright metals and the luster colors are likely to be spoiled by dust and lint, so it is best to have a separate, clean, closed work area. The material tends to cluster around impurities and cause spots of deep color surrounded by circles of colorless glass. Directions for thinning and mixing must be followed to prevent spoiling the ware.

1. Commercial gold luster is painted on a vessel prior to refiring in the oven. Painting is one method of applying metallic and vitrifiable colors. Follow the manufacturers suggestions for firing the materials.

2. During firing the oil is burned off and the metal forms a loose bond with the glass. Best results are obtained in and electric oven or in a "muffle" gas oven (an oven where the flame does not make contact with the ware).

Staining Glass

There are two metals that can be used to stain glass—silver and copper. "Muds" or a slurry of the metal salts, clay, and water are applied to the glass surface, then fired in the oven. During the firing the silver or copper exchange places with the alkali flux in the vessel surface.

Silver Stain. Silver staining is an area that recently has received a great deal of study, but the processes and results have changed little from those used in ancient times. The process involves "mudding" the glass vessel with the slurry mentioned. After firing, the excess "mud" is removed by scrubbing and washing.

The ancient process was probably first used in ceramics by the Persians and later used on glass. This method makes use of a base exchange to introduce the colorant into the glass at a temperature below the softening point of the glass. By repeated "jumps" from the glass to the slurry, the silver (Ag) and sodium (Na) exchange places.

The kind of silver compound has little effect on the results—there is no "best" silver compound to use, although chlorides and nitrates seem to be the most commonly used. The amount of silver salt in the paste varies from 5% to 20% by weight. Also, the composition of the glass does not have any great effect on the reaction, although studies indicate that minor constituents, such as iron oxide (FeO), do help the process.

Copper Staining

Copper staining or "red etching" is a comparatively recent development. The process is far more complicated than silver staining, and the reduction with copper must be thoroughly controlled. Copper therefore requires at least two separate firings, sometimes even three.

Kinds of Glass for Copper Staining. Unlike silver, the results of copper staining are influenced by the alkali oxides present in the glass (although minor constituents have little effect). The stain works best on potash glasses. When used on a mixed alkali glass, a minimum of 6% potassium oxide (K_2O) is needed. Replacing calcium oxide (CaO) with zinc oxide (ZnO) or magnesium oxide (MgO) is also generally found to be favorable.

There have been some successful attempts to produce copper stain on soda-lime glasses. In general these call for several firings. One of the most successful methods uses cuprous chloride ($CuCl_2$) vapors in contact with the hot glass surface for several hours. This produces a cuprous-ion containing glass covered with a surface "bloom" of sodium chloride (NaCl). After cooling, the salt is washed off and the vessel again heated and reduced. The time/temperature relationship of these heatings produces a variety of colors—from reds with no metallic luster to very deep reds with strong metallic luster.

Silver and Copper Combination Stains. When both copper and silver are used in the same slurry, time/temperature is important, but indications are that zinc and chlorine may also play a part in the color produced. Temperatures in excess of 600°C. either produce a metallic appearance or burn out the color completely.

On a soda-lime glass, when 0.17 silver (Ag), 58.0 copper (Cu) and 41.9 zinc (Zn) is present in the slurry you can get an effective amber. 5.0 Ag, 39.8 Zn, and 55.0 Cu makes the best green stain, and 13.6 Ag, 36.2 Zn and 50.3 Cu provides the best red stain. Also noted at some temperatures are combination effects. With the green color at 560°C., a pink coloration forms under the green and is visible from the opposite side of the glass. When red is used, the underside shows a very dense green color. The most consistent and easily produced color however, is some form of straw amber.

1. An overall covering of a slurry of clay, metal salts, and water is painted on a glass vessel. You could also make a selective design rather than an overall stain. This "mud" is allowed to dry before the vessel is refired to the annealing temperature of the glass.

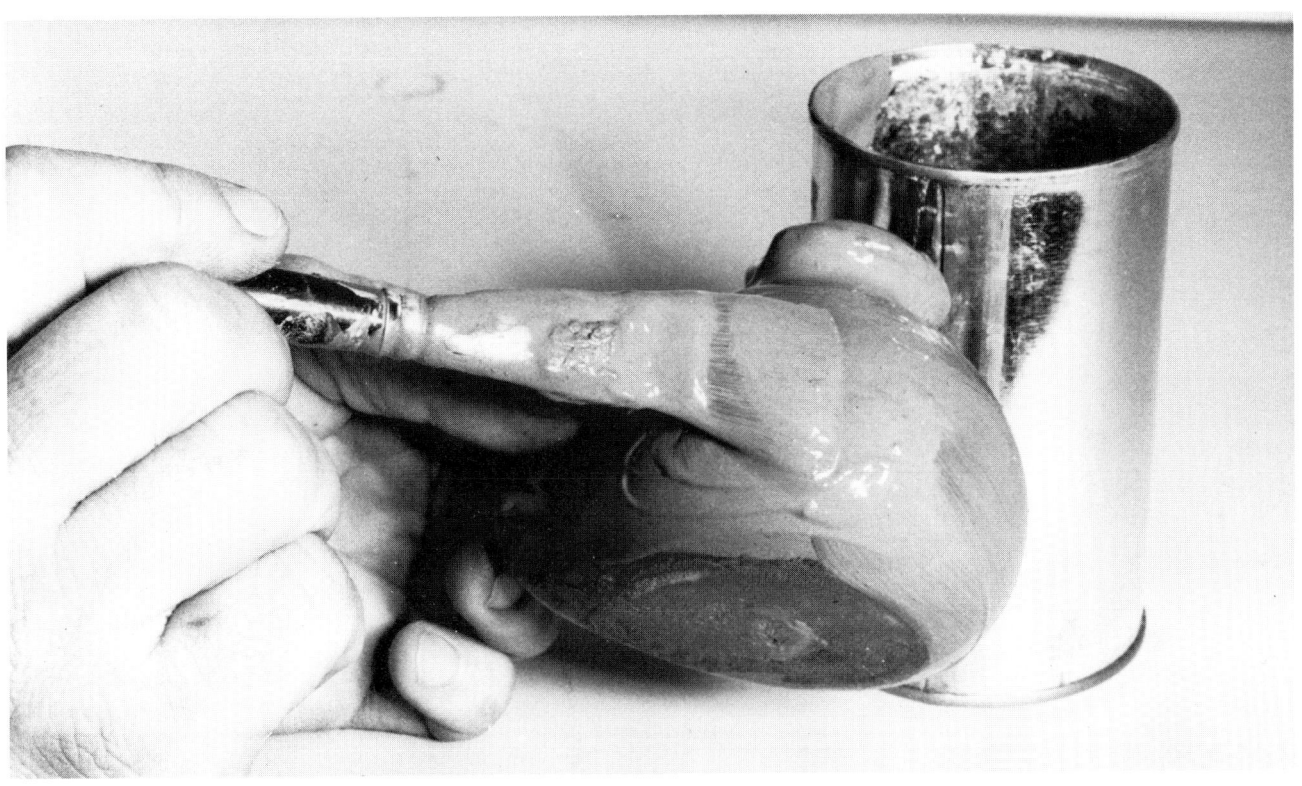

2. During the firing the metal salts (copper and/or silver) in the "mud" exchange places with the alkali flux in the glass surface. After cooling and removal from the oven, the remaining clay is washed off the glass. The color of the stain depends on the metal salts used, the type of glass, and the temperature of the firing.

DECORATING AND FINISHING 161

Iridescence

I have included iridescence in this chapter, but many iridescent glasses are produced either by introducing chemicals into the annealing oven at the end of the work day, or by reheating the vessels to annealing temperatures and introducing the chemicals into the atmosphere of the oven. The method I use is to selectively iridize pieces individually, after forming at the furnace and before annealing.

Iridescence is a surface ion exchange in which metal replaces the material in the glass surface and produces a refractive effect ("Newton Rings" or "Rainbows"). This effect is known under a number of popular names ("Carnival Glass" "Aged Glass," etc.).

Of prime consideration is the poisonous nature of the chemicals used and the released caustic fumes, so selection of equipment is important. Spraying is an effective way of iridizing, but the chemicals attack most metals. Do not use a commercial paint spray gun because most will literally be dissolved by the chemicals.

I have used an old-fashioned "lung powered" art fixative sprayer attached to a compressor hose. This works well and can be replaced at minimum cost. Keep the concentrated fumes away from motors, blowers, and the like. Basically, a large garbage can is mounted horizontally with a hole cut in one side and a bucket hung at the front for collecting excess chemicals that condense in the can. The sprayer is attached to a compressor (do not use this system on "lung power" since the fumes are very caustic). The compressor motor may be controlled by either a hand or foot electric switch. The sprayer is aimed through the hole in the side of the can. A small exhaust fan is mounted on top of the can to carry the fumes away from you as you work.

Chemicals for Iridescent Effects. I have had success with a water solution of tin chloride sprayed on the hot glass that is then reheated in a reducing flame. The process may be repeated a number of times to produce the desired amount of iridescence.

Very successful effects have been produced by artists using a spray solution of equal parts of hydrochloric acid, tin chloride, and iron chloride. Other chemicals mentioned are titanium chloride, vanadium tetrachloride, and various uranium and cadmium compounds. Purer chemicals (particularly tin chloride) generally produce the best results, and the process is usually most effective over darker glasses.

Carder's Iridescent Effects. Although Tiffany's name is most often associated with these "artificially aged" glasses, Carder was producing a variety of such glasses at about the same time. Elaborate spraying techniques were described by Mr. Carder in a recorded interview before his death.

Iridescence Produced by Fuming. I have already mentioned that iridescence (usually a light coating) can be produced by adding the chemicals to the lehr (gas or oil fired *not* electrically). The fumes are largely enclosed in the oven, with the exhaust safely taking care of escaping gasses. Another method is to heat the salts and expose the hot vessel to the fumes. The vessel is alternately heated and fumed several times. This method is rather wasteful however, because unused fumes cannot be reclaimed and are dangerous if an exhaust system is not used. It is best to heat the compounds at or on the furnace so the furnace exhaust will remove the fumes. I recently visited a glass studio in a large, well-known university, and most all the windows had a clouded coating of iridescence. Needless to say the effects on the students' lungs were probably similar.

Other Methods. Although I have not tried this method (and really cannot say I recommend it), passing mention should be made of yet another technique used to artificially age or iridize glass. In this method the glass is buried in animal waste for several months. Although I cannot vouch for the success of this method, there are several potters who have used the technique on low fire pottery and swear by the effects! If the method has nothing else of value, at least it does away with poisonous fumes!

1. This is a close-up of a hot glass vessel on the pontil prior to spraying with iridizing compounds.

2. A view of a simple and safe method of spraying chemicals on the hot glass.

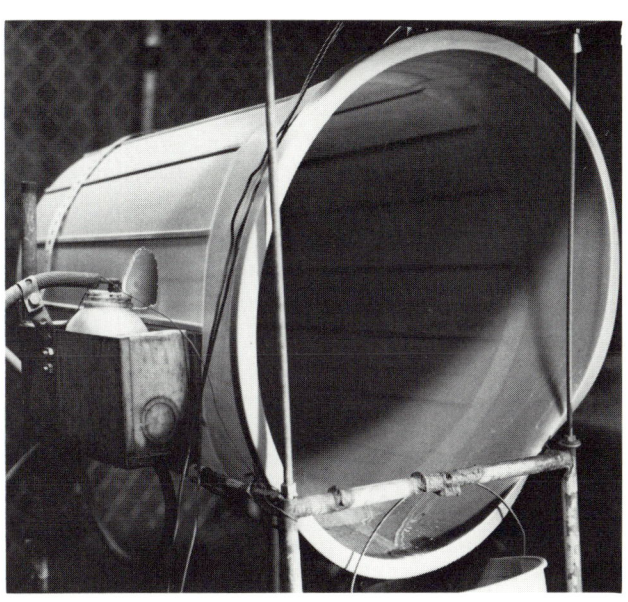

3. The hot vessel on the pontil is put into the can near the sprayer and the iridizing compounds sprayed on. The vessel is then reheated.

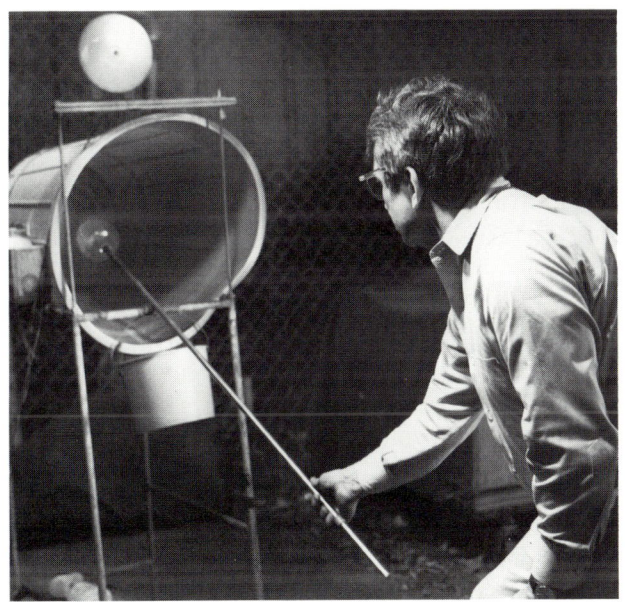

4. Here the vessel is partially iridized. The spraying/heating process may be repeated several times until the desired "aged" effect is achieved.

DECORATING AND FINISHING 163

Mirroring Glass

Silver is used extensively in producing mirrors. The process (in reality there are several methods) that is used to make the common flat mirror can also be used to coat the surface of your blown ware. The process precipitates metallic silver from ammoniacal solutions by use of a reducing agent (such as Rochelle salt) and can be done on almost *any* material including leather and wood.

In most mirrors the thin deposit of silver is backed by painting to protect the fragile coating. For your purposes it will probably be necessary to repeat the process several times to build up the silver deposit. Then you can apply a protective coat of lacquer or paint.

After the first metal coat is on, it is possible (with the proper electrical equipment and supplies) to electroplate the glass to increase the silver deposit or to coat the glass surface with other metals (nickel, chromium, etc.). This is a complicated process requiring expensive equipment.

The demonstration shows the steps in mirroring the interior of a vessel. The chemicals used are poisonous and caustic (besides the ammonia mentioned, nitric acid and various tin compounds are often part of the mirroring solutions) so be sure to follow the directions of the manufacturer and pay particular attention to any caution.

1. Dilute the concentrated mirroring solutions according to the directions of the manufacturer. Mark each bottle (the labeled bottles shown are in reality all clear liquids) according to the classifications in the directions. Clean the vessel to be mirrored with distilled water (dirtier vessels may need to be rinsed with acids).

2. Mix equal amounts of each solution in a measuring cup. Pour the mixture quickly into the vessel to be mirrored.

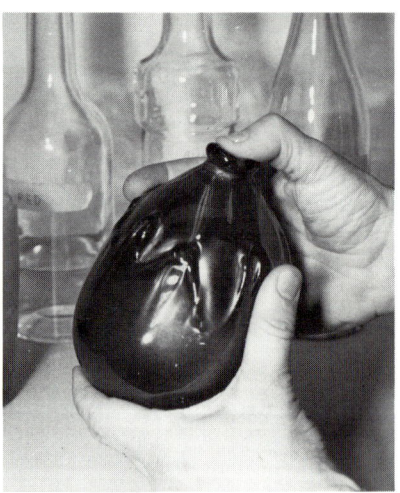

3. Shake the vessel (keep the mouth covered with a stopper or your finger) to coat the interior. It may be several minutes before the mirroring becomes noticeable.

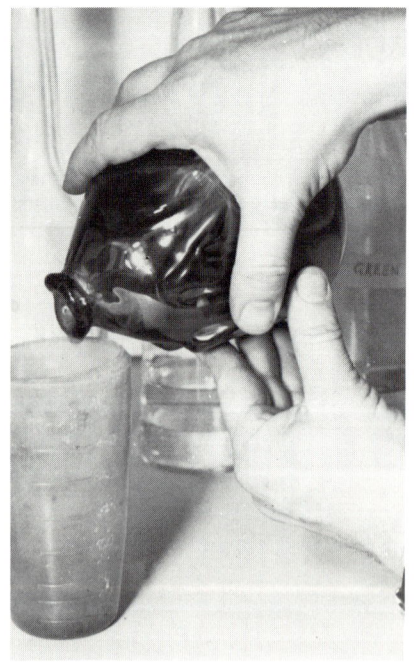

4. Discard the remaining solution in the vessel, turn the vessel over, and allow it to drain. Wash your measuring cap thoroughly before using again. Note: the mixed solutions usually stain the skin and nails brown if kept in contact for any length of time. Also pay particular attention to cautions given by the manufacturer.

Sulphide Surface Colors

A surface effect that is seldom used today but offers great potential is using colored sulphides. Basically the process is similar to some already described in that hot glass is exposed to vapors that combine with materials in the glass surface. In this instance the vapors are sulpher (and need of course, proper ventilation) and the colors possible are zinc for white, antimony for reds, cadmium for yellow, and iron for black. Although sulphide glasses were once an important part of Bohemian glass production, the colors produced were primarily mixtures in the glass composition. Although there is little reference in the field to using these materials for surface color, I think it is a fertile field for your investigations.

Flocking Glass

Flocking glass deserves mentions because of its great popularity among beginners in glass. Esthetically it has little basis for use on glass, but it is nevertheless popular. The process is the same as that used to decorate wallpaper, turntables etc. A glue is applied and finely powdered, colored "flocking" (powdered wool, cloth, etc.) is made to adhere to the glass.

Various hobby stores sell kits that can be used for flocking. The fad has become so popular—particularly on the West Coast—that some university glass departments devote entire rooms to this activity. It should be noted that some serious and deserving sculptural effects have been produced using the flocking material to cover junction lines between two pieces of joined glass, as well as to produce stark textural contrast between shiny, smooth glass and fuzzy areas.

Removing Part of the Surface

The following design techniques are concerned with removing a portion of the vessel after annealing and cooling. They offer the glass artist a wealth of possibilities. Some of the decorations are dependent on the handling the vessel received during forming at the furnace, while others are independent of such preplanning. The glass surface may be removed to reveal a different glass beneath, or to change the optical effect of the glass. Some of the decorations barely scratch the surface, while others will cut right through the glass wall.

Some of these techniques are also used for finishing glass. Although many of the tools and procedures are the same, I will nevertheless treat finishing in the last part of this chapter. Please bear with any repetitions this may cause.

Cutting and Finishing Machines

Because much of this equipment is used for several types of operations, I will briefly describe them here before presenting their various uses. The example I show are industrial machines, however craftsmen with ingenuity have managed to build less elaborate machines for their individual needs.

Glass Lathe. The term "glass lathe" has two meanings in glasswork. In laboratory lampworking the glass lathe is a complex horizonal rotating device with a multitude of burners. It is used for the production of complicated laboratory glassware and is of little importance to you at this point.

The glass lathe we will discuss is basically a horizontal driveshaft to which you can attach a variety of sizes and kinds of abrasive wheels, cork and felt polishing wheels, abrasive cones, etc. A water tray with sponge or a water drip arrangement must be made for most of your work with the lathe. The speed on some models can be varied between 100 rpm. to 2500 rpm. The photograph shows one model of such a glass lathe, but it is possible to make a less complicated, less expensive device for some of your glass needs.

Diamond Glass Saw. The diamond glass saw is usually a diamond impregnated blade that is water lubricated and mounted on a table saw. It is really a larger version of the saw used for cutting stones in lapidary workshops or in geology study. It serves a number of cutting functions with glass.

The glass lathe is a variable-speed horizontal driveshaft with several spindle sizes (making it possible to use a variety of abrasive wheels, cones, cork, and felt polishing wheels). The speeds may vary from 100 to 2400 rpm. to allow many types of decorating and finishing operations. As with most horizontally driven shafts on glass tools, the lathe runs "backwards" to most other types of power tools.

The diamond glass saw is a diamond impregnated blade, water cooled and lubricated, mounted on a table. The blade rotation is from the top down as you face the front of the machine. In this small commercial model, the water is in the trough below the table top, and the guard on the blade serves to catch the water splashed off the blade.

Grinder, Grinding Mill, or Rougher. The grinder is a horizontal steel wheel with a drip water attachment and grit of some type. A small version of this machine is used in lapidary work. The larger the wheel head the greater the versatility possible, but no matter what the size, these machines all work on the same principle. Water drips into a trough filled with grit (usually silicon carbide or aluminum oxide), which in turn drips the mixture of water and grit on the revolving steel wheel. The centrifugal force of the wheel spinning spreads the mixture out over the surface of the wheel head.

As a substitute for the grinder, some craftsmen have used a potters wheel with a makeshift drip arrangement, but this is not advisable if the wheel head is aluminum or any other soft alloy.

Polisher or Smoother. This is similar to the grinder in appearance, however the steel head may be replaced with a stone or felt wheel. The polishing material is usually fine-grain pumice that is fed to the head by dripping water.

Edger and Beveler. The edger-beveler is also a horizontal power-driven shaft mounted with grinding and polishing stones. Unlike the lathe, this machine does not allow for a variety of sizes and types of wheels because the wheels are semi-permanently mounted. In general they have a large diameter and are at least 1" wide. The stones available are a roughing stone (usually silicon carbide), a smoothing stone (usually aluminum oxide of somewhat fine grain), and a cork polishing wheel.

The wheels are mounted above a water tray that "feeds" the water to the stone through a sponge. The water acts as both a coolant and as a lubricant for the friction that develops when the glass is brought in contact. Commercially this machine is used to grind and finish the edge of sheet or plate glass, but it can be used for a variety of applications in your work (as can other commercial machines).

The grinder is a horizontal steel wheel with a drip water and grit feed trough. The centrifical force of the wheel rotating spreads the grinding mixture over the wheel surface. The glass is held in contact with the steel wheel, grit, and water and is ground flat.

This is a commercial smoother with a large (24" x 3" thick) horizontally-mounted natural stone. Its operation and design is similar to that of the rougher.

The edger-beveler is a horizontal, power-driven shaft on which are semi-permanently mounted vertical roughing, smoothing, and cork polishing wheels. In this commercial model the wheels are all 12" x 1¾". Water, the coolant and lubricant, is stored in the metal troughs below the wheels and is fed to the wheels through sponges located in the water.

DECORATING AND FINISHING 167

Cut Glass (Ground)

The term "cut glass" is confusing because of its many meanings. As you have seen, it is possible to "cut" hot glass with shears when working from the furnace. The small tool used to "cut" sheet glass for windows, etc. is called a glass cutter, but it scores the glass (which is then broken, not cut). A diamond (or other hard abrasive) impregnated blade can be used to cut glass, but this is not what we think of as "cut" glass.

The traditional "cut" glass is produced by grinding the glass with an abrasive wheel. This process of holding the glass against a revolving abrasive wheel to produce incised grooves or facets is one of the oldest forms of decorations known.

The shape of the vessel evolves first, then the decoration is literally "cut-out" of this shape by direct grinding. The resulting thickness and angle of the facets have optical possibilities that are hard to produce in any other way.

Using the Edger-Beveler. The ground glass grooves are translucent and are called "gray cuts" when left unpolished. The photographs show a vessel being cut and polished on the edger-beveler. If the cutting on either the rougher or smoother stones were the last of the process, the design would be a gray cut. Polishing the scratch marks produces the brilliance assoicated with "cut-crystal" or "rock-crystal." Authentic "cameo glass" is glass that has been ground to various levels to form a relief decoration. Both gray cut and polished cuts are used in the cameo designs.

1. The vessel is held against the roughing stone until the desired amount of glass is removed. It is usually better to take off only a bit of glass at a time—rotating from cut to cut. This prevents spot buildups of heat (from friction) that could crack your glass or destroy the symmetrical arrangement of your cuts.

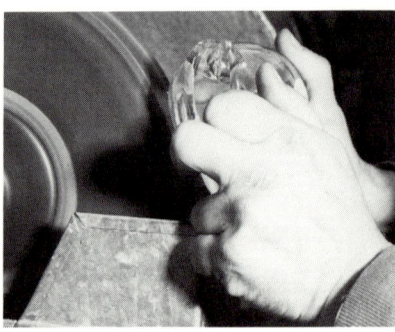

2. The vessel is next moved to the smoothing stone to remove most of the scratch marks left by the roughing stone. Wash the vessel before changing stones to remove any coarse grit that may have been picked up. If the shape permits, the vessel should be rotated to help remove directional scratches that may be evident on the gray cuts.

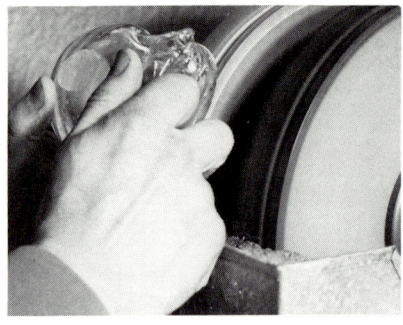

3. If a polish cut rather than a gray cut is desired the vessel should be thoroughly washed and then worked against the cork polishing wheel. Note: most vertically-mounted glass machinery runs "backwards" (from the bottom up toward you) to keep the water on the wheel as it makes contact with the vessel and also to cut down on water spray.

Using the Glass Lathe. The lathe is the most versatile tool for producing cut glass because a large variety of types, sizes, and shapes of stones are available. Generally speaking there are three shapes commonly used—the hollow cut (a round edge), the bevel cut (V-shaped edge), and the panel cut (flat edge). Except for the panel stone, the shapes described (as well as special shapes) are formed by "dressing" the stones with a diamond point tool.

There are a variety of wheel shapes that can be used on a glass lathe for cut glass decorations. The three basic shapes are a bevel (V-shape), a panel (flat), and a hollow (round).

1. All forming of the wheels on the lathe, due to the direction of rotation, is done from the back of the machine. The tool is held firmly against a support and the diamond tip starts the cut at the edge of the panel wheel. Note: wear goggles and a respirator mask!

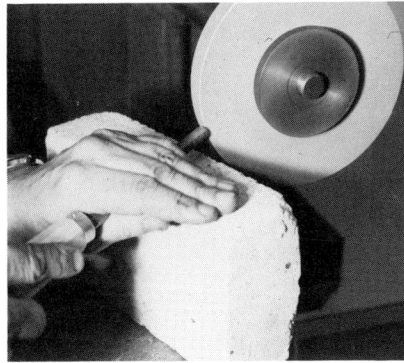

2. The cut is worked from the edge to the center of the panel and back. Repeat the process from the opposite side of the wheel to form a point at the center.

3. Finish forming the point at the center of the bevel with both sides sloping to the edges. Note: as you use any of the wheels you will periodically find it necessary to "true" them with the diamond tool.

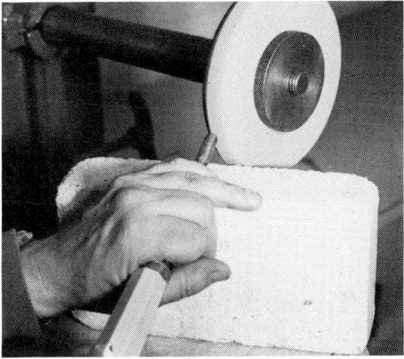

I will also demonstrate a bevel cut stone being used to gray cut a vessel. As with the beveler-edger, water is picked up from the can by a sponge that in turn deposits the water on the grinding wheel. The water keeps the friction of the abrasive against the glass from producing enough heat to break the glass because of thermal shock.

Cut glass decorations are direct, offer unique effects, good control, comparative safety, and good material/design relationship, but the equipment is expensive and is becoming hard to buy. It may be possible for you to modify some of the standard workshop equipment, however, by introducing water as coolant lubricant and by modifying the speed of the machine where needed.

1. The glass is cut and polished working from the front of the machine. A can of water and a sponge is fixed so the revolving grinding wheel picks up water as it passes over the sponge. This water acts as a coolant and a lubricant as the abrasive action of the wheel wears (cuts or grinds) the glass surface.

2. The vessel is moved so proper placement is made for the second cut on the vessel. For deep cuts it is best to take small "bites" out of the glass rather than a prolonged cut at each spot. This helps prevent rapid abrasive heat build-up.

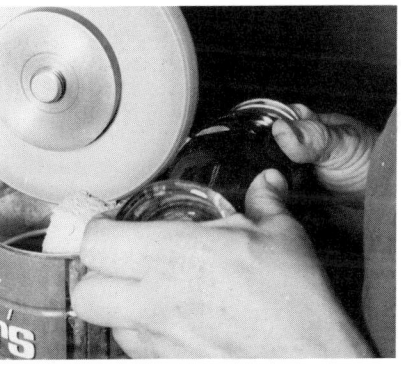

3. Further cuts are made on other parts of the vessel. After completing work on the grinding wheel, the pattern produced is known as a gray cut (cutting without polishing). As with most decorations that remove glass, it is possible with cased vessels to produce color variations.

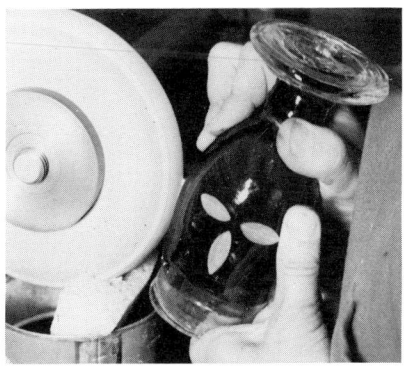

Engraving

Engraving is done with a power driven shaft fitted with various sizes and thicknesses of copper discs and used with a mixture of oil and abrasive powder (usually silicon carbide or emery dust). The abrasive dripped from a piece of leather onto the disc. The disc sizes vary from 1/8" to 3" or more in diameter. The smaller the disc the more intricate a line you can get. A thicker disc is used to produce a series of lines that cloud a larger area of the glass. The speeds for the tools vary from 490 rpm. to 2400 rpm. Because of the amount of time involved in hand engraving, and the skill required by the artist, this process is becoming less and less popular. Also the tools and equipment are very hard to find. The photograph shows Erwin Eisch engraving a vessel on an antique machine picked up in a junk shop.

As with many of these cold-glass techniques, the special optical effects produced by seeing through the glass to the design on the opposite wall can be both an advantage and a hindrance to the artist. In the case of geometric line designs, or other designs that allow for the constantly changing pattern as the vessel is moved, the effect can be pleasing. If the transparent surface of the glass is used as a substitute for an opaque piece of paper to reproduce a drawing, however, the results can be far from effective.

Other Tools for Engraving. Craftsmen have successfully used rather simple, cheap tools for a variety of effects on glass. The simplest of these is a diamond-tipped marking "pencil" that is commonly available on the market. The diamond point scratches a shallow line in the glass surface and, accepting the limited type of line possible, can be used for various drawn effects on the vessel.

There are also a variety of small electric vibrating tools on the market. If you use a diamond point (usually available for an extra charge), these can be used with a little more ease than the pencil.

The small flexible shaft used in jewelry can also be used with the proper tip. Diamond tips are the best to use on glass, but a variety of small abrasive tools (silica carbide, aluminum oxide, etc.) can also be used.

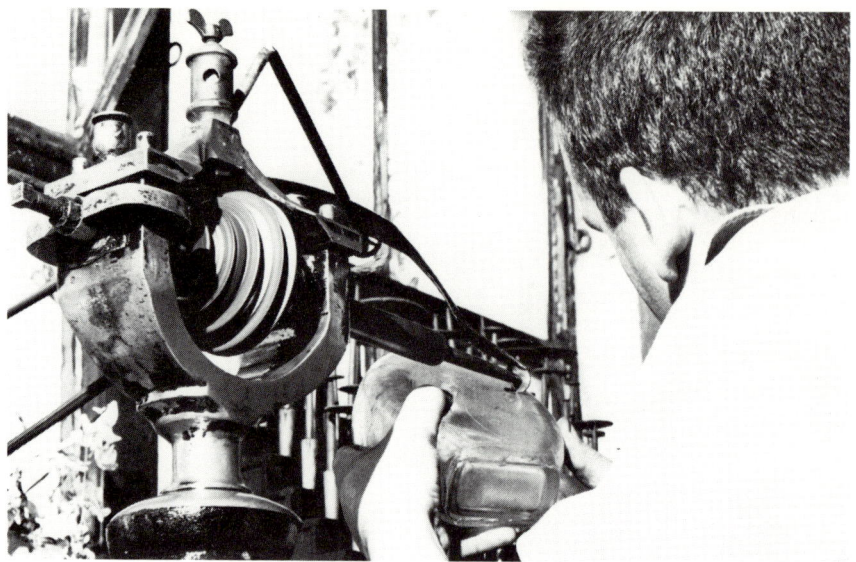

Here Erwin Eisch is engraving a bottle using an ancient engraving machine (really a smaller version of the glass lathe modified to accept mounted copper discs). The design on the vessel is produced by a mixture of oil and grit fed to the various sizes of copper discs mounted in the shaft on a small piece of leather. Photo by Bob Florian.

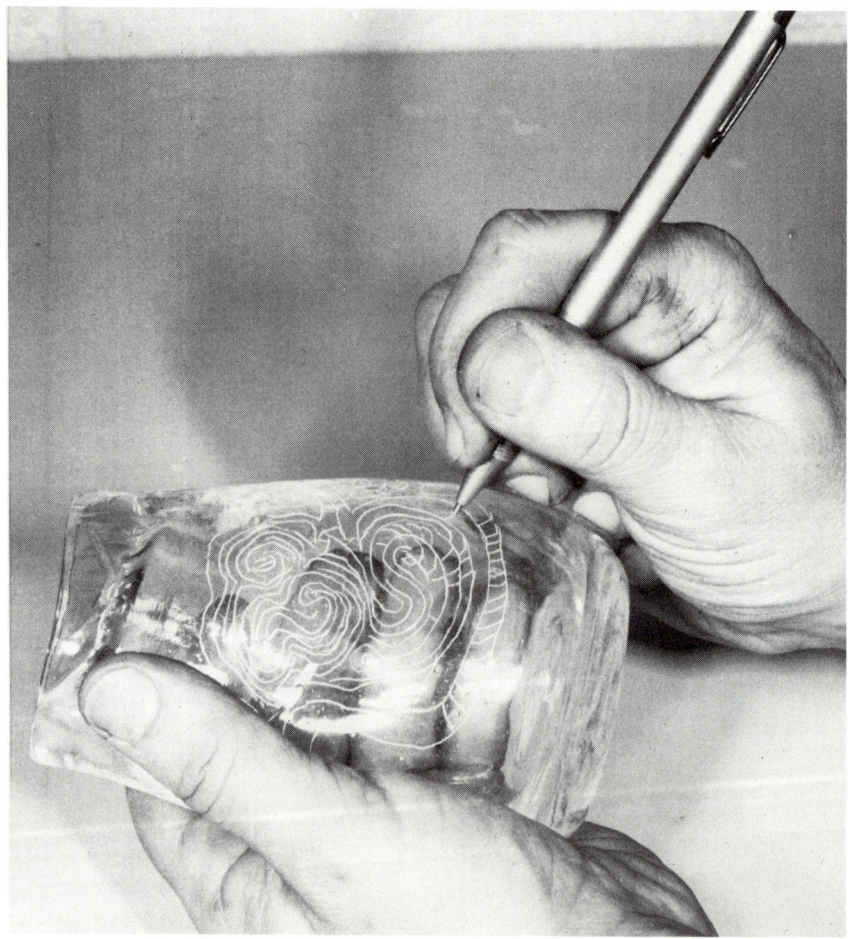

There are other tools that can be used to produce scratch lines on the glass surface. These include diamond tips (and other abrasive tips) for the jewelers flexible shaft, hand-held electric vibrating tools, and as shown here, a diamond-tipped "pencil." As with any cutting, grinding, or scratching methods, the type of glass (hardness and brilliance) plays as important a part in the success of the final product as does the skill of the artist.

Sandblasting

Sandblasting or sandcarving is done by blowing coarse sand (or other abrasive compounds) against the glass surface with compressed air. The area hit by the sand is pitted and worn to form a translucent rather than a transparent surface. Resist materials are used to produce designs. Soft rubber or lead foil are used commercially for these resist masks. For your own use you will find that masking tape and even some types of paper work satisfactorily because high pressures are not required. Selective masking can provide variety in both shading and in the depth of the cut surface. The coarseness of the sand affects the texture of the glass, but in general the surface is similar to that produced by grinding (gray cut).

The health hazard in sandblasting is caused by the fine abrasive dust. It is best to do this blasting in a closed space with good ventilation. Wear a face mask and protective clothing.

1. Sandblasting or sandcarving is done by blowing abrasive dust (silica sand, silicon carbide, aluminum oxide, etc.) against the glass surface to pit or mark it. The pressure of the air, size and kind of abrasive, and duration of the "blasting" produce the final design quality. Areas that are not to be pitted are "masked-out" with masking tape, rubber cement, sheet rubber, or lead foil.

2. Wear a respirator mask and goggles if you are working with an enclosed ventilated container where the "sand" is shot against the glass. For use with heavy-duty industrial blasting units, a plastic or rubber "tent" with built-in arm and hand covering (gloves) is used. Continued breathing of the abrasive dust causes silicosis, so proper protection and ventilation should be used when using the sandblaster.

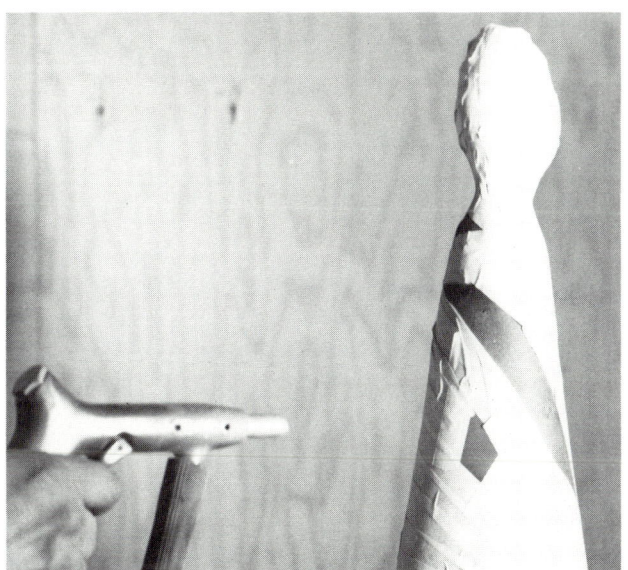

3. After blasting the resist material is removed to reveal the design areas.

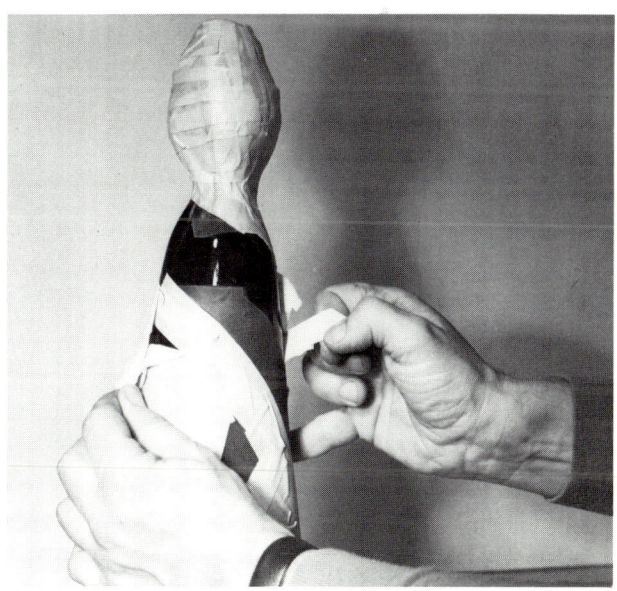

DECORATING AND FINISHING 171

ETCHING

Most of the acids used for etching metal (nitric, hydrochloric, etc.) have little or no effect on commonly-used glasses, but hydrofluoric acid attacks glasses rapidly. The surface produced by the acid depends to a large degree on the type of glass (glasses with calcium oxide are eaten away to a very rough surface, while lead glasses are smoother). Most of the etching formulas use this acid in one form or another. The solution and fumes given off by this acid are highly poisonous, caustic, and can cause permanent damage to the bone marrow. Great care must be taken when storing, handling, and using this acid.

Using hydrofluoric acid for etching glass gives possibilities ranging from rather shallow surface etching (similar to engraving or sandblasting) to very deep acid cuts. These deep cuts can provide sculptural effects, expose layers of inner glass, and can be used for a variety of combination effects.

The process is similar to that used to etch metals. A resist ground (usually a wax compound) is applied to the areas that will not be etched. The resist can be applied by painting, stenciling, silkscreening, etc. The amount of time in the bath depends on how deep you want the etch to go. Very deep etching produces sculptural effects and is called "acid cut back."

Washing off the acid with water and removing the resist ground either with boiling water or solvents may be enough to complete the process, or polishing of some surfaces may be desired.

FROSTING

A far safer method of shallow etching on glass can be done with a variety of commercially available compounds. These are ready-to-use mixtures containing ammonium bifluoride or some other fluorine compounds. Although these materials are used in school situations, they are still potentially harmful. Rubber gloves and face masks may be called for with some of them, and proper ventilation is needed to carry the fumes away. The photographs show the steps in frosting a simple design on a glass vessel using a commercial frosting compound.

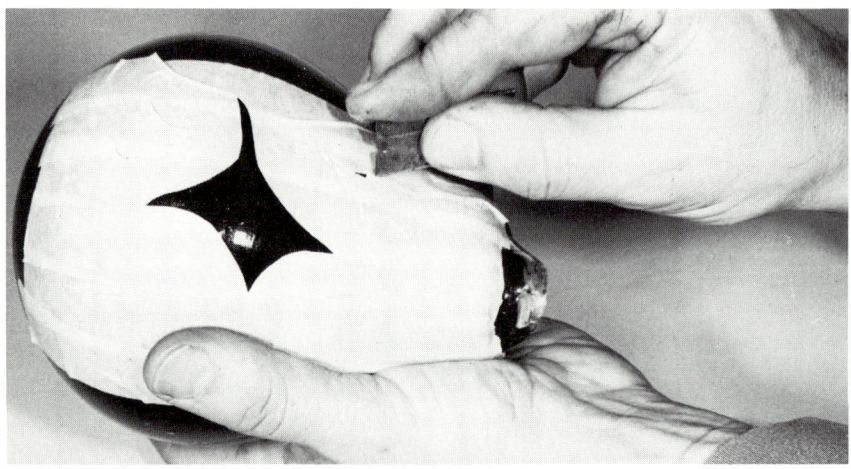

1. The portion of the vessel to receive the frosted design is covered with masking tape, and a razor blade is used to cut away the areas to be frosted. These areas are then peeled from the surface.

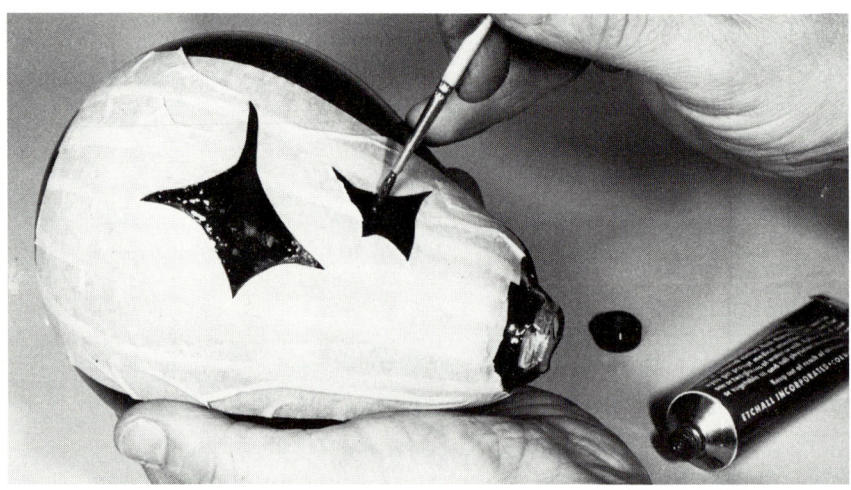

2. The frosting compound is painted on the exposed areas, allowed to dry, then washed clean under running water. A second coat may be applied and the process repeated. Note: The fumes are caustic, so use the compounds only in a ventilated area.

3. Remove the resist material to expose the "frosted" design.

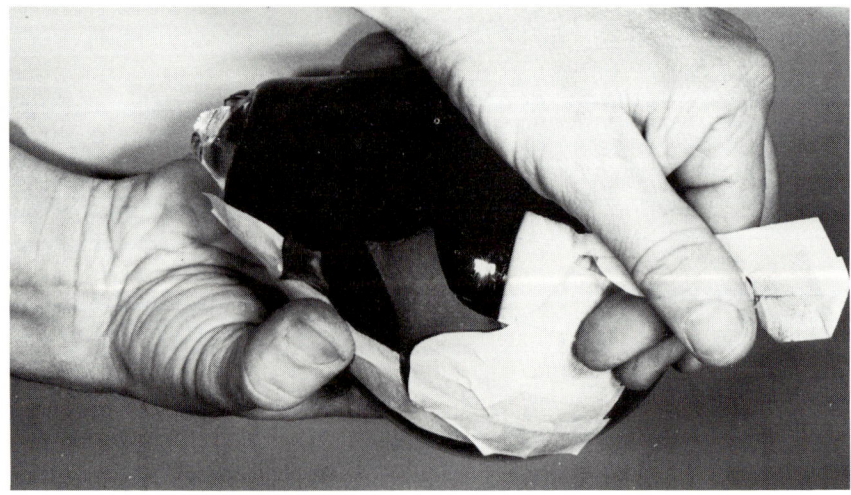

POLISHING

Polishing glass can be used with other decorative processes, or it can be used for finishing the ware without relation to any decorative effects. Polishing operations help to remove marks, pits, or scratches on the glass surface. The polishing changes translucent glass to transparent glass by removing surface conditions. With glasses that have high refractive qualities (lead, barium, etc.), polishing helps bring this out.

There are several methods of polishing glass. They are different in both the material and technique used, as well as the stage in production when the polishing is done.

Fire Polish. You have already used fire polish when working the glass at the furnace. It can be used on glass to make a lip free from sharp edges. The term explains the process—the flame polishes the glass. In fire polishing the lip of the vessel, the glass becomes liquid and the surface tension of the now liquid glass seeks to form a ball of glass or a rounded edge. In the fire polishing you have done at the furnace the resulting lip is usually wider than the wall of the vessel. The sharp edge of the vessel is removed without removing glass, but rather by "bunching it up."

Fire polishing is used repeatedly by the glass artist to form and finish his ware. It is also used commercially—to remove sharp edges on the glass. When the sculptor finishes glass pieces produced by "lost-wax" casting (please see a good sculpture book on lost-wax casting for details on the process) he many use fire polish to finish the surface on the piece.

Chemical Polishing. Acid or chemical polish has replaced mechanical polishing in industry to a large degree. The chemicals used for acid polishing are concentrated sulfuric acid and hydrofluoric acid, with proportions varying from 3 parts sulfuric to 1 or 2 parts hydrofluoric. Both these chemicals are highly caustic, and the fumes produced are very dangerous. The polish works rather fast (depending on the composition of the glass being polished). The usual procedure is to hold the ware in the acid for about 10 to 30 seconds, alternating this with water baths. This is repeated until the required polish is complete. The acid mixture quickly dissolves a thin layer of the glass surface, leaving it smooth. If kept in the acid for too long a time the glass with be unevenly attacked. Areas not to be polished are covered with a protective coat of wax. Because of its speed and the large areas it can polish, this acid polish is popular in industry. For your use, *great care* should be exercised.

Mechanical Polishing. Mechanical polishing is done on the cold, annealed vessel. The same machinery as used for grinding the glass can be used for polishing by changing the wheels. As with polishing most things, glass polishing is most effective when procedures follow an established pattern—working from rough to fine grinding compounds or wheels. It must be noted that although some glasses take on brilliant refractory qualities when polished, others hardly polish at all.

When polishing is used on vessels that have been decorated by grinding, a disc of cork the same size and shape is mounted on the shaft. As it rotates, the cork "blank" is cut to duplicate the shape of the grinding stone used for decoration.

The cork wheel is rotated against the ground decoration that it fits. Felt wheels can be used for polishing glass, as well as various polishing powders such as pumice, putty powder (fine tin oxide or lead/tin mixtures), rouge, and cerium oxide. In general the speeds used for polishing operations are slower than grinding speeds.

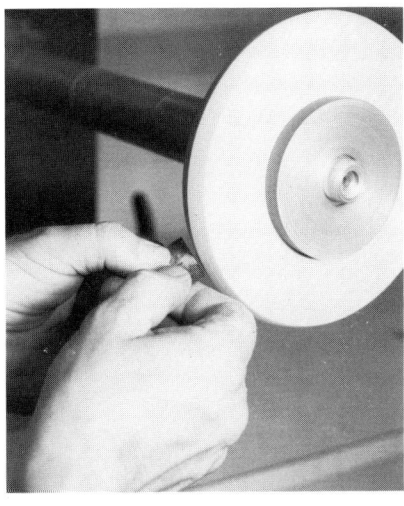

A panel-edge cork wheel is mounted on the lathe, and a razor blade (or other cutting tool) is used to form the cork into the shape of the grinding wheel (bevel). This operation is done from the back of the machine.

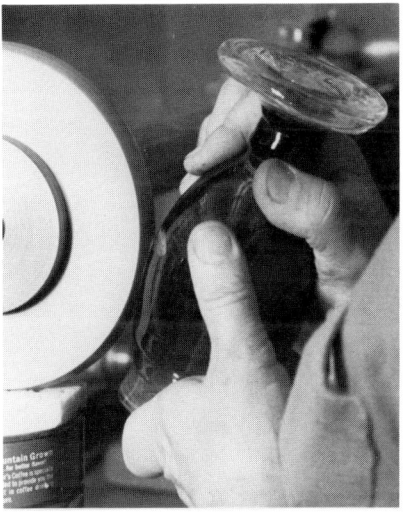

Working from the front of the machine, arrange a clean sponge (do not use the same can, water, or sponge that was used for grinding) in a can of water so the sponge deposits water on the revolving polishing wheel. Be certain that all traces of abrasive are removed from the vessel before attempting to polish. The wheel is revolving up toward you while polishing. Fit the bevel cork wheel into the gray cuts made previously and polish the scratches out. The type of glass as well as your equipment decides on the refractory brilliance of your facets.

DECORATING AND FINISHING

Finishing Glass

Most glass worked at the furnace has a pontil attached for the final hot forming operations. This "sticking up" process leaves a pontil mark on the base of the vessel. Some artists feel this mark should be left on the vessel as a form of identification of the craftsman. "A good pontil mark is the sign of a good artist."

If the mark is sharp, or if the vessel is not level, some type of finishing work may be needed. This could vary from simply filing sharp edges with a fine file to using some heavy industrial equipment. For even the simplest filing and chipping, as well as the use of any power equipment, be sure to *always* use a protective eye covering.

The Diamond Glass Saw. If extremely large amounts of bond are left on the vessel from the pontil you can use a glass saw to cut the glass. The photographs show the saw being used to cut such glass from the base of a piece. It is important that the blade be well lubricated with water when cutting. If a drip type of arrangement is used, make sure the water is adjusted for a full, even flow. In the sequence illustrated the diamond blade is lubricated by a reservoir of water under the arbor. The water level must be high enough for the blade to pick up the water as it revolves. The guard on the blade serves to keep the water from splashing excessively. The saw can be used for other operations (cutting sculptural forms, heavy glass rod, etc.) as well as for finishing work.

The Grinder. The grinder can be used for leveling the base on most blown forms. The glass to be ground is moved against the wheel and the grit grinds the glass. It is important to move the vessel over the entire head so the grit does not score "hills and valleys" in the grinder head. It is also important to hold the vessel as level as possible. The grinder can grind very fast, and the beginner may find that he must choose between a vessel that stands lopsided or one that stands with a hole in the bottom! If available, the edger-beveler shown earlier can be used for some such finishing work, and the large water-lubricated belt glass sander used in car window glass factories is also effective.

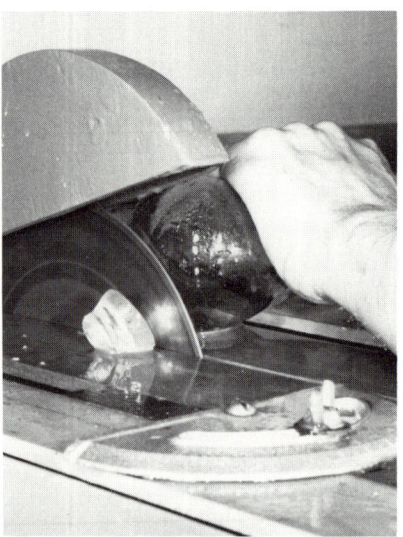

The glass saw can be used for cutting glass either for decorative or practical purposes. Here a large section of bond glass from the pontil is being cut off the saw. With the glass vessel held firm and level, the glass is pushed into the saw. The speed of the cut is determined by the condition of your blade, speed of your saw rotation, and type of glass. Note: if the saw begins to cut slowly (or not at all), or if the blade sparks against the glass, it may indicate that the blade has been impregnated with glass. To clean the diamond edge slice a section off of a common ceramic brick. Continue the cut by pushing the vessel until the section is cut free. Wear glasses when using the saw and be certain there is plenty of water on the blade.

The water drip valve is set to drain through the trough of grit carrying the mixture to the revolving metal grinding head. The vessel bottom is held firmly against the head and moved from center to edge and back again in an arc (to prevent "hills and valleys" from being ground into the grinder head) until the bottom is level.

Polisher. In most instances the rough ground base is sufficient, however if a polish is desired it may be necessary to go through a series of grit sizes working from coarse (30 or 60 grit) to fine (400 to 600 grit). It might be mentioned that the grit size classification refers to the number of holes in a screen in one square inch. After the fine grinding, the glass is polished with pumice, cerium oxide, or other compounds. Factories have a special sequence of steps in their polishing based on the hardness of the glass, its refractive qualities, and the volume of production.

In general the indivdual artist will not have need for much elaborate and expensive equipment. The jump from 60 grit to 400 grit to pumice is used successfully by some artists for polishing a variety of glasses.

It is important make sure in any polishing sequence that *all* the coarser compounds are *completely* washed off before moving to the next finer grit. The intermediate steps in some factories involves a separate grinding for each of the following: 60, 120, 220, 320, 400, 600, and then on to pumice, cerium oxide, and other compounds. Needless to say, this is seldom justified for the individual glass artist.

Glass Lathe. You have already seen the glass lathe used for decorations on glass. If the pontil mark is sharp and located in a concave indentation of the vessel base, you may want to use a cone shaped grinder or a small hollow stone grinder to remove the mark. If desired, the previously described polishing operations can be used to finish the pontil mark.

It might be noted that in the absence of the glass lathe, craftsmen have devised ways to use small grinding stones mounted in drill presses or even in hand-held electric drills. In this way either cones or small grinding wheels are effective.

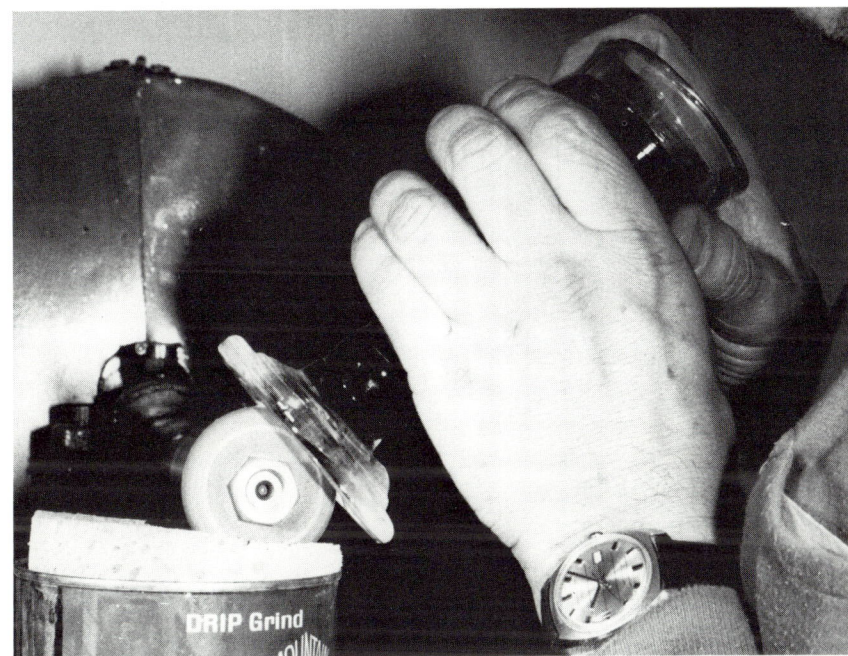

A small hollow ground wheel can be used for removing the pontil mark on the vessel base. The same can of water and sponge arrangement is used as was used when cutting glass decoratively. The vessel base is rotated against the revolving wheel to produce a concave indentation. This identation can be polished with cork or felt wheels if desired.

The rough finish on the glass bottom is usually sufficient, however the bottom can be polished if desired. This entails grinding with successively finer grits. Be certain to wash the vessel and grinder before proceeding to the next finer grit. Final polishing is done on the polisher with water/pumice (or other compounds).

DECORATING AND FINISHING 175

Appendix

Tiffany Romp III (Left) and *Brancusi Inspired* (Right) by Robert Fritz. Free-blown glass, 11" and 17" high. The piece on the left was fumed with stannous chloride, and it has a concave center with two projections. The piece on the right is slightly fumed smoky glass, and its concave center has only one projection.

Materials for Building the Furnace and Oven

Here is a fairly complete list of the materials necessary for building the furnace and oven shown in Chapter 1. You may find that you need extra nuts, bolts, etc., or you may want to replace some of the materials I suggest (metal instead of transite, metal banding rather than threaded tie-rods and nuts, etc.). Although sizes are suggested here, remember to adjust to your particular set-up.

REFRACTORY AND INSULATION BRICK FOR FURNACE AND OVEN

Insulating Firebrick
(at least 2300°F.):
   225 Straights
   27 No. 1 Arch

Hard Firebrick (1st quality):
   5 Straights
   2 bricks 18″ x 6″ x 2½″
   3 bricks 4½″ x 13½″ x 2½″
   26 Splits

Hard Firebrick
(used or less than 1st quality, suggested if you use a cement block stand:
   25 Straights

Cement Block (used for furnace stand):
   37 blocks, 15½″ x 7½″ x 7½″ (standard)

Castable Refractory
(at least 2800°F):
   about 35 lbs.

OTHER FURNACE MATERIALS

Angle Iron for Corner Brace:
   4 pieces 29″ x 1½″ x ⅛″ (or heavier)

Angle Iron for Shelf:
   1 piece 27″ x 1½″ x 1½″ x ⅛″

1 piece 27″ x 1½″ x 1½″ x ⅜″
2 pieces 10″ x 1½″ x 1½″ x ⅛″
2 pieces 5″ x 1½″ x 1½″ x ⅛″
2 pieces 6″ x 1½″ x 1½″ ⅛″

Continuous-threaded tie-rod:
   4 pieces 24″ x ¼″ (or heavier)
   4 pieces 22½″ x ¼″

Nuts and Washers:
   16 (at least) to fit tie-rod
   14 (at least) extra thick, larger than the tie-rod (nuts or washers)

Transite (or substitute):
   2 pieces 27″ x 20″ x ¼″ (or heavier)
   1 piece 27″ x 21″ x ¼″
   1 piece 23¼″ x 23¼″ x ¼″ (for floor)
   1 piece 12″ x 12″ x ⅛″ (for under tank)

OTHER DOOR MATERIALS

Angle Iron:
   2 pieces 6″ x 1½″ x 1½″ x ⅛″ (or heavier)
   1 piece 4½″ x 1½″ x 1½″ x ⅛″
   1 piece 1½″ x 1½″ x 1½″ x ⅛″

Bolts and Nuts:
   1 bolt 3½″ x ⅜″ and nut to fit
   3 nuts ½″ (for door clamp)

BURNER SUPPORT MATERIALS

Continuous-threaded Pipe (common):
   2 pieces 10″ x ¾″

Electrical (*not* plumbers) Pipe Coupling:
   2 pipes ¾″

Metal Clamps (2) or Plumbers Metal Tape with Nuts and Bolts

A Common Pipe 24″ x ½″

OTHER OVEN MATERIALS

Angle Iron for Corner Bracing:
   4 pieces 24″ x 1½″ x 1½″ x ⅛″
   2 pieces 28″ x 1½″ x 1½″ x ⅛″
   1 piece approx. 40″ x 1½″ x 1½″ x ⅛″

Continuous-threaded Tie-rod:
   4 pieces 38″ x ¼″ (or heavier)
   6 pieces 30″ x ¼″

Nuts and Washers:
   20 (at least) to fit tie-rod
   14 (at least) extra thick, larger than the tie-rod (nuts or washers)

Transite:
   2 pieces 36″ x 22″ x ¼″ (or heavier)
   1 piece 26½″ x 24″ x ¼″
   1 piece 39″ x 29″ x ¼″

OTHER DOOR MATERIALS

Angle Iron:
   2 pieces 20″ x 1½″ x 1½″ x ⅛″
   2 pieces 16″ x 1½″ x 1½″ ⅛″

Metal Strap:
   1 piece 19½″ x 1″ x ⅛″

Nuts and Bolts:
   6 (at least) ¼″

Transite:
   1 piece 18″ x 18″ x ¼″

Pipe (for hinge):
   2 pieces 1″ x 2½″ long
   2 pieces 1½″ x 2″ long

BURNER MATERIALS

The materials for the furnace and oven burners are listed in the text along with instructions for their construction.

Materials Used in Glass Making

Minerals	Formula	Description
Aluminum Alumina Oxide (Calcined)	Al_2O_3	This oxide lowers the coefficient of expansion, adds thermal stability, reduces devitrification, produces a harder surface on the finished glass, increases "toughness" and durability, decreases "brittleness," increases the index of refraction, produces high viscosity and greater chemical durability, and lowers the annealing temperatures (when substituted for CaO). The oxide is needed in fluorine opals and influences the solubility of opacifying agents such as TiO_2 and SnO_2. Amounts over 4% usually result in a glass difficult to melt and work. Glasses high in CaO melt more easily with additions of this oxide, while glasses high in Na_2O melt with difficulty when Al_2O_3 is added. Al_2O_3 can be added from other sources besides calcined alumina, including other forms of alumina and feldspars. The oxide is the simplest to use as far as calculations 90, however it is harder to melt than when introduced in mineral (feldspar, cryolite, etc.) form and is more expensive.
Alumina Hydrate	$Al_2O_3 \cdot H_2O$ $Al(OH)_3$ $Al_2(OH)_6$	Although these materials can be used in glass melts, in general the calcined form or the feldspars are preferred.
Antimony Oxide	Sb_2O_3	*Poisonous.* This is an effective decolorizer, fining agent, and oxidizing agent. In amounts less than 1% it appears to help in melting and working the glass.
Apatite	$Ca_4(CaF)(PO_4)_3$ or $Ca_4(CaCl)(PO_4)_3$	*See* Calcium Phosphate
Aplite		*See* Feldspar Chart

Minerals	Formula	Description

Arsenic Oxide
    Arsenious Acid
    White Arsenic
	As_2O_3	*Poisonous.* A fining, decolorizing, oxiding agent usually used with nitre (or other oxidizing agents). Decomposes at final stages of melting to provide needed "fining" action. Arsenic glasses are prone to solorization. It oxidizes iron, sulfur and carbon and stabilizes colors (particularly selenium and cerium). It improves the brilliance of the glass but is not effective with "rare earth" decolorizers.

Barite	$BaSO_4$	See Barium Sulphate. A natural ore used to produce barium carbonate. This is an active flux that reduces the annealing time. Like other barium oxide containing compounds, this increases toughness and brilliance, helps to prevent devitrification, etc. When barium sulphate exceeds 1% in the batch it produces scumming of the melt.
Barium Carbonate	Ba_2CO_3	*Poisonous.* Amounts less than 1% help in fluxing the batch, increases toughness, density, and brilliance, and helps reduce devitrification. It is similar to CaO and MgO in its effect on the melt. Glass quality of high barium glasses (10% or more) come between lime and lead glasses (brilliance, density, durability, toughness, etc.). A great advantage over lead glasses in that barium glasses can be melted in direct flame.
Barium Oxide	BaO	This oxide lowers the liquidous temperature, decreases tendency to devitrification, and improves color and brilliance of the glass. The oxide can be used to replace CaO and PbO, and in most of its effects falls between these oxides. It increases: fluidity at high temperatures (but not as extreme as CaO) and setting time (but not as much as CaO), but is less prone to devitrification than CaO. It produces easy-melting glasses, imparts considerable density, and has a high refractory index (but in none of these as much as does PbO). In general, in amounts around 3% or 4% it improves working and quality. In amounts over 10% it is detrimental to melting, working, and is hard on the refractories. The common source of the oxide is barium carbonate.

Barium Sulphate
    Barite
    Barytes
    Heavy Spar
	$BaSO_4$	A source of BaO and a fining agent in melts, helping to sweep bubbles out of the melt at high temperatures (fine).

Barytes		*See* Barite
Borax		*See* Sodium Biborate

Minerals	Formula	Description
Boric Acid	H_3BO_3	A source of B_2O_3 without any alkali (sodium). Although used in technical glasses, fiberglass and the like, it is not commonly used in many freeblown batches. It intumesces (swells) at a lower temperature than borax, however there is a greater loss of B_2O_3. In general it is less economical to use than borax.
Boric Oxide	B_2O_3	This oxide can replace SiO_2 as a glass former, although such silica-free glass has no real commercial use as yet. The oxide improves the chemical resistance of the glass, reduces thermal expansion, and improves resistance to thermal shock. It reduces devitrification, increases mechanical strength, and scratch hardness, helps in melting operations (lower liquidous temperature), reduces the working range, increases impact and tensile strength, produces more brilliant glass, better colors, and a smoother glass surface. The most common source of the oxide is sodium biborate (borax).

Calcium Aluminum Silicate
    Calumite
    Slag
		Industrially this silicate is widely used in glass-melting. Its formula shows that it can be adapted to almost any glass formula. In theory the material increases the melting rate since the Al_2O_3 and CaO are already chemically combined. This results in less batch segregation and improved homogeneity. Commercially the slag from blast furnances (calumite) in a milled condition is used in glass batches as sources of alumina, silica, lime, and magnesia. The formula varies, however the material has the advantage of being readily soluble in the batch.

Calcium Carbonate
    Whiting
    Limestone
    Chalk
    Calcite
    Calspar
    Cliffstone
    Paris White
	$CaCO_3$	The chief source is CaO in many glass melts, although lime and dolomite are also used extensively.

Calcium Fluoride
    Fluorspar
    Fluorite
	CaF_2	This is primarily an opacifying agent. It melts at a lower temperature than most chemicals containing CaO and produces a beneficial stirring action. It also adds glossiness and aids in decolorizing.

Calcium Oxide
    Burnt lime
    Calcined lime
	CaO	The oxide adds stability and permanence, hardness, tenacity, viscosity, and it reacts quickly with silica in the melt. Viscosity decreases at high temperatures but "sets" rapidly on cooling. The advantages of CaO tend to drop rapidly after 12% is added to the glass. It becomes hard, brittle, and difficult to melt.

Minerals	Formula	Description
		There is a tendency to rapid devitrification without some MgO. Too little CaO (without substitution of some kind) produces an easily-melted glass that is water soluble. The material, burnt lime, has the advantages of being of minimum weight and bulk and has organic matter removed. Its disadvantages are that it is dusty and caustic, and it requires special storage precautions since it hydrates rapidly, thus providing an inconsistent composition. Common sources for the oxide other than the above material are calcium carbonate and hydrated lime, as well as some feldspars.
Calcite		*See* Calcium Carbonate

Calcium Phosphate
  Bone Ash
  Apatite
  Tri-Calcium Phosphate
	$Ca_3(PO_4)_2$	Primarily an opacifying agent. The mineral "apatite"—a natural calcium phosphate—is used in commercial opal glasses. The impurity calcium fluoride helps in opal production.

Calcium Sulphate
  Plaster of Paris
  Gypsum
	$CaSO_4 \cdot 2H_2O$
	$CaSO_4 \cdot \tfrac{1}{2}H_2O$
		Possible substitute for "salt-cake" furnishing some CaO. Gypsum has the advantage of ease of storing without caking (as does salt-cake). It is a source of SO_2 gas, and as such is a fining agent, provides O_2 for oxidizing, and acts as an anti-scumming agent.

Calspar		*See* Calcium Carbonate
Calumite		*See* Calcium Aluminum Silicate
Caustic Potash		*See* Potassium Hydroxide
Chalk		*See* Calcium Carbonate
China Clay		*See* Kaolin
Cream of Tartar		*See* Potassium Bitartrate
Cryolite Kryolith	Na_2AlF_6	Small amounts of cryolite act as an excellent flux, and the fluorine adds a beneficial bubbling action. It melts easily and decreases glass viscosity. Its primary use is in the production of white and opal glasses. The high cost is a disadvantage. Amounts in opal glasses vary between 4% to 13% by weight. Small amounts (less than 1%) lower the viscosity of the glass and aid in fining clear and colored glasses. The compound helps in decolorization of the glass. Cryolite opals do not burn out as easily as fluorspar opals. This is the best source of added alumina without added cords.

Minerals	Formula	Description

Cullet
    Second Melts
    Broken Glass
    Scrap Glass
		Glass that has been melted and cooled. A standard item in most glass batch melts, added in amounts varying between 10% to 75%, with 20% being close to the average. Cullet assists in melting, however dirt (particularly organic material) requires additional oxidizing agents. Dirt in the cullet can also add alumina. In many instances additional alkali is added to melts using large amounts of cullet. The cullet should be similar to the composition of the batch.

Dolomite (Burnt)	$CaO \cdot MgO$	This is produced by heating dolomite lime ($CaO \cdot MgO \cdot 2CO_2$). Its advantages over hydrated dolomite are reduced weight and bulk (lower shipping expenses), freedom from organic material, and faster melting. It hydrates, therefore special storage provisions must be made although "dead-burned" dolomite hydrates rather slowly. The material is dusty.
Dolomite Hydrated Dolomite	$CaO \cdot MgO \cdot 2CO_2$ $CaCO_3 \cdot MgCo_3$	A double carbonate that can vary in composition, although in calculations 30.4% CaO and 21.9% MgO are generally used. It is a stable compound in storage and usually relatively free from dust. It is non-caustic. It prevents "soda bloom" in the melt, adds luster to the ware, reduces thermal expansion, and "fines" more rapidly than straight lime glasses.
Feldspar	See Feldspar Charts for Composition	These are the major sources of Al_2O_3 in glass batches. These alumina silicates of potash, soda, or lime are rarely pure, but rather are mixtures with one another. The actual composition should be obtained from the manufacturer or from analysis. In general they are cheap sources of other oxides (SiO_2, K_2O, etc.). Potash spars find their greatest use in glass, although most feldspars are standard glass materials. They do not volatalize so there is little waste. Melting points vary between 1100°–1200°C.
Flint		*See* Silica Dioxide
Fluorine	F_2	Fluorine forms no stable oxides and is used to produce opal and opaque glasses through processes that are not entirely understood. Compounds of fluorine used in glass in small amounts help in mixing and fluxing the glass and reducing viscosity in early stages of melting. Common sources of the material are calcium fluoride, sodium alumina fluoride, and sodium silica fluoride.
Fluorspar		*See* Calcium Fluoride

Minerals	Formula	Description
Fluorite		*See* Calcium Fluoride
Glass Sand		*See* Silica Dioxide
Glaubers Salts		*See* Sodium Sulphate
Gypsum		*See* Calcium Sulphate
Heavy Spar		*See* Barium Sulphate *or* Barite
Kaolin China Clay	$Al_2O_3 \cdot 2SiO_2 2H_2O$	Although it is possible to use kaolin as a source of Al_2O_3, this is seldom done since Fe content is often high and composition is likely to vary.
Lead Oxide Litharge	PbO	*Poisonous.* This oxide increases the density and refractive index of the glass. The glasses have long working ranges, excellent color, are easy melting, and are capable of taking a brilliant polish. The glass is soft and easily scratched, with low acid resistance, and low weathering. They require special furnace design and firing control. The common sources for the oxide are litharge, red lead, and the various lead silicates. The material lead oxide is an important source of lead in glassmelting. Its melting temperature (888°C.) is higher than that of lead silicates. Litharge offers a reliable composition with a high content of lead per pound and is cheaper than most silicates of lead. It is dusty, volatilizes, and sticks to handling and mixing equipment.
Lead Oxide (Red) Red Lead	Pb_3O_4	*Poisonous.* A valuable source of PbO in glassmelting. It decomposes at about 500°C, releasing 25% of its oxygen, and is therefore a valuable oxidizing agent. The composition is seldom constant since the PbO roasting is seldom complete. The material is dusty and sticky.
Lead BiSilicate Alsilox	$PbO \cdot 0.03Al_2O_3 \cdot 1.95SiO_2$	Although this compound was developed for use in low-fire ceramics, it has characteristics that make it desirable for glassmelting. It is insoluble and granular, therefore safer to handle than litharge. It has a high viscosity and low rate of volatilization. On a pound for pound basis, the cost of the PbO is usually higher than other lead silicates or oxides. The Al_2O_3 is advantageous in improving chemical durability and glass quality. This is the least poisonous of the lead compounds. The material has a constant and dependable composition, low impurities, combines readily with other materials in the melt, there is very little segregation, less tendency to reduction, etc.

Minerals	Formula	Description
Lead Monosilicate Lead Silicate	$3PbO \cdot 0.67SiO_2$	*Poisonous.* The first of the lead silicates to be marketed, and of the three it is the most economical source of PbO. It is comparatively free from dust and insoluble, therefore safer than litharge or red lead. It has low impurities, high lead, constant composition, is vitreous, combines readily in the batch, and segregation is low. Volatilization is low thereby reducing the health hazard.
Lead Silicate (Tri-Basic)	$PbO \cdot 0.33SiO_2$	*Poisonous.* Developed primarily as a glass and frit ingredient, this product has the lowest viscosity of the three lead silicates but is slightly soluble in water.
Lepidolite "Lithium Mica"	$LiF \cdot KF \cdot Al_2O_3 \cdot 3SiO_2$	A lithia (potassium) aluminum fluorsilicate mineral. It is used in a variety of glasses primarily for its lithia content and for Al_2O_3 in an easily-melted form. It lowers the coefficient of expansion, reduces devitrification, increases refraction and hardness of finished glass, etc.
Lime (Burnt)	CaO	*See* Calcium Oxide
Lime (Hydrated) Masons Lime Slaked Lime	$CaO \cdot H_2O(Ca(OH)_2)$	This is the most readily available source of CaO and probably the cheapest. Although usually less pure than other sources of CaO, lime can be used in glassmelting. It is a stable composition easily stored, finely powdered, and easily calcined in the furnace during melting.
Limestone		*See* Calcium Carbonate
Litharge		*See* Lead Oxide
Lithium-aluminum Silicate Petalite	$Li_3 \cdot Al_2O_3 \cdot 8SiO_2$	Used to introduce both lithia and alumina into the glass in an easily-melted form.
Lithium Carbonate	Li_2CO_3	Principle means of direct introduction of Li_2O into the melt. The high cost of lithium carbonate prevents its extended use.
Lithium Oxide	Li_2O	This oxide has a strong fluxing action on the glass melt, increases the melting speed, increases the working range, and decreases the thermal expansion. Compared to the other alkali fluxes (sodium and potassium) it is expensive. Chief sources of this oxide for glassmelting are the mineral lithia-alumina-silicates (lepidolite, etc.) and lithium carbonate.
Magnesium Carbonate Magnesite	$MgCO_3$	Chief source of MgO without CaO, but since MgO is seldom used without at least as equal amount of CaO, the carbonate has rather limited use in glass—it is also expensive.

Minerals	Formula	Description
Magnesium Oxide	MgO	This oxide is of the greatest value when used to substitute for a part of the CaO in the glass batch. A ratio of 1 to 3.5 MgO to CaO is ideal. This mixture lowers thermal expansion, decreases devitrification, prevents soda bloom, speeds fining, increases the melting rate, lowers annealing temperatures, and makes an easier-working glass. High MgO glasses have a high tendency to cordiness. Without CaO the glass is more difficult to melt and work than straight CaO glasses, and even up to a 1 to 1 ratio the glass is more difficult to melt than with straight CaO glasses. The chief sources are dolomite and magnesium carbonate.
Nephelene Syenite	$K_2O \cdot 3Na_2O \cdot 4Al_2O_3 \cdot 9SiO_2$	A complicated feldspar with consistent formula and high AL_2O_3. It is becoming more popular with melters because of low Fe_2O_3 and its low melting temperature.
Nitre		See Potassium Nitrate
Paris White		See Calcium Carbonate
Pearl Ash		See Potassium Carbonate (Hydrate)
Petalite		See Lithium-Aluminum Silicate
Phosphorous Pentoxide	P_2O_5	This is a glass former like silica dioxide, however the glass produced is usually soft and lacks chemical durability. P_2O_5 is primarily of interest in the production of phosphate opals. Chief sources for use in glass are calcium phosphate, the various sodium phosphates, and natural phosphoric acid minerals.
Plaster of Paris		See Calcium Sulphate
Potassium Bitartrate Cream of Tartar	$KHC_4H_4O_6$	This chemical, used in small amounts, is a reducing agent in some ruby glasses.
Potassium Carbonate (Calcined)	K_2CO_3	The preferred source of K_2O by glass melters. Most forms presently available are dust free, however they will hydrate in humid atmosphere so special storage precautions must be taken (airtight container).
Potassium Carbonate Hydrated Borax Pearl Ash	$K_2CO_3 \cdot 1\frac{1}{2}H_2O$	A source of K_2O with a variable composition depending on how much H_2O it has picked up (it is deliquescent). Percent references generally refer to the amount of dry carbonate contained and not to the amount of K_2O.
Potassium Hydroxide Caustic Potash Potassium Hydrate	$KOH\ (KOH)_2$	A possible source of K_2O. It is corrosive to handle, hygroscopic, and therefore requires special storage facilities. Its composition varies.

Minerals	Formula	Description
Potassium Nitrate 　Saltpeter 　Nitre	K_2NO_3	Used when K_2O in strong oxidizing is required. It is usually quite pure and non-hygrosopic. It is an excellent flux but is hard on furnace refractories.
Potassium Oxide	K_2O	This is an alkali flux similar in its action to that of Na_2O. There is no marked thermal expansion as in Na_2O glasses. The oxide increases chemical durability, diminishes the tendency towards devitrification, increases viscosity, requires higher temperatures, and improves the appearance and brilliance of the finished glass. Mixed Na_2O and K_2O glasses are more durable than single-alkali glasses. Sources of the oxide are potassium carbonate, potassium nitrate, and some feldspars.
Potassium Sodium Tartrate 　Rochelle Salt	$KNaC_4H_4O_6 \cdot 4H_2O$	This chemical is sometimes used as a reducing agent in ruby glasses.
Potter's Flint		*See* Silica Dioxide
Quartz		*See* Silica Dioxide
Rochelle Salt		*See* Potassium Sodium Tartrate
Salt Cake		*See* Sodium Sulphate
Saltpeter		*See* Potassium Nitrate
Sand		*See* Silica Dioxide
Silica Dioxide Sand 　Silica 　Flint 　Quartz 　Glass Sand 　Potter's Flint	SiO_2	The major glass former in the majority of common glasses, making up 65%–75% of the batch in more than 95% of all glasses melted. Purity should be about 99.5% with less than .1% Fe_2O_3. Because of the large amount used in common glass formulas even minor amounts of impurity in the silica can change the color of the glass produced. Silica dioxide possesses a high degree of desirable qualities, such as freedom from devitrification, resistance to attack by water or by acids, and low coefficient of expansion. Alone it is difficult to melt, free from bubbles, or work, therefore other oxides are added as flux and to reduce viscosity. The larger the grain size the longer it takes (and more heat required) to melt. Uniform grain size is also important. The smaller grain sizes tend to contain more impurities—primarily iron (larger surface area in proportion to weight).
Soda Ash		See Sodium Carbonate

Minerals	Formula	Description
Sodium Biborate 　Hydrated Sodium Tetraborate 　Borax 　Bydrated Borax 　Decahydrated Borax	$Na_2B_4O_7 \cdot 10H_2O$	The most common source of B_2O_3 in general use and one of the purest raw materials available. Readily available and cheap because of its many industrial uses. The material looses water (effloresces) in extreme dry conditions so should be stored in airtight containers. Because of high water content transportation is more costly than anhydrous borax and more heat is required in early stages of melting to drive off the water. Borax has the advantage of initial low melting temperatures so it begins reacting with other chemicals and acts as a flux. The excess water tends to hold the batch together. The steam released promotes a mixing action in the melt. One part borax supplies the same amount of B_2O_3 as .53 parts anhydrous borax.
Sodium Biborate Anhydrous 　Sodium Tetraborate 　Anhydrous Dehybor 　Anhydrous Borax 　Dehydrated Borax	$Na_2B_4O_7$	This is produced by heating ordinary borax to above 325°C. to drive off the water. It has greater bulk when compared to hydrated borax and lower shipping costs. It takes in water readily so must be stored in airtight containers. It does not foam in the melt and is not as easily available as ordinary borax.
Sodium BiCarbonate 　Bicarbonate of Soda	$NaHCO_3$	A rather uneconomical source of Na_2O. It breaks down on heating to form sodium carbonate. One part of $NaHCO_3$ supplies as much Na_2O as .63 Na_2CO_3. One part Na_2CO_3 supplies as much Na_2O as 1.56 $NaHCO_3$.
Sodium Carbonate 　Soda Ash	Na_2CO_3	The most common alkali-supplying material in general use. It is readily available since it serves so many uses in industry.
Sodium Cyanide	Na_2CN	*Poisonous.* This is a delinquescent, water soluble chemical used in minute amounts (less than 1/10th of 1%) as a reducing agent in some ruby glasses.
Sodium Nitrate 　Chile Saltpeter 　Soda Niter	Na_2NO_3	This is an excellent source of Na_2O and available in a "food" grade for industrial purposes. This material has the lowest melting point of any of the commonly-used glass materials, gives a bubbling action in early stages of melting to help mix the various materials, and it gives off large amounts of oxygen into the furnace atmosphere which aids in oxidizing organic impurities. Substitutions of 1% or 2% Na_2NO_3 in the formula for the Na_2CO_3 called for is usually beneficial. For ease of conversion: 1 part of soda ash supplies the same amount of Na_2O as 1.61 parts of Na_2NO_3, and one part of Na_2NO_3 is equivalent to 0.62 soda ash. The material is a strong oxidizing agent and should therefore be stored away from inflammables of all types in a waterproof container.

Minerals	Formula	Description
Sodium Oxide	Na_2O	This oxide is the most common alkali flux used in glass melting. It produces easy-melting glass, lowers the viscosity, reduces resistance to chemical attack, lowers mechanical strength, increases thermal expansion, corrodes furnace linings, etc. The chief sources are sodium carbonate, sodium nitrate, and some feldspars.
Sodium Phosphate (and related phosphates)	$NaPO_3$	There are a number of rather complicated compounds of sodium and phosphorous oxide, most of which are useful as opacifying agents. I have used several of these. They have several advantages over calcium phosphates. These materials are readily available (since they are used for so many purposes in industry). They are also less expensive than the calcium compounds. The theoretical composition of the material is 30.4% Na_2O and 69.6% P_2O_5. More commonly available tri-sodium phosphate ($Na_2HPO_4 \cdot xH_2O$) is available in a number of crystal forms varying from $2H_2O$ to $12H_2O$. A fairly common form, $Na_2HPO_4 \cdot 10H_2O$, contains 19.3% Na_2O and 22% P_2O_5. This material is usually available from cleaning supply houses. Anhydrous sodium tri-polyphosphate ($Na_5P_3O_{10}$) is used in a variety of industries and although usually more expensive, the tri-polyphosphate probably proves more practical since it contains about 42% Na_2O and 56% P_2O_5.
Sodium Tetraborate		*See* Sodium Biborate
Sodium Sulphate Salt Cake Glaubers Salts	Na_2SO_4	This is primarily used to prevent "silica scum." About 2% or more of the sodium in the sulphate form is often added in commercial melting for this reason. It may be used with powdered coal to reduce the sulphate to sulphite, however large amounts of carbon produce sulfides (amber) colors. The material usually contains large amounts of iron impurities. Adding the sodium in the form of sulphate instead of carbonate makes for a harder-melting batch that is also harder on the refractories.
Spodumene	$Li_2O \cdot Al_2O_3 \cdot 4\,SiO_2$	A lithia material with the largest amount of lithia of any of the natural lithia-alumina-silicates. Although not a traditional glass material, it is an effective source of lithia.
Tin Oxide	SnO_2	This has limited use in glass except in production of rubies (gold and copper). Theoretically, the tin (at least in copper rubies) is a reducing agent. It is also of some use in production of opal glasses and is usually introduced into the glass in the oxide form.

MINERALS	FORMULA	DESCRIPTION
Titanium Oxide	TiO_2	The use of this oxide in glassmelting is in a state of development. Though not commonly used, it is similar to lead and increases the index of refraction. It is not considered a colorant, but it has a pronounced effect on certain colorants (iron, copper, uranium, cerium, etc.). It can be introduced into the glass in impure forms (rutile) or in the oxide form.
Whiting		*See* Calcium Carbonate
Zinc Carbonate	$ZnCO_3$	This is a source of zinc oxide in glassmelting.
Zinc Oxide	ZnO	This oxide increases the melting temperature of the glass, increases the brilliance of the glass, and is beneficial to most colorants. When substituted for CaO, it increases the working range, reduces devitrification, and increases chemical resistance of the glass. It is the only colorless network former that has an affinity for sulfur—making it important in colored sulphide and selenide glasses (rubies) and opal-opaques.

TABLE 1: SELECT COMMON CHEMICALS AND FELDSPARS

Material	Minerals (given as chemical formulas)								
	SiO_2	Al_2O_3	K_2O	CaO	Na_2O	MgO	Li_2O	F_2O_3	
Apatite	----	tr.	----	----	54.0	tr	----	.15	P_2O_5–40.5 F_2–2.25
Aplite	6.00	24.0	2.5	6.3	5.67	----	----	.4	
Bone Ash	----	----	----	----	54.2	----	----	----	P_2O_5–45.8
Buckingham Spar	65.5	19.5	12.4	2.6	.2	.2	----	tr	
Burnsvill N.C. 261-H Spar	68.8	17.4	11.2	2.1	.2	tr	----	.09	
Burnsvill N.C. NCY Spar	67.9	19.0	4.9	6.2	1.5	tr	----	.05	
Cornwall Stone	71.1	16.8	6.6	2.3	1.6	.05	----	.16	CaF_2-Tr.
Cryolite	----	12.8	----	32.9	----	----	----	----	
Custer Spar	68.5	17.5	10.4	3.0	.3	tr	----	.08	
Eureka Spar	69.8	17.1	9.4	3.5	tr	----	----	.1	
Fluorspar	----	----	----	----	71.8	----	----	----	F_2–48.7
Kingman A-3 Spar	71.5	16.3	7.5	4.0	.4	tr	----	.08	
Kingman Potash Spar	66.2	18.4	12.0	2.7	.1	tr	----	.08	
Kona F4 Spar	66.8	19.6	4.8	6.9	1.7	tr	----	.04	
Lepidolite	55.0	25.0	9.0	1.0	----	----	4.0	.05	
Middleton Conn. C-6 Spar	67.1	19.1	5.9	6.6	.9	tr	----	.05	
Monticello Ga. 261-F Spar	67.8	17.6	11.0	2.6	.5	tr	----	.06	
Nepheline Synenite	60.2	23.5	5.1	10.6	.3	.1	----	.077	
Oxford Spar	69.4	17.0	7.9	3.2	.4	----	----	.09	
Petalite	77.0	17.5	tr	tr	tr	tr	4.3	----	
Plastic Vitrox	75.5	14.8	6.8	.3	.22	.2	----	.09	
Pyrophylite	75.4	20.3	tr	tr	.02	----	----	.3	
Spodumene	62.9	28.4	.7	.5	.1	.2	6.8	.5	
Spruce Pine #4 Spar	67.9	19.0	4.9	6.2	1.5	tr	----	.05	
Tri-Soda Phosphate	----	----	----	19.3	----	----	----	----	P_2O_5–22.0
Volcanic Ash	72.5	11.5	7.91	1.8	.7	.07	----	1.2	

Table 2: Conversion Factors

Raw Material	Chemical Formula	Molecular Weight	Oxide Supplied	Material to Oxide	Oxide to Materials
Alumina (Calcined)	Al_2O_3	102.0	Al_2O_3	1.000	1.000
Alumina (Hydrated)	$Al_2O_3 \cdot 3H_2O$	156.0	Al_2O_3	0.654	1.530
Barium Carbonate	$BaCO_3$	197.4	BaO	0.777	1.288
Barium Sulphate	$BaSO_4$	233.4	BaO	0.657	1.523
Borax (Anhydrous)	NaB_4O_7	201.3	B_2O_3	0.692	1.445
			Na_2O	0.308	3.247
Borax (Hydrated)	$Na_2B_4O_7 \cdot 10H_2O$	381.4	B_2O_3	0.365	2.739
			Na_2O	0.163	6.154
Boric Acid	H_3BO_3	61.8	B_2O_3	0.563	1.776
Calcium Carbonate	$CaCO_3$	100.1	CaO	0.757	1.321
Calcium Fluoride	CaF_2	78.1	CaO	0.718	1.392
Calcium Phosphate	$Ca_3(PO_4)_2$	310.2	CaO	0.542	1.844
			P_2O_5	0.458	2.185
Cryolite	Na_2AlF_6	210.0	Na_2O	0.443	2.258
			Al_2O_3	0.243	4.118
°Dolomite	$CaO \cdot MgO \cdot 2CO_2$	184.4	CaO	0.304	3.290
			MgO	0.219	4.574
°°°°Lead Bisilicate	$PbO \cdot 0.03Al_2O_3 \cdot 1.95 SiO_2$	299	PbO	0.650	1.538
			SiO_2	0.340	2.941
			Al_2O_3	0.010	100.0°°
Lime (Hydrated)	$CaO \cdot H_2O$	74.1	CaO	0.757	1.321
Litharge	PbO	223.2	PbO	1.000	1.000
Lithium Carbonate	Li_2CO_3	73.9	Li_2O	0.404	2.473
Magnesium Carbonate	$MgCO_3$	84.3	MgO	0.478	2.092
Potassium Carbonate	K_2CO_3	138.2	K_2O	0.682	1.467
Potassium Nitrate	K_2NO_3	101.1	K_2O	0.466	2.147
Red Lead	Pb_3O_4	685.6	PbO	0.977	1.024
Sodium Carbonate	Na_2CO_3	106.0	Na_2O	0.585	1.710
Sodium Nitrate	Na_2NO_3	85.0	Na_2O	0.365	2.743
Sodium Phosphate	$NaPO_3$	102.0	Na_2O	0.304	3.290
			P_2O_5	0.696	1.437
Sodium Tri-Poly Phosphate	$Na_2P_3O_{10}$	367.8	Na_2O	0.420	2.380
			P_2O_5	0.560	1.785
Tri-Sodium Phosphate	$Na_2HPO_4 \cdot 12H_2O$	322	Na_2O	0.193	5.181
			P_2O_5	0.220	4.545
Zinc Carbonate	$ZnCO_3$	125.4	ZnO	0.649	1.541
Zinc Oxide	ZnO	81.0	ZnO	1.000	1.000
°°°Kingman Potash Spar	$K_2O \cdot Al_2O_3 \cdot 6SiO_2$	557	SiO_2	0.662	1.510
			Al_2O_3	0.184	5.434
			K_2O	0.120	8.333
			Na_2O	0.027	37.037°°
				0.523	1.912

° The combined total of both oxides in dolomite.

°° Generally speaking these amounts are most likely not significant although you can use the figures in your calculations.

°°° For substitution of other spars see Table 1.

°°°° Since this is a glass (mixture) the Formula and the Molecular Weight are theoretical figures supplied by the manufacturer.

TABLE 3: CHANGING THE PERCENTAGE OXIDE TO BATCH MATERIAL

Amount of Oxide needed x CF (Conversion Factor of Oxide to Material) = Material Amount

ex. (Na_2O) 18.0 x (CF) 1.710 = 30.8 sodium carbonate

TABLE 4: CHANGING THE BATCH MATERIAL TO PERCENTAGE OXIDE

Amount of Batch Material x CF (Conversion Factor of Material to Oxide) = Oxide Amount Percentage

ex. (Na_2CO_3) 30.8 x (CF) 0.585 = 18.0 Sodium Oxide

TABLE 5: COLOR SCALE FOR VISUAL MEASURING OF TEMPERATURE

Color	Degrees F.	Degrees C.
Barely Visible Red	900	500
Cherry Red	1400	750
Orange	1650	900
Yellow	2000	1100
Light Yellow	2400	1300
White	2800 and above	1500 and above

TABLE 6: CONVERSION FORMULA

Centigrade to Fahrenheit

$X°C \times \frac{9}{5} = Y$ $\qquad Y + 32 = Z°F$

Fahrenheit to Centigrade

$X°F - 32 = Y$ $\qquad Y \times \frac{5}{9} = Z°C$

TABLE 7: CONVERSION FACTORS FOR MATERIALS AND OXIDES

If a material is not included on the charts of Conversion Factors you can calculate the Material to Oxide factor in two ways:

I. Using the Chart of Molecular and Atomic Weights:

$$\frac{\text{Weight of Oxide}}{\text{Weight of Material}} = \text{Conversion Factor}$$

I will use sodium carbonate (Na_2CO_3) as an example for this first method. During the melting of the batch the sodium carbonate breaks down into sodium oxide and carbon dioxide, thus—

$$Na_2CO_3 = Na_2O + CO_2.$$

Most of the sodium oxide goes into the glass and most of the carbon dioxide is given off into the furnace atmosphere. The weights are established from atomic weight charts; sodium is 23 x 2 atoms = 46, carbon 12, oxygen 16 x 3 atoms 48 for a total of 106. The weights of most commonly used compounds are included in charts that simplify calculations, and some molecules have easily remembered values such as carbon dioxide (CO_3) which is 44. In this example the sodium oxide (Na_2O) is 62 and the carbon dioxide is 44. The weight of the oxide supplied to the melt (62) and the total weight of the chemical (106) are the figures used in the computations

$$\frac{(\text{Weight of Oxide})\ 62}{(\text{Weight of Material})\ 106} = (\text{Conversion Factor})\ 0.585$$

Soda ash is a fairly simple chemical with a fairly simple reaction under heat. Other chemicals can be more difficult. It is usually necessary to know what happens to the chemical in the melt. The two sides of the equation will usually be equal but not always, since a chemical may lose elements to other chemicals in the melt or pick up elements from other chemicals.

II. Using the Percent of Oxide Added by the Material:

$$\text{Percent of Oxide} \times .01 = \text{Conversion Factor}$$

Studying the Conversion Factor charts show that the Percent of Oxide by Weight and the Material to Oxide Conversion Factor are related. If the percent by weight is known the CF is simple to establish. Take sodium carbonate for example. The percent of sodium oxide (Na_2O) in sodium carbonate (Na_2CO_3) is 58.5 therefore:

$$58.5 \times .01 = .585\ CF$$

The percentage of the oxide often appears on the bag of chemicals, can be supplied by contacting the manufacturer, found in percentage tables, or can be calculated.

TABLE 8: BATCH EXPRESSED IN TERMS OF 1000 POUNDS OF SAND

Mention should be made of a practice once common in glassmelting (and still used in some instances): expressing the batch material amounts in relation to 1000 lbs. (or parts) of sand. In order to express our first batch in terms of 1000 lbs. of sand we multiply all the weights by 1000 and divide by the weight of the sand.

$$\text{Sand} \quad 71.5 \times 1000 = \frac{71500.0}{71.5} = 1000\ \text{lbs.}$$

$$\text{Soda Ash} \quad 30.8 \times 1000 = \frac{30800.0}{71.5} = 431\ \text{lbs.}$$

$$\text{Lime} \quad 13.9 \times 1000 = \frac{13900.0}{71.5} = 194\ \text{lbs.}$$

TABLE 9: 1000 POUNDS OF BATCH CONVERTED TO PERCENTAGE OXIDE FORMULA

When comparing older batch formulas it is often advantageous to convert the batch formulas based on 1000 lbs. of sand to a percentage. There are several ways to do this. Again using our first batch:

1. Multiply the batch amounts by the Material to Oxide CF:

$$\text{Sand } 1000 \times 1.00 = 1000.000$$

$$\text{Soda } 431 \times 0.585 = 253.735$$

$$\text{Lime } 194 \times 0.757 = 146.858$$

2. Total the results: 1400.593, or 1401

3. Divide the answers in 1 by the total in 2 to obtain the percentage of each oxide:

$$\frac{1000}{1401} = 71.4 \text{ SiO}_2$$

$$\frac{254}{1401} = 18.1 \text{ Na}_2\text{O}$$

$$\frac{147}{1401} = 10.6 \text{ CaO}$$

TABLE 10: FIGURING THE OXIDE TO MATERIAL CONVERSION FACTOR

To calculate the Oxide to Material Conversion Factor use this formula:

1. $$\frac{100}{\text{Percent of Oxide}} = \text{Conversion Factor}$$

or

2. $$\frac{\text{Weight of Material}}{\text{Weight of Oxide}} = \text{Conversion Factor}$$

Again let us use sodium carbonate as examples (the minor discrepancies are due to insignificant variations from the original).

1. $$\frac{100}{58.5} = 1.710$$

or

2. $$\frac{106}{62} = 1.710$$

APPENDIX 195

TABLE 11: PERCENT OF OXIDE SUPPLIED TO THE MELT BY GLASS BATCH MATERIALS

Some chemicals behave rather simply when heated in the melt (ex. sodium carbonate – Na_2CO_3 = sodium oxide – Na_2O + carbon dioxide CO_2). Others are more complicated (ex. lead carbonate – $2PBCO_3 \cdot Pb(OH)_2$ = lead oxide – $3PbO$ + carbon dioxide $2CO_2$ + water – H_2O). Some pick up chemicals from other materials in the melt, products of combustion, or the atmosphere (ex. calcium fluoride – CaF_2 = calcium oxide – CaO + fluorine – F_2). And some do not change at all (ex. lead oxide – PbO = lead oxide – PbO). A knowledge of what happens in the melt is essential in figuring the use of the material. Below is an example of how to calculate the percent of oxide in a glass batch material in a step-by-step sequence using a fairly complicated material.

Sodium Tri-polyphosphate (Anhydrous) $Na_5P_3O_{10}$

Molecular Weight: to be established

Oxides Supplies: Na_2O and P_2O_5

Percent Supplies to be established

One mole (the molecular weight of a substance expressed in grams) of $Na_5P_3O_{10}$ will not convert to sodium oxide (Na_2O) and phosphorous pentoxide (P_2O_5) however 2 moles (10 sodium—6 phosphorous—20 oxygen) break down when heated to produce 5 Na_2O and $3P_2O_5$ (10 sodium—6 phosphorous—20 oxygen):

$$2\ Na_5P_3O_{10} = 5Na_2O + 3P_2O_5$$

Having established what takes place in the melt we can calculate the percentage of each oxide. To find the molecular weight multiply the atomic weight (See Table 12) by the number of atoms:

$$2\ (Na_5 + P_3 + O_{10}) = 5\ (Na_2O) + 3\ (P_2O_5)$$
$$2 \times (23 \times 5 + 31 \times 3 + 16 \times 10) = 5 \times (23 \times 2 + 16) + 3 \times (31 \times 2 + 6 \times 5)$$
$$2 \times (115 + 93 + 160) = 5 \times (46 + 16) + 3 \times (62 + 80)$$
$$2 \times (368) = 5 \times (62) + 3 \times (142)$$
$$736 = 310 + 426$$
$$736 = 736 +$$

310 and phosphorous pentoxide P_2O_5) weights 426. With these figures we calculate the percentage of Of the total weight of the material (2 moles of $Na_5P_3O_{10}$ at 368 each) 736 sodium oxide (Na_2O) weighs 310 and phosphorous pentoxide (P_2O_5) weighs 426. With these figures we calculate the percentage of each oxide:

$$\frac{310}{736} \times \frac{100}{1} = 42 \text{ percent } Na_2O$$

$$\frac{426}{736} \times \frac{100}{1} = 58 \text{ percent } P_2O_5$$

Note: the manufacturer gives the molecular weight as 367.86 and the P_2O_5 percentage as a minimum of 56%. The manufacturers information is preferred. When the actual accuracy differs from the mathematical accuracy, the actual is used.

TABLE 12: ATOMIC WEIGHTS OF COMMON ELEMENTS

Element	Symbol	Atomic Weight
Aluminum	Al	26.9
Barium	Ba	137.4
Boron	B	10.8
Calcium	Ca	40.1
Carbon	C	12.0
Fluorine	F	19.0
Hydrogen	H	1.0
Iron	Fe	55.8
Lead	Pb	207.2
Lithium	Li	6.9
Magnesium	Mg	24.3
Nitrogen	N	14.0
Oxygen	O	16.0
Phosphorous	P	30.9
Potassium	K	39.1
Silicon	Si	28.1
Sodium	Na	22.9
Sulphur	S	32.1
Tin	Sn	118.7
Titanium	Ti	47.9
Zinc	Zn	65.4

Glass Recipes

In this section I will present several formulas for melting batchglass. Comments about the glass or its needs for melting, etc. will follow the formulas. In most instances I have personally melted these glasses—if I have not the glass will be so identified. There may be a "name" to identify the simpler glasses, however most will be identified by letter and number code. Those starting with Kula are mine. Formulas from other sources will usually be spelled out. The letters and numbers may identify the kind of glass, its number in a sequential experimental series, etc. This is not really important to you since it is offered here simply as a means of identification.

Most of the recipes will be presented as a suggested batch amount, either on the basis of 1000 lbs. of sand, or based on a batch developed from the percentage oxide followed by the approximate percentage oxide. When I feel it necessary, I may give more than one batch recipe. The fining decolorizing agents are generally left out (since they depend so much on your materials), however they are included with formulas received from other craftsmen and at times with suggestions in my glasses.

Kula/SI/6

Sand	65.0	SiO_2	65.0
Soda Ash	31.6	Na_2O	18.9
Potassium Carbonate	9.4	K_2O	6.4
Dolomite	7.8	CaO	5.9
Lime	4.8	MgO	1.7
Borax	2.7	PbO	1.0
Barium Carbonate	1.2	B_2O_3	.9
Litharge	1.0	BaO	.9

An excellent glass for most standard colorants: the batch could be adjusted for at least one alkali nitrate, arsenic, and antimony.

Carder Clear Base

Sand	120	SiO_2	70.2
Soda	56	Na_2O	21.5
Whiting	20	CaO	6.6
Sodium Nitrate	11	K_2O	1.6
Potassium Carbonate	4		

In melting this glass I used 8.7 lime hydrate in place of the limestone, plus .1 arsenic and .1 antimony. The Carder formula calls for (in addition to the batch materials) .6 arsenic, .4 manganese dioxide, and .6 antimony. The glass is easy-melting, easy-working, and has a wide working range. Colorants suggested by Carder (none with the manganese as decolorizer) are Azure (copper oxide 1.360); rosa (0.36 selenium); champagne (1.0 cadmium, 0.5 sulfur, 0.9 colorfornic (sic ?), 0.7 selenium). Compare this to the Murano glass and also to some of the glasses used for Christmas tree ornaments!

White (Clear) Attributed to Murano

Sand	100	SiO_2	72.5
Soda Ash	43	Na_2O	20.1
Calcium Carbonate	15	CaO	6.1
Sodium Nitrate	5	B_2O_3	1.0
Boric Acid	2.5		

Modified and melted by me

Sand	100
Soda	43
Lime hydrate	11
Sodium Nitrate	5
Borax	4

With the changes I made (borax) the sodium oxide has been increased slightly, but the change is not shown in the oxide formula. This is an easy-working, easy-melting glass similar to that attributed to Carder except for minor oxide changes. The original calls for 30% cullet with the batch, .2 arsenic, .3 antimony, and .004 selenium. Some of the suggested colors: sea green (.1 copper oxide and .2 potassium bichromate); red (2.0 manganese dioxide); hub (sic) green (.2 manganese dioxide and .1 copper oxide); straw (2.5 iron oxide and 2.5 manganese dioxide); ruby red (.450 selenium, 1.0 cadmium sulphide). (No antimony or arsenic in the last, however no mention is made of the sodium nitrate!).

Kula/SL/14

Sand	57.2	SiO_2	68.0
Soda Ash	27.4	Na_2O	16.9
Feldspar (Potash)	16.3	CaO	6.0
Lime	6.1	K_2O	2.9
Dolomite	4.6	Al_2O_3	2.9
Sodium Nitrate	2.7	BaO	1.0
Potassium Nitrate	2.2	ZnO	1.0
Barium Carbonate	1.3	MgO	0.9
Zinc Oxide	1.0		

With .1 arsenic, .1 antimony, .01 manganese dioxide, and .01 powdered blue, this is basically a soda/lime glass with small amounts of the other materials added to improve glass and working qualities. It has good clarity and color and is a good glass for beginners and school situations.

Rocky Mountain Glass Works Clear Glass
(Courtesy of Joe Harmon)

Sand	400	SiO_2	74.0
Soda	160	Na_2O	19.2
Raw Lime	40	CaO	5.6
Sodium Nitrate	26	B_2O_3	.5
Borax	6.75	BaO	.5
Barytes (Barium Carbonate	4. (3.4)		

An excellent glass. Mr. Harmon's formula calls for .75, manganese dioxide, 1.5 arsenic oxide, and .25 powdered blue. The real "secret" is the use of barytes (a barium sulphate ore) that is an active flux that helps to "sweep" bubbles out of the melt (fine) at high temperatures. My substitution of the barium carbonate is therefore not a real test of this glass—but it worked well.

Balos Clear Soda/Lime

			Theoretical	Actually Melted
Sand	58.0	SiO_2	67.0	67.0
Soda Ash	20.3	Na_2O	14.5	12.8
Feldspar	13.6	CaO	7.0	6.9
Lime	9.2	ZnO	7.0	7.0
Zinc Oxide	7.0	Al_2O_3	2.5	2.5
Borax	5.5	B_2O_3	2.0	2.0
		K_2O	----	1.6

A good, easy-melting glass with working range somewhat shorter than the "heavy" soda glasses (Carder, Murano, etc.). The modification (substitution of K_2O for some of the Na_2O) was done because of the available feldspar.

Kula/SZ/E 32

Sand	1000	SiO_2	63.8
Sodium Carbonate	308	ZnO	15.3
Zinc Oxide	250	Na_2O	12.1
Borax	100	K_2O	4.9
Potash	108.9	B_2O_3	2.2
Feldspar	50.	CaO	1.4
Lime	25.	Al_2O_3	0.5
Dolomite	12.5	MgO	0.2

This is a reduction form of the *Kula/SZ/1E* glass. Excellent yellow opals are produced with 18.3 cadmium sulphide and 4.7 sulfur and a good orange to red ruby with 9.8 sulfur, 2.0 sodium selenite, 15. selenium and 4.7 sodium chloride (fining agent). The glass is clear until struck. As with many high zinc glasses, this is somewhat more "stiff" after cutting with shears, etc., tending to keep sharp edges unless *strongly* fire polished.

Kula/SZ/IG IV

Sand	1000.0	SiO_2	68.5
Soda Ash	373.0	Na_2O	16.0
Zinc Oxide	160.5	ZnO	10.8
Borax	54.0	B_2O_3	1.4
Potash	28.5	K_2O	1.3
Kryolite	20.0	CaO	1.3
Dolomite	13.5	MgO	.3
Lime	13.5		.3
Bone Ash	10.0	P_2O_5	.2
Sodium Chloride	5.0		

This is an effective reduction glass for ruby production. The bone ash, in theory, helps in the formation of the cadmium/selenium ruby. The kryolite (fluorine) and salt (chlorine) free gasses to help in the mixing and fining that is usually done by the nitrate (oxygen) in normal melts. The colorants were 18 cadmium sulphide, 15 selenium, 2 sodium selenite, and 20 sulfur for the test run. Most of the tests struck opal—yellow through orange.

Kula/CAS/55B

Sand	1000	SiO_2	67.20
Soda Ash	380	Na_2O	17.30
Zinc Oxide	150	ZnO	10.00
Borax	80	B_2O_3	2.00
Cryolite	40	K_2O	1.30
Potash	30	P_2O_5	.67
Bone Ash	20	CaO	.67
Sodium Chloride	10	Al_2O_3	.67

A very effective base glass for ruby glasses. Unlike the glasses recommended in most of the literature, this is not a potash glass but it works nonetheless. Figured in the calculations are cryolite and salt even though they are, in this glass, fining and mixing materials. This may be justified for the cryolite (since a little over 1% of Na_2O is added), but hardly for the salt. Colorants have been experimented with and in general the "shotgun" method (B) has been more consistent than A.

A		B	
Selenium	20	Selenium	5
Cadmium sulphide	26	Sodium Selenite	5
		Zinc Selenite	5
		Selenium Dioxide	5
		Cadmium Sulphide	26

This glass is usually yellow and yellow/orange in the early stages of working, then light reds, dark reds, and opaque reds, and finally a light transparent "green."

WHITE (CLEAR) ATTRIBUTED TO MURANO

Sand	100	SiO_2	72.5
Soda Ash	43	Na_2O	20.1
Calcium Carbonate	15	CaO	6.1
Sodium Nitrate	5	B_2O_3	1.0
Boric Acid	2.5		

Modified and melted by me

Sand	100
Soda	43
Lime hydrate	11
Sodium Nitrate	5
Borax	4

With the changes I made (borax) the sodium oxide has been increased slightly, but the change is not shown in the oxide formula. This is an easy-working, easy-melting glass similar to that attributed to Carder except for minor oxide changes. The original calls for 30% cullet with the batch, .2 arsenic, .3 antimony, and .004 selenium. Some of the suggested colors: sea green (.1 copper oxide and .2 potassium bichromate); red (2.0 manganese dioxide); hub (sic) green (.2 manganese dioxide and .1 copper oxide); straw (2.5 iron oxide and 2.5 manganese dioxide); ruby red (.450 selenium, 1.0 cadmium sulphide). (No antimony or arsenic in the last, however no mention is made of the sodium nitrate!).

KULA/SL/14

Sand	57.2	SiO_2	68.0
Soda Ash	27.4	Na_2O	16.9
Feldspar (Potash)	16.3	CaO	6.0
Lime	6.1	K_2O	2.9
Dolomite	4.6	Al_2O_3	2.9
Sodium Nitrate	2.7	BaO	1.0
Potassium Nitrate	2.2	ZnO	1.0
Barium Carbonate	1.3	MgO	0.9
Zinc Oxide	1.0		

With .1 arsenic, .1 antimony, .01 manganese dioxide, and .01 powdered blue, this is basically a soda/lime glass with small amounts of the other materials added to improve glass and working qualities. It has good clarity and color and is a good glass for beginners and school situations.

ROCKY MOUNTAIN GLASS WORKS CLEAR GLASS
(Courtesy of Joe Harmon)

Sand	400	SiO_2	74.0
Soda	160	Na_2O	19.2
Raw Lime	40	CaO	5.6
Sodium Nitrate	26	B_2O_3	.5
Borax	6.75	BaO	.5
Barytes	4.		
(Barium Carbonate	3.4)		

An excellent glass. Mr. Harmon's formula calls for .75, manganese dioxide, 1.5 arsenic oxide, and .25 powdered blue. The real "secret" is the use of barytes (a barium sulphate ore) that is an active flux that helps to "sweep" bubbles out of the melt (fine) at high temperatures. My substitution of the barium carbonate is therefore not a real test of this glass—but it worked well.

BALOS CLEAR SODA/LIME

			Theoretical	Actually Melted
Sand	58.0	SiO_2	67.0	67.0
Soda Ash	20.3	Na_2O	14.5	12.8
Feldspar	13.6	CaO	7.0	6.9
Lime	9.2	ZnO	7.0	7.0
Zinc Oxide	7.0	Al_2O_3	2.5	2.5
Borax	5.5	B_2O_3	2.0	2.0
		K_2O	----	1.6

A good, easy-melting glass with working range somewhat shorter than the "heavy" soda glasses (Carder, Murano, etc.). The modification (substitution of K_2O for some of the Na_2O) was done because of the available feldspar.

Kula/SL/1F-

Sand	70.0	SiO_2	70.00
Soda Ash	22.2	Na_2O	14.98
Dolomite	9.2	CaO	4.70
Borax	5.5	PbO	3.00
Litharge	3.0	B_2O_3	2.00
Potassium Carbonate	2.9	MgO	2.00
Sodium Nitrate	2.7	K_2O	1.90
Lime	2.6	BaO	1.10
Barium Carbonate	1.3	ZnO	1.00
Zinc Oxide	1.0		

An improved soda/lime that can be melted in an open tank despite the lead content. The flame should be neutral and oxidizing. Colors are good with standard colorants—.1 lead chromate, green (yellow in thin sections), .02 cobalt oxide, gaudy blue, etc.

Christmas Tree Ornament Glass

Sand	68.00	SiO_2	68.00
Soda Ash	26.51	Na_2O	22.00
Lime Hydrate	9.50	CaO	7.20
Alumina, Calcined	3.1	Al_2O_3	3.1

I have not melted this glass. It is offered for comparison purposes since this glass (by most modern standards) is considered to lack durability for most uses except tree ornaments.

Kula/MA+/31

Sand	60.8	SiO_2	68
Sodium Carbonate	23.2	Na_2O	15
Feldspar	10.8	K_2O	5
Dolomite	4.6	ZnO	4
Zinc Oxide	4.0	CaO	3
Potassium Carbonate	3.9	Al_2O_3	2
Sodium Nitrate	2.7	MgO	1
Borax	2.7	B_2O_3	1
Potassium Nitrate	2.1	BaO	1
Lime Hydrate	2.1		
Barium Carbonate	1.3		

This is an easy-working, easy-melting glass with little tendency to devitrify. The potash and zinc help the color and brilliance of the glass. This is similar to the glass used in the text except for the B_2O_3 and ZnO change. Use fining agents in the actual melt.

Kula/MA+/10

Sand	1500	SiO_2	65.8
Sodium Carbonate	500	Na_2O	14.5
Borax	200	K_2O	8.2
Potash	200	CaO	4.2
Feldspar	200	BaO	3.1
Potassium Nitrate	100	B_2O_3	2.9
Sodium Nitrate	100	Al_2O_3	1.5
Barium Carbonate	100	MgO	0.9
Dolomite	100		
Lime Hydrate	100		
Antimony Oxide	2		
Arsenic Oxide	2		

Despite the low SiO_2, this is an effective glass with acceptable durability and good colors in oxidation. 16.6 chromium oxide and 8.4 copper carbonate produce a very bright green; other bright colors can be expected with the standard colorants and mixtures of these colorants.

Carey's Kansas Volcanic Ash Glass

Kansas Volcanic Ash	30.78
Talc	16.85
Flint	14.85
Barium Carbonate	10.36
Arsenic	9.70
Borax	9.20
Soda Ash	8.98
Zinc Oxide	2.70
Dolmite	1.70
China Clay	1.36
Flourspar	.07

The above is a batch formula exactly as supplied by Mr. Carey for an experimental glass he has melted using a local volcanic ash. I have not melted the glass. The analysis of this ash is included in Table 1. In his note he makes mention of a volcanic ash in the area of Dillion Montana that contains little or no iron that he feels would make a beautiful glass.

Kula/6E+/K1F

Flint	60.0	SiO_2	60.0
Sodium Carbonate	27.3	Na_2O	17.8
Potassium Carbonate	14.7	K_2O	10.0
Borax	11.0	B_2O_3	4.0
Dolomite	9.2	PbO	3.0
Litharge	3.0	CaO	2.8
		MgO	2.0

This is a low silica, high alkali glass that can be melted in an open tank despite the lead content. It has a very easy-melting, easy-working, wide working range, and excellent color (to oxidize add at least one alkali nitrate). With copper, tin, and a secondary reducing agent (sodium cyanide, Rochelle salts, etc.) this can product an excellent copper ruby that, of course, should be cased.

Kula/ZCR/1C Red

Sand	1500	SiO_2	60.6
Sodium Carbonate	600	Na_2O	14.8
Zinc Oxide	300	ZnO	11.1
Potash	260	K_2O	7.4
Borax	200	CaO	2.8
Feldspar	200	B_2O_3	2.1
Lime	100	Al_2O_3	1.4

This glass was melted in a small test furnace and struck to a red and red/orange, somewhat "opal" or "cloudy." The colorants were 15. selenium, 15. cadmium sulphide, and 7. sulfur. The color was more likely the result of thermal history of the melt than the colorant form or relationship.

Kula/SZ/1-E

Sand	1000	SiO_2	63.0
Sodium Carbonate	300	ZnO	15.0
Zinc Oxide	250	Na_2O	14.0
Borax	100	K_2O	4.9
Potash	100	B_2O_3	2.2
Feldspar	50	CaO	1.4
Lime Hydrate	25	BaO	.6
Potassium Nitrate	12.5	Al_2O_3	.6
Sodium Nitrate	12.5	MgO	.2
Barium Carbonate	12.5		
Dolomite	12.5		

This glass could be called a soda/zinc glass. Melting is not as easy as with some of the high soda glasses, but colors are excellent. To help in fining add .2 arsenic and .2 antimony. Particularly brilliant are the uranium yellows. Oxidize strongly when melting and working.

Kula/SZ/E 32

Sand	1000	SiO_2	63.8
Sodium Carbonate	308	ZnO	15.3
Zinc Oxide	250	Na_2O	12.1
Borax	100	K_2O	4.9
Potash	108.9	B_2O_3	2.2
Feldspar	50.	CaO	1.4
Lime	25.	Al_2O_3	0.5
Dolomite	12.5	MgO	0.2

This is a reduction form of the *Kula/SZ/1E* glass. Excellent yellow opals are produced with 18.3 cadmium sulphide and 4.7 sulfur and a good orange to red ruby with 9.8 sulfur, 2.0 sodium selenite, 15. selenium and 4.7 sodium chloride (fining agent). The glass is clear until struck. As with many high zinc glasses, this is somewhat more "stiff" after cutting with shears, etc., tending to keep sharp edges unless *strongly* fire polished.

Kula/SZ/IG IV

Sand	1000.0	SiO_2	68.5
Soda Ash	373.0	Na_2O	16.0
Zinc Oxide	160.5	ZnO	10.8
Borax	54.0	B_2O_3	1.4
Potash	28.5	K_2O	1.3
Kryolite	20.0	CaO	1.3
Dolomite	13.5	MgO	.3
Lime	13.5		.3
Bone Ash	10.0	P_2O_5	.2
Sodium Chloride	5.0		

This is an effective reduction glass for ruby production. The bone ash, in theory, helps in the formation of the cadmium/selenium ruby. The kryolite (fluorine) and salt (chlorine) free gasses to help in the mixing and fining that is usually done by the nitrate (oxygen) in normal melts. The colorants were 18 cadmium sulphide, 15 selenium, 2 sodium selenite, and 20 sulfur for the test run. Most of the tests struck opal—yellow through orange.

Kula/CAS/55B

Sand	1000	SiO_2	67.20
Soda Ash	380	Na_2O	17.30
Zinc Oxide	150	ZnO	10.00
Borax	80	B_2O_3	2.00
Cryolite	40	K_2O	1.30
Potash	30	P_2O_5	.67
Bone Ash	20	CaO	.67
Sodium Chloride	10	Al_2O_3	.67

A very effective base glass for ruby glasses. Unlike the glasses recommended in most of the literature, this is not a potash glass but it works nonetheless. Figured in the calculations are cryolite and salt even though they are, in this glass, fining and mixing materials. This may be justified for the cryolite (since a little over 1% of Na_2O is added), but hardly for the salt. Colorants have been experimented with and in general the "shotgun" method (B) has been more consistent than A.

A		B	
Selenium	20	Selenium	5
Cadmium sulphide	26	Sodium Selenite	5
		Zinc Selenite	5
		Selenium Dioxide	5
		Cadmium Sulphide	26

This glass is usually yellow and yellow/orange in the early stages of working, then light reds, dark reds, and opaque reds, and finally a light transparent "green."

Kula/CAS/55G

Sand	67.2	SiO_2	67.2
Soda Ash	24.4	Na_2O	14.6
Zinc Oxide	11.4	ZnO	11.2
Borax	1.9	CaO	1.9
Dolomite	1.8	K_2O	1.2
Lime	1.8	B_2O_3	0.7
Potash	1.8	MgO	0.4

Although this formula started out as a mistake, it works so well there is little reason to go into details on that mistake. In general the "carrot" orange color has been avoided in the early stages of working this recipe. I doubt if this is because of the formula, but rather because of differences in heating and the speed of working the glass (thermal history). Very bright, brilliant reds were produced with: .4 selenium, .4 selenium dioxide, .4 sodium selenite, .4 zinc selenite, .5 sulfur, and 1.5 cadmium sulphide.

Carder White Milk Glass

Sand	90	SiO_2	62.9
Soda Ash	25	Na_2O	17.4
Cryolite	23	K_2O	7.6
Potash	16	ZnO	6.2
Zinc Oxide	9	Al_2O_3	3.8
Whiting	6	CaO	2.3

This is a fluorine milk glass that is an opaque white if worked soon after fining. The cryolite is an excellent way to introduce both the needed Al_2O_3 and the F_2. The whiteness of the glass is further helped by the zinc oxide. As with most such fluorine glasses, this will tend to turn clear with long soaking periods in the furnace, develop cords, and dissolve the refractories.

Kula/OF/2

Sand	74	SiO_2	67.2
Soda	25	Na_2O	11.2
Potash	15	K_2O	8.5
Lepidolite	10	Al_2O_3	6.8
Spodumene	10	CaO	4.9
Pelalite	10	Li_2O	1.0
Feldspar	10		
Fluorspar	10		
Cryolite	5		

This is a rather complicated fluorine opal batch using equal batch amounts of the three lithia-alumina-silicates. Any one of these could be used for the Al_2O_3 (with a change in the lithia, etc.). The glass is a very long-working, easy-melting glass that is not as white as the Carder glass melted under the same conditions. Evidently even the 1% lithium oxide has a beneficial effect on the working range and fluid quality of this glass.

Kula/OP/5A

Sand	63	SiO_2	63.0
Soda Ash	20	K_2O	12.3
Potash	18	Na_2O	11.9
Bone Ash	12	CaO	6.5
Tin Oxide	1	P_2O_5	5.4
		SnO_3	1.0

This is a fairly easy-melting opal that strikes very white, and unlike the fluorine shows little tendency to lighten with longer soaking periods.

Kula/OP/5B

Sand	63	SiO_2	63.0
Sodium Carbonate	20	Na_2O	12.0
Bone Ash	12	CaO	6.5
Potassium Carbonate	9	K_2O	6.1
Zinc Oxide	6	ZnO	6.0
Tin Oxide	1	P_2O_5	5.5
		SnO_3	1.0

Colorwise this glass is a slightly less warm white than the previous formula, however this could be cause by either the thermal history or the purity of the ingredients used.

Kula/OP/2+

Sand	1200	SiO_2	60.0
Soda Ash	312	Na_2O	17.3
Sodium Tri-polyphosphate	376	P_2O_5	10.5
Lime	204	CaO	7.6
Potassium Nitrate	94	K_2O	2.2
Zinc Oxide	30	ZnO	1.5
Sodium Nitrate	16		

This is an opal/opaque glass that usually requires rather hot working temperatures—there seems to be some tendency to devitrification (or at least an over abundance of the glass emulsification). Colors added are predictable before striking but usually are toned somewhat after striking "white"—11.2 copper carbonate makes a light "baby blue," 1.4 cobalt oxide makes a blue that tends some toward a purple after striking, 5.6 nickle carbonate produces grays (but not unpleasant), 22 iron oxide makes a rather pleasant very light blue-green, and 44 titanium dioxide produces only a slight increase in the whiteness noted. Note: lead chromate and manganese dioxide mixtures will not produce the usual browns and ambers with this glass (they produce grays to light blues) however 11.2 selenium, .3 cadmium sulphate and 5.6 sulfur produce an excellent tan (fire as for a ruby and modify the oxidizers in the formula). In this glass the cheaper sodium phosphate and lime has been used instead of bone ash.

Kula/OP/5D

Sand	63	SiO_2	60.0
Sodium Carbonate	35	Na_2O	19.5
STP°	20	P_2O_5	8.8
Dolomite	8	CaO	6.0
Potash	5	K_2O	3.2
Tin Oxide	1	MgO	1.7
		SnO_2	1.0

An effective opal phosphate using a commercial phosphate/lime fertilizer° as the source of the P_2O_5! The cost is reduced greatly using such a product. The material also contains iron and sulfur (possibly beneficial to plants but of no help in producing a white glass). It is impossible to get a white, however the effective light blue opal is a good color and a good base for other colorants.

Lead Potash Glass (Alfred University)
Courtesy of Andre Billeci.

Sand	55.75	SiO_2	55.75
Lead Oxide	30.75	PbO	30.75
Potash	20.75	K_2O	14.51
Sodium Nitrate	.82	Na_2O	.30
Antimony Oxide	1.30	SbO_2	1.30

These are the figures given by Mr. Billeci. I have not melted it, however he has used the formula at Alfred for years and attests to its excellence. The theoretical formula varies from those I have used in this book in that the fining agents are included in the computations.

Kula/LEP

Sand	11.2	SiO_2	56.0
Litharge	6.2	PbO	31.0
Potassium Carbonate	3.0	K_2O	13.0
Potassium Nitrate	1.2	Na_2O	1.0
Sodium Nitrate	.6	B_2O_3	.4
Borax	.2		

This is, more or less, my standard lead/potash glass with most all colorants. It is a very easy-melting, easy-working glass with good clarity and some tendency toward cordiness. Colors are brilliant with most standard colorants. I have used this formula as is for gold rubies using .01 tin chloride, .01 sodium cyanide, .01 antimony oxide, .01 silver nitrate, and .01 gold chloride. The *theoretical* gold to tin ratio and colors produced are 1:10 maroon, 1:5 rose, and 1:4 light purple. Th cost of the materials has prohibited my doing more detailed work with the gold ruby.

Japanese Lead Glass Formula
(Courtesy Iwata Glass)

Sand	55.00	SiO_2	55
Lead	25.00	PbO	25
Potash	19.00	K_2O	13
Sodium Nitrate	5.48	CaO	3
Calcium Carbonate	5.35	Na_2O	2
Boric Acid	1.77	B_2O_3	1
Zinc Oxide	1.00	ZnO	1

I have not melted this glass—the figures are those supplied by the factory. Indicated fining agents are .2 antimony oxide, and .2 arsenic oxide.

Kula/BAL/14

Sand	68.0	SiO_2	68
Barium Carbonate	12.9	BaO	10
Lithium Carbonate	12.4	Li_2O	5
Dolomite	9.6	K_2O	5
Sodium Carbonate	6.8	Na_2O	5
Potassium Carbonate	5.9	CaO	3
Sodium Nitrate	2.7	MgO	2
Potassium Nitrate	2.2	Al_2O_3	2
Alumina (Cal)			2.0

This is barium glass high in lithium oxide. Colors are bright and strong, using standard colorants. The batch could be improved by introducing the Al_2O_3 from one or more of the lithia-alumia minerals (petalite, lepidolite, etc.). This would improve melting and fining. Although complicated (since this would change the sand, lithium, etc. calculations) it might well be worth the trouble for the possible melting benefits and even an improvement in cost.

Kula/ST/2N+

Sand	67.0	1000	SiO_2	67.0
Soda Ash	27.3	310	Na_2O	16.9
Dolomite	9.2	138	TiO_2	7.0
Titanium Dioxide	7.0	105	CaO	2.8
Potassium Carbonate	4.2	63	MgO	2.0
Sodium Nitrate	2.7	40	K_2O	1.9
Barium Carbonate	1.3	20	BaO	1.0
Zinc Oxide	1.0	15	ZnO	1.0

The above batch is shown on the basis of 1000 lbs. of sand and in the usual form used in this book. This glass is one of a series using titanium dioxide as a major ingredient. This oxide seems to shorten the working range a bit, but has a beneficial effect on color. I found that 36 cerium oxide produced a light yellow, 36 cerium and 7 manganese dioxide produced a light amber, and uranium produced very bright yellows.

Glossary

Acid Cut Back. Dissolving the glass surface with hydrofluoric acid to form a decorative relief design.

Acid Polishing. Polishing the glass surface with acid mixtures (usually hydrofluoric and sulphuric).

Alabaster Glass. A white transluscent glass similar in appearance to the natural variety of granular gypsum called "alabaster" that diffuses light without opal color.

Alexandrite. The property of some glasses to appear one color in artificial light and another color in natural light, or a similar effect when the thickness of the glass varies.

Alkali. The oxides of sodium, potassium or lithium.

Annealing Point. The temperature at which the internal stress in glass is substantially relieved in 15 minutes. In general the upper end of the annealing range.

Annealing Range. The range of temperature in a glass during which strains are removed. It is assumed to be between the annealing point (A.P.) and the strain point (St.P.). The annealing range depends on the glass composition and other variables.

Arch. The curved roof of the furnace spanning the interior.

Aventurine. A glass containing colored, opaque crystals that glisten.

Baffle Wall. A wall within the furnace used to deflect gases and flames.

Barium Glass. A glass containing significant amounts of barium.

Batch. The mixture of raw chemicals in specific proportion that are to be melted into a glass.

Bead. The enlarged, rounded edge of a glass vessel usually produced by fire polishing.

Blister. A large bubble usually resulting from improper gathering of the glass.

Blocking. 1. Shaping a gather of glass in a cavity of wood, paper, metal, graphite, etc. 2. Mixing the molten glass by sinking organic matter (wood, potato, etc.). 3. Firing the furnace at comparatively low temperatures.

Bloom. A film produced when smoke and gases affect the surface of the glass.

Blown Glass. Glassware formed by air pressure from within the piece.

Blow Pipe. A hollow metal tube used for gathering and blowing glass (same as blowing iron).

Body. The consistency of molten glass that makes it workable.

Boil. 1. Activity in the melt caused by escaping gases. 2. A gas bubble larger than a seed.

Borate Glass. A glass in which the essential glass former is boric oxide (B_2O_3) instead of silica (SiO_2).

Borosilicate Glass. Silicate glasses having at least 5% boric oxide (B_2O_3).

Burner Block. A refractory block with an opening through which fuel and air (or flame) is admitted to a furnace.

Calcined. A substance that is heated to drive off water.

Campaign. The life of the tank or crucible.

Cane. Solid glass rod.

Cased Glass. Different colored glasses gathered on top of one another.

Charge. The batch or cullet for melting, or the actual loading of the furnace itself.

Check. A crack in the surface of a piece of glass.

Chemical Durability. The resistance of the glass to chemicals.

Chill Mark. The wrinkled surface on the vessel resulting from uneven cooling during forming.

Closed Pot. A pot in which the glass contained is protected from the flame.

Cooling Down. The time after opening the furnace until the glass is cool enough to work.

Cooling Rate. See setting rate

Cord. A defect within the glass due to inhomogenteity. It is visible because of a difference in refraction between the composition of the cord and the main body of the glass.

Crackled. A surface decoration produced by chilling the glass in water and reheating to partially smooth the cracks and relieve the strains.

Crystal. Any colorless transparent glass.

Cullet. Melted batch glass that has been cooled and can be remelted. Any waste or scrap glass.

Cut Glass. The decorating process of abrasive grinding of the surface followed by polishing.

Cycle. The time between the first load of batch and working out.

Day Tank. A tank in which a batch of glass is melted overnight for the next days' work.

Decolorizing. The production of a colorless looking glass by adding small amounts of complimentary colorants.

Devitrification. Crystal formation in glass.

Dichroic. Glass that is "two-colored," usually one color in reflected light and another color in transmitted light. See Alexandrite Effect.

Drag Ladle. Gathering molten glass from the furnace and dropping it in water to produce cullet for future melts.

Durability. See Chemical Durability

Engraving. Use of carborundum powder and oil on a revolving metal disc to produce hand-cut letters, figures, etc. on a glass surface.

Etch. To dissolve the surface of the glass with an agent, usually hydrofluoric acid, for decoration.

Fill. The unit charge of batch into the tank or pot.

Fined. A glass melt that is thoroughly mixed and is without bubbles.

Finish. The time at which the molten glass seems free of bubbles.

Fire Cracks. Cracks caused by spot temperature changes.

Fire Over. To let the furnace soak at working temperature.

Fire Polish. To smooth the vessel surface by heating in a flame.

Flash. A thin layer of colored or opaque glass applied to the surface of the vessel.

Flint Glass. A lead-containing glass.

Fluorescence. The reversal of light absorption—radiant energy transformed into light of longer wavelengths.

Flux. A chemical that promotes melting.

Flux Block. The refractories in the furnace that hold the molten glass.

Flux Line. Corrosion line in the tank at the point where the glass level usually meets the atmosphere.

Foam. A layer of bubbles on the surface of molten glass.

Fold. See Lap

Freeblown. See Offhand Glass

Frosted. Decorative treatment of the glass surface to make it look like frost (etched, sandblasted, etc.).

Fuming. See Iridescence

Gaffer. A master glassblower.

Gall. Surface scum on the melted glass caused by molten sulfates.

Gather. 1. Glass taken from the furnace on pontil, gathering iron, or pipe. 2. To remove glass from the furnace on a pipe, pontil, or gathering iron.

Glass. A molten mixture of various inorganic compounds that on cooling forms a random pattern rather than a set of crystalline structure.

Glassblowing. Forming glassware by air pressure from within the piece.

Glory-Hole. An opening in the furnace or a separate heat container used for reheating ware while working glass.

Hard Glass. A glass difficult to melt—high melting temperature, high viscosity, hard to scratch or of good durability.

Hot Spot. The zone of highest temperature in the furnace.

Iridescent. An ion exchange in which metal replaces material in the glass surface to produce a refractive effect called "Newton rings" or "rainbow."

Jacks. A tool made of spring steel, usually with two metal blades connected at the top, used to form hot glass.

Knot. Glass defect in the form of a vitreous lump.

Lampworking. Production of objects by melting together tubes and rods of glass over a burner.

Lap. 1. A fold in the surface of a glass piece. 2. A tool used to polish glassware.

Lead Glass. Glass containing a substantial amount of lead oxide.

Lehr. A long annealing oven in which ware is constantly conveyed through the annealing range and down to room temperature.

Lime Glass. A glass containing a substantial portion of lime—usually with soda and silica.

Liquidous Temperature. The temperature at which crystals form in cooling glass or, when heated, the temperature at which crystals dissolve.

Long. A comparative term used to describe a glass with a wide working range (slow-setting).

Luminescence. The emission of light not caused by incandescence.

Marver. 1. A flat surface on which a gather of glass is rolled, shaped, and cooled. 2. The procedure of rolling a gather of glass on the marver.

Melt. Molten glass in the furnace.

Melting. To liquify the glass-forming ingredients by heat.

Metal. Molten glass.

Milk Glass. An opaque white glass.

Mix. Interchangeable with "batch" or "charge."

Moil. Scrap glass remaining on the pipe or pontil after the piece is complete.

Mold. A form into which glass is blown to make a shape.

Muffle. An enclosure in the furnace protecting the contents from the flame and gas.

Obsidian. A natural glass.

Offhand. Process of forming glass without use of a mold (freeblown, in the air, from the melt).

Opalescent Glass. Transluscent white or colored glass. When viewing a lamp filament through this glass the filament appears with a sharp outline that is reddish in color.

Opal Glass. A glass that does not directly transmit light. When viewing a lamp filament through this glass the outline of the filament cannot be detected.

Oxidizing Agent. A compound that releases oxygen to other batch chemicals in the melt.

Phosphate Glass. A glass in which the essential glass former is phosphorous pentoxide rather than silica dioxide.

Pig. A rest at the furnace door for the blow pipe and pontil.

Plain. Glass free from bubbles (fine).

Polariscope. An optical instrument for measuring or showing stress and strain in glass.

Pontil. An iron used to hold the vessel during fire polishing and finishing.

Port. Any opening in the furnace for flame or exhaust gases.

Pot. A seamless refractory vessel for holding molten glass.

Pot Furnace. A furnace containing one or more pots or crucibles of glass. These can be open to direct flame or closed.

Pounds Pressure. A measurement of pressure in the gas line determined by pounds per square inch.

Punty. See Pontil.

Raw Batch. A glass charge with no cullet.

Raw Cullet. A glass charge of only cullet.

Reboil. The reoccurrence of seeds in molten glass after having appeared fined.

Reducing Agent. A compound that lowers the oxygen content of other batch materials in the melt.

Refining. See Fining

Refractory. Material that can be heated to high-temperatures.

Rock Crystal. Highly polished, hand-cut, transparent glass.

Running Batch. Continuous remelting of cullet with raw batch of the same composition.

Sagging. Heating sheet glass on a mold to reproduce the shape of the mold. The glass does not reach the molten stage.

Scum. Unmelted materials floating on the molten glass.

Seeds. Small bubbles in the glass.

Setting Rate. The length of time it takes the molten glass to cool to the point at which it is no longer workable.

Sharp Fire. A short, strong, oxidizing flame.

Shear Mark. A cooling scar on glassware from cutting tools.

Short. A comparative term for fast-setting glass.

Silica Glass. Pure silicon dioxide glass.

Soft Fire. A reducing, long, yellow flame.

Softening Point. Refers to the elongation of a specified sized glass strand or fiber at a set rate.

Soft Glass. 1. A glass easy to melt or a glass with a low melting temperature. 2. Glass easily scratched or of poor durability.

Solarization. A change in a glass as a result of exposure to sunlight.

Stable. 1. Glass that does not devitrify. 2. Glass that is resistant to weathering.

Stain. Color applied and fired to near annealing temperature; unwanted "marks" on the finished vessel.

Sting Out. Hot air and flame exhausting from the furnace due to internal pressure.

Stones. Any non-glassy material imbedded in a piece of glass caused by improper grain size in batch material, devitrification, or refractory material.

Strain. Elastic deformation due to stress.

Stress. This is a condition of tension or compression in glass.

Striking. Appearance of color or opacity due to cooling or reheating to form different matrix arrangements.

Tank Block. See Flux Block.

Tank Furnace. A furnace in which the walls serve as the glass container and in which the flame is usually in direct contact with the glass surface.

Thermal Endurance. Relative ability of glassware to withstand sudden changes in heat and cold.

Working Range. The period when the glass is cool enough to gather out of the furnace yet hot enough to work.

Bibliography

BOOKS

Books on glass generally fall into two categories: those that are of a technical nature—dealing with glass, glass equipment, industry, etc., and those dealing with the history of glass (including esthetic opinion). I have listed none that deal generally or specifically with history since the field is so vast it would require a separate book. What I have included are books that I have found (with concerted effort) helpful in understanding glass. Probably the most important of these are the Weyl book and first volume of the set edited by Tooley—both unfortunately now out of print.

Glasses.
London: Borax Consolidated Limited.
New York: United States Borax and Chemical Corp.
(50 Rockefeller Plaza,
New York, New York 10020) 1965

Kulasiewicz, Frank I.
Offhand Blown Glass as a Contemporary Craft.
Ann Arbor, Michigan:
University Microfilm, 1972

Labino, Dominick.
Visual Art in Glass.
Art Horizons Series.
Dubuque: William C. Brown, 1968

Littleton, Harvey K.
Glassblowing.
New York: Van Nostrand
Reinhold Company, 1971

Morey, W.
The Properties of Glass.
New York: Reinhold
Publishing Corp., 1954

Scholes, Samuel R.
Modern Glass Practice.
New York: Industrial
Publications, Inc., 1952

Shand, E. B.
Glass Engineering Handbook.
New York: McGraw-Hill
Book Co., 1958

Tooley, F. V. (ed.).
Handbook of Glass Manufacture.
Vol. 1 and 2.
New York: Glass
Publishing Co., 1960

Waugh, Sidney.
The Art of Glass Making.
New York: Dodd, Mead & Co., 1938

Weyl, Woldemar A.,
Coloured Glasses.
London: Wm. Dawson
and Sons, Ltd. 1959

PUBLICATIONS

Ceramic Industry,
5 S. Wasbash Avenue,
Chicago, Illinois 60603
Of particular interest is the January issue of this industrial magazine which contains a rather complete listing of glass chemicals (as well as ceramic chemicals). This issue is an excellent reference source.

Ceramics Monthly,
4175 N. High St.,
Columbus, Ohio 43214
Periodically this magazine runs articles on glass, glassblowers, etc. Generally useful to the beginner.

Craft Horizons,
29 West 53rd St.,
New York, New York 10019
In recent years this magazine has been transformed into a review journal on craft (and near craft) shows in the United States. There are articles on the general crafts area and craftsmen with, from time to time, coverage of some glass-related areas.

Glass Art Magazine,
486–49th St.,
Oakland, California 94609
A new magazine devoted to all forms of glassworking, glass artists, informa-

tion on exhibitions, shows, reprints of important material on glass, materials and tools, etc. Recommended.

COLOR SLIDES OF CONTEMPORARY WORK IN GLASS

American Craftsmen's Council,
44 West 53rd Street,
New York, New York 10019
They offer a wide variety of slides on all of the crafts including a limited amount on glass. Write the Council for information.

Douglas Grimm,
2424 Sycamore St. No. 6,
West Rattlesnake,
Missoula, Montana 59801
A rather complete record of contemporary American ceramics with a growing offering in the field of glass. Write Mr. Grimm for information.

RECORDINGS

Conversations with Carder on Steuben his American Art Glass,
Recorded Interview, 1963
The Fieldstone Porch,
Stamford, Connecticut 06900.
A most interesting "live" recording made by the late Frederic Carder recalling glass in America in the early part of this century.

Of Special Interest to British Readers

BOOKS

Davis and Middlemas.
Coloured Glass.
Herbert Jenkins, 1968

Heddle, G.M.
Manual on Etching and Engraving Glass.
Alec Tiranti, 1962

Maloney, F.J. Terence,
Glass in the Modern World.
Aldus Books, 1968

Polak, Ada.
Modern Glass.
Faber & Faber, 1962

Shuler.
Glass Forming.
Pitman Publishing, 1971

PUBLICATIONS

Crafts Magazine,
28 Haymarket,
London SW17 47Z

Design Magazine,
The Design Centre,
Haymarket, London SW17 47Z

Glass Directory & Buyers Guide,
Fuel & Metallurgical Journels Ltd.,
John Adam House,
17-19 John Adam St.,
London WC2N 6JH

COLOUR SLIDES OF CONTEMPORARY WORK IN GLASS

Craft Advisory Committee,
12 Waterloo Place,
London SW1
They hold slides of the work of selected craftsmen listed in the Index of Craftsmen.

Suppliers List

In general you will find a local source of many bulk items is most economical. The prices of chemicals are often largely transportations costs. If a local ceramic supplier purchases in bulk amounts you may very well find his price more than competitive on items like potters flint, feldspars, etc. In any case, get a transportation estimate from suppliers any distance from you and include this in your cost before deciding on a source.

Do not forget to check local industrial chemical suppliers for things like phosphates and nitrates that have wide industrial usage (McKesson Chemical Co. and Van Waters and Rogers Co. have dealers in most parts of the country—check the phone directory for companies like this to see how much help they can be). Soda ash is usually available from swimming pool suppliers, lime from some hardware stores, and local paint manufacturers often use large amounts of glass chemicals (silica, iron oxides, etc.) however, their needs are such that you may be paying for the *color* of the unfired material rather than for the chemicals.

The above advice holds true for furnace building supplies (particularly firebrick and other heavy items). Check with local cement factories, foundries, etc. to see where and when they order their insulation and refractory materials. I have found very sympathetic ears among such companies.

If you decide to use scrap glass, consider very seriously the cost of shipping glass "marbles" halfway across the country when the manufacturer is only a quarter of that distance! The glassworker in New Mexico would seldom be foolish enough to purchase Arizona feldspar from New York. Cullet buyers have often neglected considerations of such practicalities. There was for a while the idea that a particular glass was "the" glass and the only one useful—nonsense! Some of the easiest-working glass I have seen was "doctored" local window-glass scraps.

I have included some addresses of suppliers and manufacturers. The list is far from complete for the reasons mentioned above and because I know it would be impossible to keep an up-to-date listing for *all* local suppliers. In the case of heavy refractories, write the main company and ask for the address of a local supplier (or even a local purchaser). For heavy-duty glass equipment purchases, you may find you will have to contact the Chicago area manufacturers, however they too may have a dealer closer to your area.

GENERAL SUPPLIERS

There are at present at least two companies that are attempting to offer special service to the glassworkers in this country. With some items they compete and with others they compliment. Their addresses are below with a brief description of what they carry. Please contact them for specifics and prices, etc.

Drykiln Design
P. O. Box 7527
Oakland, California 94601

Hand tools of all types (jacks, tweezers, shears, tongs, etc.), pipes, gathering irons, pontils, stands and racks, wood blocks with handles, cork polishing wheels, asbestos gloves, glass drills, benches, furnaces, cullet (read terms and conditions of sale!) that is delivered anywhere in this country with no extra freight or packing charge, ovens, glory-holes, etc.

Paoli Clay Company
Route 1
Belleville, Wisconsin 53508

Hand tools of all types (jacks, tweezers, shears, tongs, etc.), pipes, pontils, marvers, benches, pyrometers and thermocouples, electric oven controls, heavy-duty rougher-grinders, selected publications on glass, fiberglass marbles, etc.

Burners

I am not listing suppliers since in most instances you can do a better and safer job making burners *for your needs* instead of a scaled-down version of some industrial burner.

Chemicals

Ceramic Color and Chemical Co.
P. O. Box 2975
New Brighton, Pennsylvania 15066

Hommel, O. Co.
P O. Box 475
Pittsburg, Pennsylvania 15200

Stewart Clay Inc.
133 Mulberry St.
New York, New York 10013

Trinity Ceramic Supply Inc.
9016 Diplomacy Row
Dallas, Texas 75235

Van Howe Co.
1185 South Cherokee Ave.
Denver, Colorado 80223

Westwood Ceramic Supply Co.
610 Venice, California 92091

Cullet

If you are really interested in going this route, try recycling local scrap and writing some of the factories in West Virginia, etc. for information on what they are willing to supply you with.

Bassichis Co.
2323 W. 3rd St.
Cleveland, Ohio 44113

C & C Cullet Supply
Marietta, Pennsylvania 17547

Johns-Manville Fiber Glass Inc.
1810 Madison Ave.
Toledo, Ohio 43624

Electric Heating Elements and Heat Measuring Devices

Fairchild, W. H.
712 Centre St.
Freeland, Pennsylvania 18224

Paragon Industries Inc.
Box 10133
Dallas, Texas 75207

Skutt & Sons
2618 S.E. Steele St.
Portland, Oregon 97202

Electric Motors

Use any local source for small cheap, shaded pole—motor such as W. W. Grainger, Dayton, etc.

Furnaces and Ovens

A. D. Alpine Inc.
11837 Tenle St.
Culver City, California 92030

Glass Tools (Hand)

I have not listed Mexican, German, Italian, Dutch, etc. manufacturers.

Red Hot Tools
3558 Maple Avenue
Oakland, California 94602

Sabine, Frank M.
211 Wisconsin Street
Excelsior Spring, Missouri 64024

Glass Tools (Heavy-Duty Power)

These companies also handle replacement blades, polishing and grinding wheels, abrasive compounds, etc.

Buehler Ltd.
2120 Greenwood
P. O. Box 1459
Evanston, Illinois 60204

Lawrence, C. R. Inc.
1425 Tonne Road
Elk Grove Village, Illinois 60007

Sommer and Maca Glass Machinery Co.
5501 W. Ogden Avenue
Chicago, Illinois 60650

Grinding and Cutting Supplies (Blades, Wheels, etc.)

Avco Felker Corp.
1900 S. Greenshaw Blvd.
Torrance, California 90501

Sample Marshall
63 Park Avenue
Lyndhurst, New Jersey 07071

Polariscopes

Polarizing Instrument Co., Inc.
110 S. Buckhout St.
Irving-on-Hudson, New York 14081

Refractories and Insulation Materials

Most of the refractory companies have their main plants in Missouri, with other plants and offices spread across the country. Contacting the main plant can put you in touch with local factories and/or distributors.

A. P. Green Refractory Products
Mexico, Missouri 65265

Walsh Refractories Corp.
101 Ferry St.
St. Louis, Missouri 63147

Wellsville Firebrick Co.
West Hwy. 19
Wellsville, Missouri 63384

Suppliers for British Readers

Asbestos Products

Beldam Asbestos Co. Ltd.
Lascar Works,
Hounslow, Middx.

Jencons (Scientific) Ltd.
Mark Road,
Hemel Hempstead, Herts.

Burners

Glass Machinery Manufacturing Co. Ltd.
Imperial Works,
Perren Street,
London, N.W. 5

Heathway Machinery Co. Ltd.
Uxbridge Road,
Hillingdon, Middx.

Blow Pipes and General Glassmaking Tools

Armytage Bros. (Knottingley) Ltd.
P.O. Box No. 10,
Foundry Lane,
Knottingley, Yorks.

Glassworks Equipment Ltd.
Park Lane
Halesowen,
Worcestershire B63 2QS

Chemicals

Chance Bros. Ltd.,
Glass Works,
Smethwick,
Warley, Worcs.

Johnsom Mathey & Co. Ltd.
74 Hatton Garden,
London, EC1P 1AE

C.E. Ramsden & Co. Ltd.,
Foley Colour and Chemical Works,
Fenton,
Stoke on Trent, Staffs.

Electric Heating Elements and Heat Measuring Devices

Electrothermal Engineering Ltd.,
270 Neville Road,
London, E7 9QN

Kilns & Furnaces Ltd.,
Keele Street,
Tunstall,
Stoke on Trent, Staffs.

Morganite Electroheat Ltd.,
Point Pleasant,
Wandsworth,
London, S.W. 18

Electric Motors (Fans)

Alldays Peacock & Co. Ltd.,
Sydenham Road,
Birmingham, B11 1DH

Buck & Hickman Ltd.,
P.O. Box No. 74,
2 & 4 Whitechapel Road,
London, E.1.

Sturterant Engineering Co. Ltd.,
Hamlyn House,
Highgate Hill,
London, N.19 5PP

Furnaces and Ovens (Lehrs)

General Glass Equipment Co. Ltd.,
50 Argyle Crescent,
Portobello,
Edinburgh, EH15 2QD

Glassworks Equipment,
Park Lane,
Halesowen, Worcs.

Grinding and Cutting Supplies

Agate & General Stonecutters Ltd.,
25 Hatton Gardens,
London, E.C.1

Carborundum Co. Ltd.,
P.O. Box 55,
Trafford Park,
Manchester, M17 1HP

Shaw Abrasives (Diamond) Ltd.,
Waterloo Road,
London, NW2 7UN

Refractories and Insulation Materials

Carborundum Co. Ltd.,
P.O. Box 55,
Trafford Park,
Manchester, M17 1HP

Morganite Refractories,
5 Grosvenor Gardens,
London, SW1W OBQ

Price Pearson Refractories Ltd.,
P.O. Box No. 9,
Moor St.,
Brierley Hill, Staffs.

Index

Alumina, 96
Aluminum oxide, 96
Angel swings, making, 128
Annealing: definition, 46; methods, 46–47, 80–83, 118–119
Annealing oven: controls for, 81; lighting, 81; loading, 82; temperature, 46; turning off, 82; types, 47
Annealing oven, building: base, 48; burner, 56; door, 53–55; roof arch, 51–52; walls, 49–50

Barium oxide, 99
Batch melt. *See* Cullet
Bench, 64; illus., 102
Bernstein, William, 70
Billeci, Andre, 87
Bingham, John M., 151
Biniarz, Robert, 14, 145
Blocking, 110
Blocks, 66
Blower: air control, 71–72; markings on, 72
Blow pipes, 62–63; forming on, 111; keeping hot, 102
Borax, 96
Boro-silicate glass, 86
Boylen, Michael, 94, 151
Brejcha, Vernon, 88, 149
Bridges. *See* Angel swings
Buffoni, Nino E., 12

Burner: building, 34–39; lighting, 74; types, 72
Burner block, casting, 24–25

Cadmium selenium, 153–155
Calcium carbonate, 93
Calcium oxide, 99
Carbon amber, 155
Carpenter, Jammie, 151
Casing, 121
Chile saltpeter, 93
Chromium, 143
Cleaning tools, 60
Clocking devices, 12
Closed shapes, making, 114–115
Cobalt, 143
Cold glass additions, 132
Colorants: adding, 141; composition, 142; types, 142
Commercial glass, requirements, 85–86
Conversion factors in glass recipes, 91
Copper, 144
Crucible furnace. *See* Furnace
Crystal, 86
Cullet, 76, 89, 99. *See also* Glass

Decorating, safety factors, 157–158
Devitrification, 89
Diamond glass saw, 166; using, 174
Dudchenco, Boris, 13, 150

Edger-beveler, 167; using, 166–167
Engraving, 170

Feather edge (firebrick), 18
Feldspar, 96
Fined glass, 77
Finishing techniques, 174–175
Firebrick: breaking, 18–19; for furnace walls, 22; shapes, 18
Fire polishing, 173
Flameworking. *See* Lampworking
Flash colors. *See* Strike colors
Flint, 93
Flocking, 165
Fluorine opal glass, 89
Foot tool, 69
Freeblown glass, definition, 11
Free water, 77
Fulgurites, 85
Furnace: adjustments, 72, 75, 78; cleaning, 72; 78–79; larger, 40; lead glass, 41; loading, 76; test firing, 72; turning off, 75
Furnace, building: base, 20–21; burner, 34–39; burner block, 24–25, 37; crucible, 42–43; finishing, 30–31; front, 28–29; pot, 27; roof, 26–27; shelf, 32–33; walls, 22–23

Gas line connections, checking, 71